ii

ENVIRONMENTAL ANARCHY

Charles J. Keenan

ENVIRONMENTAL ANARCHY

THE INSIDIOUS DESTRUCTION OF SOCIAL ORDER

A LEGACY OF THE SIXTIES

————
———
——
—

By Charles J. Keenan

CAPPIS PRESS, VICTORIA, B.C. CANADA

vi

Published in Victoria, British Columbia, Canada by Cappis Press Ltd., 252 Superior St., Victoria, B.C., V8V 1T3.

Printed by Friesen Printers, Altona, Manitoba

Canadian Cataloguing in Publication Data

Keenan, Charles J. (Charles Joseph), 1922-
    Environmental anarchy

ISBN 0-919763-08-1

1. Environmental policy - British Columbia.
2. Environmental policy - British Columbia -
Citizen participation. 3. Economic development -
Social aspects - British Columbia. I. Title.
HC117.B7K43 1984   363.7'05   C84-091205-6

TO

BEAUTIFUL BRITISH COLUMBIA

FROM

WHOSE ENVIRONMENT WE MUST WREST

OUR LIVING

ACKNOWLEDGEMENT

The Author wishes to acknowledge the assistance of Ed Gould, a well known author in his own right, in editing this book. As I reflect back on the initial manuscript, and the several redrafts which followed, it was indeed a sizeable undertaking to bring the material to its present format. Both the Author and the reader, even though the latter may not know it, are indebted to Mr. Gould.

AUTHOR'S NOTE

The reader will observe, with but a few exceptions, I have refrained from naming individuals. While the use of names might well add to the credibility of some incidents in the eyes of Doubting Thomases, it would in other ways serve little purpose. It is not my desire to embarrass individuals, but instead to expose the grave shortcomings of our present day approach to environmental matters and the resulting political, economic and social impacts. Fortunately, many of those to whom unnamed reference is made no longer occupy the roles they did at the time of the events in this book. To those others still in harness I offer my apologies, if they are in anyway upset by my story. Since the activities and events described cover a span of 20 years, it is important to remember that those who presently occupy the various positions mentioned, with but one exception, are not those to whom reference has been made. For example, the present Director of Waste Management (formerly Pollution Control), the present Minister of Environment, etc., are not those referred to in this book.

Many newspapers, as well as other forms of the media, are involved in some of the deductions presented. Though I am loath to attach any credibility to media material, its use has been necessary, on two counts: firstly, the media is, regrettably, the primary and in most cases the only link between the public and the administration of the country. Whether we like it or not, the media has become an inseparable part of our daily lives. Secondly, environmentalism now provides a plethora of media events, for reasons which shall duly unfold.

As with personalities, I have generally refrained from naming media sources, especially where reporters are involved, for, at best, they are so unreliable as to be of no value in any serious discussion. In general, the media has not been used to support any of the more serious points made, but used rather to illustrate the influence it has in creating much public mischief. Only one paper is frequently mentioned by name, not because it is the villain of the piece, but rather on the contrary. *The Daily Colonist** of Victoria, to which I was a subscriber, was more objective in its attitude to the needs of society, as opposed to the social demands of the all too many leftwing publications. I take this opportunity to express my grateful thanks to *The Daily Colonist* for the references I have used to help develop a point here and there.

While I have quoted the writings of others to help clarify a point or two, I neither assume nor suggest that they agree with my thesis. In most cases I have simply used a quote where it better expresses my own thoughts than I can do. To the respective authors I am grateful. In the final analysis, the credibility of this book is to rest with the commonsense of the reader. It is written primarily for the silent

---

*In 1980, *The Daily Colonist* and the *Victoria Daily Times* amalgamated into a daily renamed *Times-Colonist,* a change which in no small way has diminished the better aspects of the editorial policy pursued by the *Colonist.*

majority, that mass of trusting people who naively believe what is presented through the media.

Nothing in this book is to be construed as suggesting that the needs of living species, be they fish, birds, mammals, or even plants for that matter, should be treated lightly or disregarded. Rather, an honest and long overdue attempt is made to put the needs of both society and nature in realistic perspective; an attempt to separate the wheat from the chaff by the consideration of the realities of life on planet earth.

In presenting this book to the reading public, I am reminded of the wise words of Omar Khayyám:

The Moving Finger writes; and, having writ,
Moves on; nor all thy Piety nor Wit
Shall lure it back to cancel half a Line,
Nor all thy Tears wash out a Word of it.

So be it!

Charles J. Keenan,
Victoria, British Columbia, Canada
September, 1984

CONTENTS

FOREWORD

There are few who will disagree that the now departed W.A.C. Bennett, former leader of the Social Credit Party (a rightwing free-enterprise body in spite of what the name implies) was one of the outstanding, if not indeed the greatest, of the Premiers of British Columbia. During his premiership, which spanned 20 years, from 1952 to 1972, Bennett continually warned, "the socialist hordes are at the gates", a reference to the NDP (New Democratic Party) which perceives state control as its goal. Unfortunately, towards the end of his regime, W.A.C. had surrounded himself with those who failed to grasp how deep-rooted and cunning were the seeds of socialism within this Province. His Cabinet, as this book makes clear, did not recognize the treachery of the politics at work, which diverted us then, as now, from pursuing our true destiny with all diligence.

Some have said that no other country has put so many obstacles in the way of resource users, as has Canada and its Provinces. It is clear the resource companies, or multi-nationals as the socialists derogatorily call them, which for years have financed resource development in our land, are being driven away by the threat of state control. It is ironical that socialism, which is so violently opposed to the activities of multi-national corporations, is itself a world-wide brotherhood, a multi-national in the truest sense.

Having lived and worked in both Great Britain and New Zealand, the writer has no illusions about the intent of socialism — the handmaiden of communism — which seeks only the power to subjugate individualism to the will of the state. There is no doubt that environmentalism and socialism are bed fellows — that our country is being taken over from within by the Fabians. Environmental pressure groups, with the influence of the academic "intellectuals", have been able to capitalize on the disorder created through the 60's and 70's to an extent few really appreciate. In an age claiming to be well-informed, it is most disconcerting to note the confusion of the public as it attempts to decipher the realities of the issues which are set out in this book. Indeed, it appears that George Orwell's *Nineteen Eighty-Four* has many forms. For solely political gains, governments have done much to create administrative chaos through reorganization of their Ministries, or Departments to the extent that it is now virtually impossible to find out who does what. The Ministry of Environment, in which I survived, is a classic example. Throughout this book will be found many examples to validate the theme of Orwell's classic.

Perhaps the most distressing aspect of the story which follows, is not so much the revelation of the anarchy in the environmental and associated political and bureaucratic scenario, but rather that the insidious symptoms identified are *equally prevalent* throughout *all* the institutions of our social structure, all the way from an ineffective justice system, through the seats of learning, the business community and down to self-serving labour unions. As we move through the 1980's a dire warning of "economic restraint" is vibrantly thrust upon our ears by politicians. This book shows how we got there, to the shame of many who now would like to claim immunity from such charges. Each reader will have to decide for himself, or herself, who is guilty and who is not.

Chapter One

THE REVELATION

In a newspaper item dated November 18, 1980, there appeared the following pronouncement:

> "Greenpeace intends to train volunteers in nonviolent confrontation for the group's intended actions in the Cowichan Estuary . . . . Residents may register for the training by contacting, or by visiting the Greenpeace office."

A year earlier, the now notorious international environmental organization known as Greenpeace Foundation, threatened to block American supertankers from entering the Straits of Juan de Fuca, a threat later attempted during supertanker manoeuvreability tests in the American portion of the Straits. All this was followed, in mid-1983, with a world-wide publicized farce involving Russian territory, when a handful of Greenpeacers perpetrated an adolescent act by "invading" Russian territory to photograph a group of obscure buildings in Siberia. An editorial put the matter this way:

> ". . . we wonder about the objectives of Greenpeace. The group sacrifices credibility whenever its members invade foreign territory to break local laws and then couples that kind of caper with confusing charges. There is a growing suspicion such stunts are staged mainly to keep Greenpeace in the news and in the money. . . ."

While the editorial quoted makes an astute point, the media cannot dissociate itself from the events quite that easily. It is the glare of the cameras and the attending headlines that sustain such acts of adolescence. The Russians, to their credit, had the good sense to treat the whole idiotic episode with the contempt it deserved by politely returning the delinquents to a freedom they did not deserve.

Launching Forth

Again, to launch this story, I draw from an editorial column headed "ECO-TWITS", which points out that:

> ". . . mindless goons posing as environmentalists are at it

again . . . its members have driven long spikes into more than 1,000 trees on scenic Grouse Mountain to thwart logging plans. . . . Has it occurred to these misguided souls that . . . their act of vandalism will fade from public memory and that one or more of those spiked logs may some day end up in a mill to shatter saw blades and maim or kill mill workers? Idiots of this ilk who believe that the end justifies the means in any environmental crusade are little better than terrorists. . . ."

On November 30th, 1980, the media offered this:

"A union representing British Columbia loggers said its members will not log the Skagit Valley to prepare it for flooding by a U.S. proposed dam."

Another item: "Guns of Riley Creek More Fearsome Than Iran", described an incident involving a confrontation between loggers and fishery conservation officers. Then there was the report of a radical group in the United States of America which had "a death list" for use against industrial pollutors. Our daily papers are full of such examples illustrating an alarming posture being taken by environmentalists towards our society.

Trained Saboteurs

The environmental attitude described led to the inevitable — an ultimate act of outright violence, an open declaration of war against progress. On May 31, 1982 the forces of anarchy broke loose with a devasting $6 million blast of destruction with the sabotage of a B.C. Hydro substation near Qualicum on Vancouver Island. Investigative experts were convinced from the nature and position of the explosive devices that it was the work of well-trained saboteurs. An anonymous caller, who claimed to have been involved in the destructive madness, made it clear that those involved were, on environmental grounds, unequivocally opposed to progress in the form of the new Cheekye-Dunsmuir power transmission line being constructed to bring much-needed energy to Vancouver Island from the hydro-power dams in the heart of British Columbia.

This was not a thoughtless act of vandalism, nor an emotional outburst by misguided, mis-informed objectors, but a dastardly plotted act of sabotage by a group of terrorists acting against our social order. While individual freedom is a keystone of democracy, the fact remains that if democracy is to work, it is essential when claiming one's rights to grant to others theirs. In a democratic society, individual preferences must, by necessity, give way to what is decided by the majority to be in the public interest. Any other posture leads to tyranny, anarchy and dictatorship.

The violent act of confrontation was the substance of an editorial in the *Times-Colonist* which in part said:

". . . in recent years there has emerged a lunatic fringe whose members clearly are unwilling to acknowledge defeat in any form. When petitions, demonstrations, appeals and letters fail, they resort to violence. If a sewer line they don't want is being built, they attempt to sabotage it. If they think a killer whale should not be in captivity, they ineptly attempt to free it, causing the animal's death. And now in the most serious such incident to date, a radical group has blown up a B.C. Hydro sub-station near Qualicum Beach, causing $6 million in damage . . . a criminally stupid, perhaps even deranged attitude of mind which believes the end justifies the means, even the destruction of public property."

The perpetrators of the above act of terrorism were caught. At the trial, on June 21, 1984, the defence presented by one of the bombers was,

"The reason I did . . . it . . . is that the Cheekye-Dunsmuir project is going to inflict large-scale, severe damage on the environment of B.C. and I consider that to be reprehensible and intolerable."

In pleading for a lenient sentence, his lawyer asked the court to take into account "his 'honourable' motives." His father was in court with a T-shirt bearing the words, "Doug's dad and proud of it".

Throughout the 60's and 70's, society was under constant attack to live in harmony with nature. A noble directive — but when the rules are spelled out, they invariably imply that the ways that built our society must be forsaken — that growth and industry are anti-social vices. One cannot but wonder where Doug's dad was in the Sixties.

Inciting Youth

In 1970, the Sierra Club martialled the academic youth, now the protagonists, through publication of a handbook, entitled *Ecotactics,* prepared for *Environmental Activists.* An introduction by Ralph Nader incited the reader by speaking of environmental pollution as "violence". In the December 1982 issue of *Maclean's Magazine* we read of a proposed "school for budding environmentalists" to be headed by an ex-FBI fugitive, Yippie leader and political radical. Our politicians, oblivious to the realities of the social destruction going on, simply go with the flow, with the inevitable damning effects which now pervade the decision-making process, as illustrated by the uranium mining moratorium.

One February morning in 1980 amid the tranquil and pleasant life in British Columbia we awoke to find, without rhyme or reason, that Premier W.R. Bennett (a son of W.A.C. Bennett) had declared that a blanket moratorium for a period of seven years had been clamped on uranium exploration and mining in British Columbia.

Although surprising, perhaps we should have been prepared.

Moratoriums are getting to be conspicuously high on the list of tactics used by inept decision-makers on their flights from reality. A few years earlier a moratorium had been placed on exploration drilling for oil off the coast of British Columbia. In 1977, there was yet another cry for a moratorium from that well-known advocate of socialism, Mr. Justice T.R. Berger when he called for a 10-year stay of execution on the Mackenzie Valley pipeline route. While Berger made the wrong choice, at least he had completed his inquiry before burdening our free society with his ill-conceived decision. On the other hand, Bennett, the advocate of free-enterprise, made his pronouncement in the midst of a Royal Commission set up to evaluate the validity of the claims of the environmentalists that mining uranium would destroy us.

There is little doubt that the Bennett regime was intimidated; the Greenpeace Foundation was threatening to demonstrate at the opening of the Legislature; the Legislative Buildings were to be scaled by mountain climbers and anti-uranium banners were to be hoisted; Bennett's hardware business in Kelowna had already been the target of picketing.

Lame Excuses

A few lame excuses, which fooled no one, were given for the moratorium. It was said by the Premier that British Columbia can continue to meet its economic goals without the need to develop its uranium resources; that plenty of other mineral and mining opportunities were available. He even went so far as to suggest that the uranium deposits were of marginal value. Those investing large sums of money obviously wouldn't agree. In justification of this calamitous decision he claimed that nuclear power was not to be a part of the government's energy strategy — that the mood of the people was against it.

> *The Province,* a Vancouver daily, put the moratorium this way: "Premier Bill Bennett has made himself the darling of the environmentalists — he went with the mood of the people even though there is scientific evidence to refute many of the concerns. But whatever the short term gain, the decision is not in the public interest, it is a capitulation to the politically astute pressure groups that must now believe they have the government on the run. It is an extraordinary precedent for any government to set. It is incredible coming from a government that says it wants to protect free-enterprise from the socialist hordes."

The mining industry, quite naturally, expressed shock and dismay at the Bennett pronouncement. Some referred to it as a "nightmare". Disbelief was expressed that the Royal Commission, which was set up to put the environmental hysteria surrounding uranium mining into perspective, was cut off in mid-stream. Scientific facts had been preempted. We were to return to ignorance and superstition, rather than knowledge and good judgment in dealing with such matters. Huge investments were destroyed, all because of the capitulation of our political structure to the forces of anarchy. To say that world confidence in the political ideology of British Columbia was shattered, would be, if anything, an understatement.

Damning Effect of Moratoriums

We, who live north of the Forty-ninth Parallel, have for sometime been frantically attempting to encourage the Americans to build an oil pipeline through British Columbia as an alternative to tanker transportation from Alaska to refineries in the State of Washington, an all-American controlled endeavour. In the light of the moratoriums on uranium mining, on the Mackenzie Valley pipeline route and the reneging on the agreement to flood an inconsequential part of the Skagit Valley, only political fools would trust those who might well resort in the future to acts of pipeline hostage-taking. That the younger Bennett still lacks the maturity and judgment of his father needs no qualification. That the environmental rabble were ecstatic with the Bennett decision goes without saying. They were instantly elevated, some swilling beer, to prominence on the magic tube, the ultimate goal of most of them.

The most damning effect of moratoriums like Bennett's is the fact that it arms the world-wide environmental movement with propaganda which can have far-reaching repercussions. The environmentalists have built their theology on intangibles, but when a government, a free-enterprise government to boot, gives, without documentation, credibility to the nebulous claims of doomspeakers, as has been done by Bennett's moratorium, then the future damage to our destiny is inestimable. The ban, incidently, was done through Order-in-Council, not by legislation. The NDP immediately demanded that it be put in legislation, a move not only designed to threaten multi-national corporations, but one that would increase state control.

Bureaucratic Disaster

To expand this introductory scenario, let us for a moment or two consider what has been happening to the bureaucracy. Going back to 1971, the free-enterprise government of W.A.C. Bennett accidently created an administrative and bureaucratic disaster for British Columbia when it innocently promulgated, in response to incessant environmental pressures, new legislation called the "Environment and Land Use Act" in which authority was given to establish a committee to be known as the "Environment and Land Use Committee", a purely political body, to be composed of Cabinet Ministers.

Today, few realize that the intent of the legislation was to provide a mechanism by which the politician could inject himself into the environmental fray without being accused of meddling. It was also to serve as a device to keep an interfering Federal Government at arm's length in environmental issues. However, no legislation, good or bad, can substitute for inept political leadership.

The purpose of the Environment and Land Use Committee was set out in the legislation, in what was a most damning admission that the political system had lost contact with reality. In section 3 were the words:

> "It is the duty of the committee to establish and recommend programs designed to foster increased public concern and awareness of the environment."

Surely those preparing the legislation were aware of the media's efforts in fostering "public concern and awareness of the environment." Just what did they hope to accomplish, other than provide, as it so happened, a ready-made platform for environmental opportunists to exploit when the socialists came to power a year later?

Earlier Experience

Those preparing the Environment and Land Use legislation failed to benefit from the earlier experience obtained in administering the pollution control legislation. The first Pollution Control Act in the Province defined pollution as "anything done . . . detrimental to . . . public interest." Administration of the Act proved to be totally impractical, because of the chaos created as a result of the "public interest" implications. After 10 years of frustrating administration, the definition had to be supplanted with one more practical.

Considering the obvious loss of contact with reality of the 1971 government of W.A.C. Bennett, it is little wonder that they were defeated at the polls in 1972. Unfortunately, they were replaced by a socialist regime, which with a vengence implemented the Environment and Land Use legislation to the letter; they created a parasitical group of humbuggers under the grandiose title of the Secretariat of the Environment and Land Use Committee, whose primary function has been "to foster increased public concern" while feathering their own nests.

What useful purpose the Secretariat served, if there was one, has been a well guarded secret. In spite of detailed investigations of the Secretariat's activities, briefly discussed within a 400 page report issued in 1975 under the title "Environmental and Land Use Policies", no reason for their being came to light. The Secretariat, composed almost entirely, if not totally, of those trained only in the social sciences was set up by Barrett's 1972-75 socialist regime to advise on resource development. The contempt shown for those with years of experience and technological know-how in resource development should not go unnoticed, as it is all part of the environmental anarchy. Inevitably, this ill-conceived group could not survive in the real world of hard times.

In mid-September, 1979, across the top of the front page of a newspaper was the headline: *KEY ADVISORY BODY DUMPED*. This was followed by a sub-headline stating: *Back to the Bad Old Days*. Under the headline we were informed that the free-enterprise government of British Columbia, which had taken over from the socialists in 1975, had decided to eliminate a "key" research and advisory body, the Secretariat. The media instantly gave prominence to the expected routine, shallow criticism of the socialists, now the oposition party: "Disbanding of the Environmental Land Use Committee Secretariat will return the days when mining and forestry interests got whatever they wanted while environmental concerns went begging."

Over the past few years a concerned section of the public has been pressing for governments to curb, or dismantle, the bulging public services. Even the press has been hammering relentlessly at this issue. How conveniently they forget. No sooner is a way conceived to achieve a cut-back than the media take it upon themselves to cast aspersions at those attempting to implement this direly needed action. An editorial in the *Times-Colonist* had this to say about the news item:

> "You don't have to be an environmental freak to be alarmed and disgusted with the provincial government's decision to disband the Environmental and Land Use Committee Secretariat. It is a bad move and a brazen political move to boot. It confirms the suspicion that this government really doesn't give a fig for a rational, carefully-balanced approach to settling legitimate and important environmental issues.
>
> "Why, then, is the Secretariat being disbanded? The most likely reason is that it has not been coming up with the answers this government wanted to hear — on questions, for example, like whether to allow development on the Cowichan estuary and whether B.C. Hydro's Cheekye-Dunsmuir transmission line should go ahead. To get rid of the Secretariat doesn't make any environmental sense. But it does make political sense."

Second Look

The confrontation with the media, to whom politicians are beholden for their elected status, chilled their bones to the marrow. They did an about turn, for reasons stemming from ignorance, in that they did not know they were right, or from lack of fortitude. The facts were that a few days later the headline ran: *ENVIRONMENTAL BODY DEATH FEAR FIZZLES*. There followed a statement attributed to the Minister of Environment that it was never his intention that the Secretariat "be disbanded or its services be curtailed . . . there has been an obvious misunderstanding. There is no intention now, and there never has been any intention, of changing the role of the secretariat."

That decisions involving environmental activities were not (and are not) being taken on the basis of fact, should by now start to be apparent to the reader. If there are still some doubts, the following should dispel them. As just presented, the political machine had stated that the Secretariat was inviolate, its proposed dissolution was all an "obvious misunderstanding". As one comes to expect in today's political arena, such assurances are meaningless.

One year later, almost to the day, in mid-September, 1980, the Government again decreed disbandonment of the Secretariat. This time, so as not to unduly raise the ire of those involved, in typical compromising political fashion, the participants were transferred to other areas of activity within the public service. While the action taken removed the direct interference of the Secretariat at the political level, it does little to solve the real problem, namely, that they continue to be a drain on the taxpayer in high-salaried and influential positions, from which their unrealistic attitudes continue to surface in many areas of the bureaucratic decision-making process.

Offensive Attacks

Over the years, the pseudo-experts within the Secretariat produced Guidelines relative to project development which say ". . . the committee may hold public hearings . . . at which the developers will be expected to defend their plans." This begs the question, "Who defends the developers?" Both the politicians and the bureaucracy have abdicated their responsibilities and now stand timorously behind the environmental wall. Why should any corporation, industry, or person be subjected to the irrational and offensive attacks for which the environmental movement is now notorious? As will be shown later, the Mining Association, at the Public Inquiries in 1972, defended its position with all the expertise available, only to be brushed aside by the socialist NDP government and its hirelings, a topic fully presented in chapter 8. One cannot help but note with chagrin that subsequent free-enterprise regimes have done nothing to correct the situation.

Battle-lines Were Drawn

On September 30, 1978, *The Daily Colonist* carried a most revealing report pertaining to the earlier mentioned Cowichan Estuary issue on Vancouver Island, over which Greenpeace were proposing to train recruits in confrontational tactics. Battle-lines were drawn: The eco-freaks were on one side, industry and developers were on the other. The issue at stake was the proposed enlargement of a wood-mill and the traditional waterfront activities that go with such an operation.

The main drive of the *Colonist's* news article was to the effect that the local environmentalists were stunned to find that the Government's impact study for the Cowichan Bay Estuary had been subjected to "political manipulation" and "tampering". Those who made the charges, among them the Sierra Club, another militant environmental group, stated:

> "There would certainly appear to be some type of collusion by the government. It would appear that the Cabinet has tampered with the original findings."

It is interesting to observe in passing that everything government does, with which they don't agree, is collusion in the eyes of the environmental cult. I had this charge thrown at me, personally, when adjudicating on the Buttle Lake mining episode. That they pretend not to understand the intent of the Environment and Land Use legislation is all too evident. Preliminary reports for this administrative body *must* remain open-ended until the politicians have their say.

Petty Attitudes

Viewed in this context there is nothing materially wrong with what happened. The mechanism of the situation is such that an inhouse confidential impact report is presented to the political level for input, as most decisions relative to society's well-being must take into account factors other than, as in this case, the petty attitudes of those using environmentalism to further their own goals.

While it is refreshing to see such informative facts in the daily paper, it is extremely difficult for the uninitiated, the great unwashed public, as it were, to make sense out of what is transpiring. Even the editorial writer in a Vancouver newspaper missed the subtlety involved when he wrote:

> "There is no law setting out requirements for environmental impact studies and public hearings, pollution control standards, inspections and the like supervised by an agency answerable to the legislature. Until we get it, proper environmental protection in British Columbia will be an impossible dream."

The posture taken is not borne out by the facts. There are already too many environmental and pollution control laws in place in this province, as shall become clear later. It is not a lack of environmental laws that is at fault, but rather the political intrigue of the socialists and the media, using environmentalism as a means of undermining and discrediting the fundamentals of our free-enterprise society.

Chapter Two

THE BIAS OF THE MEDIA

The reader will no doubt have noticed in Chapter One the many, many references to media material, particularly the printed variety. Such material obviously plays a vital role in our daily lives and influences our thinking. This is very evident in the field of environmentalism. Let us then, at the outset of this story, review this role of the media to determine what reliance can be placed on it, as the media certainly plays a substantial part in the delicate subject matter to be discussed in later chapters.

In April 1981, the news media was stunned by the announcement that one of its Pulitzer Prize winners was a fake, that a reporter had deliberately concocted a hoax to deceive the public. Editors feigned shock, some were quoted as reacting with sorrow, others proclaimed that the news media would be tarnished by the episode. One paper said: "It was a black day and the discomfort should be shared everywhere newspaper presses rumble." Another queried: "Maybe it's time for some soul-searching about the competitiveness in journalism?" A self reprimand went: "We must guard so carefully against over-eagerness. Every institution, including the press, is vulnerable to someone who does not tell the truth." In the midst of the agony, some even questioned the authenticity of "Deep Throat", the knave of the Watergate affair.

To the chagrin of the media, the above episode was quickly followed by another exposure of faked reporting in Northern Ireland. This too involved an internationally-known award-winning reporter. On his resignation, his paper excused themselves of any implication by simply saying they could not approve of ". . . his use of misleading journalistic techniques . . . implying that some things are fact when they are not."

Manipulators Control Media

Was all this self-reproach really because a member or two of the media were less than honest in reporting facts, or does it go deeper, much deeper? Could it be that the despair stems from the public expose of the deceit of the manipulators who control our daily reading material?

Is the structure of our society so fragile as to blindly accept, at face value, such totally unsubstantiated statements as, "ENVIRONMENTAL DISASTER", "ECOLOGICAL COLLAPSE" and other such doomsday phrases? How has this environmental hysteria gained acceptability, even respectability, particularly with those in higher places? To one who sat at the inner circle while these events were happening, it is amazing to me that the truth has gone so long unchallenged. But then, who dares fight the press with its fearsome unilateral control over the content of what it makes public? It can destroy with a single headline those who oppose it.

While serving its own God-like powers, the press allowed the environmentalists, under the guise of a false "motherhood" theme, to assume a prominence in our social structure they do not merit. The press, often credited with being the champion of the underdog, undertook to aid and abet the untenable and insidious plot devised by subversive minority forces to superimpose their will upon the Silent Majority. The heroic underdog is associated with right-over-wrong, the battle to correct an injustice, the fight of the oppressed against The Establishment.

Outwitted the Inept

Reflect for a moment: Where, in the name of all that is just, did the hippie fit in as an underdog? Yet who got greater front page support during the Sixties than these self-indulgent creeps who forced their way, with condonation of the press, into every segment of our society, bringing with them their outrageous, anti-social conduct? Were they — and similar pressure groups — while furthering their own ends, seeking power and authority, disrupting our social structure and violating the rights and freedoms of others, worthy of the tolerance bestowed on them? In like manner, the environmentalists have surreptitiously outwitted inept politicians who, because the environmental movement offered a source of votes, were all too willing to jump on the bandwagon without as much as a single thought for the consequences to our society.

Newspaper editors and other media editorial vehicles love to seize the slightest opportunity to play the devil's advocate — not because they want to show the other side of the story, but rather because it gives them the veiled opportunity to attack, without the moderating annoyance of dealing with realism, while in pursuit of their own pet political and social goals. This exploitation of the press has done much to undermine democracy.

Granted, the press is indisputably an indispensable part of our society. Indeed, the press is the mightiest weapon we have for social justice, thus there must be deep-felt concern for the obvious abuses of the media when, for the sake of controversy, it attacks the very foundations of our establishment. While we could indeed survive without our daily paper, the thought of such an event, to most, would be abhorrent. How else can one keep in touch with the great diverse mass of activities going on around us? While we need the press, a free press — we need even more A RESPONSIBLE PRESS.

That the press prefers to shun its responsibilities is evidenced by the unethical abuse of that popular section, "Letters to the Editor". Writers are allowed, even encouraged, to present blatantly inaccurate statements, which, when not refuted, are taken by naive readers as gospel. For example, in the *Times-Colonist* of March 4, 1983, there was a letter in which was the statement ". . . until the strait is biologically dead", a reference to the Straits of Georgia and the discharge of sewage thereto, a statement which is totally without substance. Surely, it is incumbent upon the publishers, as a courtesy to the readers, to check the credibility of such sweeping statements before publishing. Much mischief has been added to the environmental scenario through such abusive practices.

The Non-experts

In considering a media story, one must always remain cognizant of how reporters gather their "facts". In all fairness, they are confronted with an impossible task by virtue of the fact that they are, as non-experts in just about everything they cover, at the mercy of their sources. Time, too, is against them, forcing superficial treatment of what may be a complex subject. When confronted with issues involving administration of government affairs, they invariably go first to the official source, to the bureaucrat, who ends up getting stabbed in the back. When that source dries up, as it inevitably must (once bitten, twice shy and all that), they then turn to the psuedo-expert, often an academic type, who is overjoyed at the public exposure granted to one of no authority in the matter at stake. Thus, the lavish dissemination of misconceptions through the pages and sound waves of the media. The final insult in many cases arises with those reporters who suddenly see themselves in the midst of the turmoil as "experts".

Socreds "Seized" Power

In 1956, when I arrived in Vancouver, I was a little taken aback with the official name of the political party in power in British

Columbia, that is "Social Credit". I assumed that they were some type of socialistic regime, which perturbed me more than a little as I had just come from New Zealand where I had first-hand experience of the defects of socialism. In addition I had previously left an over-socialized Britain.

I was totally at a loss, upon reading the local press, to comprehend how the Social Credit party had "seized" power. With daily monotony, the press, in bold print, was making vicious attacks on the Government, leaving an unsuspecting reader like myself with little doubt that all was wrong, that the Government was assinine and that they would have a short life. Not being politically-oriented, or indeed interested in the sordid matter, imagine my surprise when at the next election they were re-elected with a greater majority — and so it went on for 20 years, until a vindictive press had its day and brought down the Social Credit Government in 1972, to be replaced by a socialistic regime which quickly wrought inevitable economic chaos.

That the bitter lesson was quickly learned in three short years was evidenced by consolidation of the free enterprise votes at the next election. Perhaps this brief sup from the cup of socialism will suffice for another 20 years, though, with the wanton growth of the public service and the blackmail tactics of their unions, we may not be so lucky as to escape the fate which appears to have befallen Great Britain.

In trying to reconcile the blatant disregard of the press for the elected representatives of the people, I soon built up a very negative feeling towards newspapers. I expected, for some naive reason, to get enough basic facts from the press to allow me to formulate my own impartial ideas. During those years which followed, I was dismayed to observe on the one hand that the people elected a Government, but on the other hand, because that Government was unacceptable to the politics of the media, the press took it upon itself to do everything in its power to pull the Government down. The power exhibited by the press was frightening and disquieting to behold.

Disillusioned By Press

Up until this time I had, because of my early teachings, placed some faith in what I read in the press. I recall distinctly one of my English teachers recommending to the class that as an aid to developing our language capabilities, we thoroughly read the daily paper, especially the editorial column, which we were assured was likely to be of great assistance in helping us to develop responsible logical criticism, as well as teaching us fundamental English. Regrettably, I must confess that time and experience have greatly disillusioned me. Obviously, my teacher was not familiar with the tactics of the media manipulators who turn facts into fiction to create sensationalism.

That our daily press manipulates the facts to serve its own ends is a sad reflection on its integrity, a topic on which it never ceases to preach to government. This bias was brought home to me with no uncertainty when I joined the ranks of the bureaucrats in the service of the people. It was painfully obvious that the press was not interested in presenting facts which would give any Government credit for any intelligence. I soon found that out when attempting to develop a rational pollution control organization: While the press thrived on all the intangibles surrounding the subject, they insensitively ignored the truth, to develop a basis on which to attack the Government. It is well-known that reporters, for journalistic reasons, seek out the worst. If material dared to infer that an ecological collapse was not imminent, it was disregarded. I was involved in the development of many press releases that never got a line of publicity, simply because they supported the Establishment.

Toughest Job

That the press can be both devious and treacherous is well known to those who come in contact with it. It operates without feelings of sensitivity towards its victims. That I had learned this lesson well is supported by the following quote from The *Vancouver Province:*

> "In his 10 years as a key figure in the British Columbia Pollution Control organization, Charles Keenan undoubtedly had one of the toughest jobs in the civil service. The Director shunned publicity. He operated, rightly or wrongly for his position, on the principle that as a civil servant he could make no pronouncements in policy areas unless directed to by his superiors."

The following event well illustrates the hard-knock learning process to which I had been subjected. In 1965, while Executive Engineer to the Pollution Control Board, I was contacted by reporters from a leading Vancouver newspaper wishing to consult with me in respect to a series of pollution articles which the paper proposed to publish. I responded that I had no wish to participate as I had grave reservations as to the intent of the articles. I strongly suspected, indeed knew, they were to be written for the sole purpose of ridiculing the Government's environmental control activities. It was no secret that the paper in question, *The Vancouver Sun,* was on a vendetta against the Government of the day.

Next day, an instruction reached me from my Minister, directing me to cooperate with the reporters. The Minister had been assured by an executive of the newspaper that the approach was to be objective, an honest attempt to present the facts. (I swore under my breath as I thought that it is indeed true that the gods first make mad, those whom they would destroy.) I protested vehemently that we had been deceived too often in the past to place any faith in reporters' assurances, be they from the editor or a minion. In spite of my protests, I was prevailed upon, on the understanding that I would be given full opportunity to review the material before it was published.

The interview duly took place, with tape recorders and all the paraphernalia that reporters use to intimidate and blackmail, but which they claim is just to help them get an accurate story, so they will not misquote — God bless them!

Totally Fallacious

True to word, the first article arrived on my desk a few days before publication. One statement immediately caught my eye as it had been discussed specifically with me. (As this is not to be a technical presentation, precise scientific terms and numbers will be avoided. Technical matters will be presented in general terms only.) The item said pointedly that the Okanagan Lake had an oxygen deficiency and inferred that industrial pollution was the cause. The argument put forward was the oxygen level in the lake was 20 per cent lower than the oxygen level in a well-aerated nearby river. Anyone with an ounce of scientific knowledge of the subject knows warm water cannot absorb or hold the same level of dissolved oxygen as a cool, flowing, well-aerated river. Indeed, the difference of 20 per cent was to be expected, especially when the surface waters of the lake reached maximum summer temperatures. The inference that the difference in dissolved oxygen content showed pollution was totally fallacious.

I immediately contacted the reporter who suggested I dispatch a letter to him pointing out the facts with pertinent quotes from scientific tables. This I promptly did. To my disbelief, when the article was duly published, it was unchanged. I was incensed. I phoned the reporter and asked what happened, as I understood that the text was to receive my approval before publication. With little ado, I was told that the bargain had been kept. I had been given the text to review before publication; there was no agreement that the text would be changed; thus ended the conversation. I had just learned that it is indeed true that the press takes what you give them and uses it to suit its own ends. Add to all this the fact that the dear old chap received a journalistic award for his articles for dedication and selfless public service! Cogitate on this for a moment: the media publishes false "facts" and the manipulator gets a journalistic award; not the Pulitzer Prize, of course.

However, there is a much more disconcerting aspect to this incident, which is succinctly stated by a well known reporter and editor of scientific material :

"It is all too easy to arouse the public's fears by sensational newspaper or television reportage. Once the public becomes alarmed, even the most lucid reasoning is apt to fall on disbelieving ears . . . They (good reporters) are vastly outnumbered by hordes of reportorial vandals whose egos dwarf their slender understanding of anything more complex than traffic accidents . . . In an age when the media is the message, it is all too easy to create myths that later defy demolition, even by experts . . . the written word carries a special authority. Once published, a statement becomes 'a fact'."

Second Time Around

Incident number two is of a slightly different nature and is presented to help understand the insensitive and callous, day to day, handling of news by the press. This episode started somewhat similarly to the one just recounted. Toward the end of 1966, a young reporter, new to the business, came in to see me with a request to have me assist him in writing yet another series of articles on environmental issues. "Oh God," I said, "not again."

Without too much ado I firmly and politely turned him down in spite of his pleas that he was new, sincere and only sought the truth. With the fiendish persistence that reporters must obviously develop to stay in business, he went the rounds. In due course I got the inevitable request from higher up to cooperate. I recall being quite resentful and hostile as I reminded my superiors of past experiences which I might add involved dozens of incidents not just the few that I am using to illustrate my thesis. However, notwithstanding protestations, I reluctantly agreed to cooperate, in what, at face value, I accepted as a lost cause. The reporter in this instance, I must admit, appeared to be sincere and impressed me as having a few of the qualities ascribed to gentlemen. (I subsequently found out that he was the son of a Canadian Ambassador. Whether this helps or not I cannot say.)

During lengthy discussions which we had on the subject of pollution, it soon became evident to me through the frankness of the reporter that a series of articles along the lines suggested by me, assuring the public that all was not as bad as presented by the environmentalists, would not be acceptable. The paper, he assured me, would not publish them as it was felt that the public had now been conditioned to expect the worst in environmental matters and that assurances to the contrary would make it look as if the reporter had been brain-washed. Verification of this is self-evident from the preamble at the head of each article which was inserted by the paper at time of publication. The preamble said:

> "The pollution of British Columbia air and water is a major threat facing the province in the century ahead. The *Times*

assigned (a reporter) to examine the many aspects of the problem.''

Volatile Issue

There is little doubt that the project was to be directed to providing a scenario of pending disaster. As a result, it was agreed that I could only cooperate with him, in name, on one article to which I had more inside knowledge than anyone else, namely, the mining activity at Buttle Lake on Vancouver Island. The subject had for sometime been a volatile ◦issue in the press.

Eleven articles in all were prepared and published in early 1967. Let us look at the headlines that went with these articles, "Pollution — Major Threat to Prosperity", "Towns Lack Muscle to Enforce Pollution Ban", "Corroded Cans Tell Story", "Giant Hog Fuel Stack Plagues People", "Inlet Nears Critical Point", "City Beaches Called Worst", "Never A Dull Moment Controlling Pollution", "Uncontrolled Wastes Menace World", "700,000 Lost Work Days" and "People Signed Death Warrant".

There is one more headline which I extracted from the above list, to illustrate the point of this discourse. It reads "TAILINGS IN BUTTLE NO HEALTH HAZARD". Now you must admit if you showed the above list to any average citizen and asked him which of the headings is out of context in the total list he would surely nominate the last. How did this happen? Who twisted the arm of the press to make a favourable comment? Here's the story:

During discussion with the reporter on the matter of Buttle Lake, I agreed to lay before him every fact available on file in my office, or in my knowledge, and that I would answer all questions on the understanding that the facts be frankly stated. In summary, the article was favourable towards the mining operation at Buttle Lake and assured the public that all possible considerations and precautions had been taken.

Misleading Headlines

I reviewed the article before publication and satisfied myself as to the content. However, I was somewhat shaken up when I asked the reporter what the headline was to be. He replied to the effect that he did not know; it was in the hands of the sub-editor or typesetter. I started to get a bit hot around the collar because I was all too familiar with the abusive use of headlines. All are aware of the fact that headlines seldom bear relationship to the content of the text beneath them. We are also all aware of the fact that many readers read only the headline, not the text.

Due to my anxiety, I enquired further as to how the headline would be chosen. I was told that when the page is being set up, the space available for the article is a major factor. When it is decided how much space is available for the article and the headline, the man responsible then scans the article and picks, out of the text, a few words to make a suitable topping. I shuddered at the thought. I pleaded with the reporter to choose a headline in advance and clear it with the editor responsible. I duly received a phone call telling me that the paper would not agree to a headline ahead of time, but he wished to assure me that the matter would be given special attention. It was agreed that the Buttle Lake article would be the second in the series.

When the first article appeared and I saw the headline, "POLLUTION — MAJOR THREAT TO PROSPERITY", all my worst fore-bodings of the press surged up within me. I phoned the reporter and again asked what assurance I could get that the headline for Buttle Lake would be in accord with the content of the article. He said he intended to be in the printing offices in the early hours of the morning when the article was being set up and he would do what he could.

Slept Restlessly

The deputy minister under whom I functioned at the time had told me on more than one occasion that I was too sensitive. As I look back on it I must agree; but at the time, because of my involvement I was determined that the truth should prevail. That night I slept restlessly. At two o'clock in the morning I left my bed and at 2:30 a.m. I was in the press offices. I managed to dig up the reporter, who by this time had no illusions about my intentions to see the thing through. Off he went to the composing room and came back beaming; the headline was to be "TAILINGS IN BUTTLE NO HEALTH HAZARD".

I went home satisfied that at least one headline in this series would be in keeping with the content of the article. The point of this incident is to illustrate the insensitive and indifferent workings of the press geared to create sensationalism, with little regard for the substance of the story or the feelings of the parties involved.

A favourite ploy of reporters is to find an issue which involves markedly different points of view. Not too difficult where environmental issues are concerned. First, one party is contacted and by some form of guile, a statement is solicited, then successively, second, third and fourth parties, likely to have opposing points of view, are solicited for comments. The earlier statements are often quoted over the phone to the later parties in the hope that such may incite some hot-tempered rebuttals. The prodding for information goes on until the reporter has the type of controversial tale wanted for printing. This too is the ploy used in many television documentaries. I was deluged with many such calls, but having been bitten once or twice, I learned to shy away from such matters. You end up, of course, losing, for the media ruthlessly pursues its goal of creating controversy by, without too much subtlety, advising its listeners or subscribers that the "victim" *refused* comment, leaving the implication that there is a cover-up or guilt factor present.

Tone of Responsibility

While editorials in most papers assume a tone of responsibility, it is regrettable that this does not get through to the subordinate levels. Of course, if the paper is committed to a vendetta then it's the devil take the hindmost. It we are to have stability in a free society it cannot be done without a responsible press.

The media like us to believe that they cater to public concerns. Every now and then they delight in getting into the poll-taking business. The purported idea behind this is to check the concerns of the man in the street, a self-defeating exercise. After all, from where does the man in the street get his opinion in the first place? The media, of course. We are trapped in a vicious circle. If the media runs a campaign of the type just described, decrying "pollution" and then seeks an opinion for their cause on the street, it is not surprising that they can find support for the polemic opinions expressed in their articles. Nor is it surprising, then, to one day pick up a newspaper and see, in the boldest of print, a headline *"Environment interest growing, B.C. survey shows."* In the next chapter is presented the bias and manipulation which can enter into such surveys, making them meaningless pieces of propaganda. At no time over the past years has there ever been a serious effort made to put both the pros and cons of environmentalism into honest perspective.

Own Causes to Further

But why should we expect honest perspective from the media; after all it has its own causes to further. In the *Times-Colonist* of August 7, 1983, there was a succinct letter from a Member of the Government side of the Provincial Legislative Assembly taking the paper to task for its outrageous indifference to accurate and understanding reporting. The paper had published a photograph over the caption, "Defiant civil servants posted solidarity signs in support of protesters". It turned out that those in the photograph were not civil servants, but hired hacks of the opposition party. Two other examples were given in the letter, one dealing with a brazen headline, all of which were simply acknowledged with a curt two line, small print, editorial note below the letter, which concluded, "We apologize." But what of the thousands of people who saw the headline and not the apology?

If the press treasures its freedom of speech, it must learn to equate its liberties with responsibility. Peter Worthington of the *Toronto Sun*

Syndicate put this in good perspective when he reminded us that one of the myths of our Western media is that "a free press guarantees a free society". He aptly explained that one cannot genuinely have a free society without a free press, but it does not follow automatically that a free press will ensure that society *remains* free. That this is frighteningly close to the truth is exemplified by another member of the *Toronto Sun Syndicate,* Lubor Zink, when he addressed himself in his column to the "leftist manipulators" of the media when asking how does a government in a free society generate public support if the manipulators of the media have a bias against the government? Zink points out that our media, schools and the entertainment industry are manipulated almost exclusively by "leftist" Utopians.

Sell Us Short

In 1968 the Canadian Broadcasting Corporation were preparing to make a film on pollution. I was invited to meet with production representatives in the office of the Chairman of the Pollution Control Board. The Chairman and I had been assured, as ever, by our Minister that the production was to be factual, an assurance I took with a pinch of salt. I had vehemently protested to the Chairman that the media, as always, would sell us short.

During discussions with the producers, it became painfully obvious at the outset that the film was intended to stress the "horrors" of pollution. The producers were looking for someone on the British Columbia scene to develop script and participate in the production. After hearing a few of my down-to-earth thoughts about the media and the environmental nonsense going on, it soon became obvious that I would not be their choice, even though I headed Pollution Control for British Columbia. The film was made and — as suspected — played the favourite theme: we are all doomed.

The whole matter of reporting issues is astutely summarized by the words of journalist Walter Lippman when he said, ". . . news and truth are not the same thing." Dictators Hitler and Stalin knew well how to exploit the media. Between them, they slaughtered innocent millions and convinced their societies of the wisdom of such acts by controlling editorial policy.

In 1981, the Kent Royal Commission, set up to investigate the alarming concentration of Canadian dailies throughout the country into newspaper chains, warned that such action was clearly the reverse of all normal concepts of freedom of the press — that it did not serve democracy, nor fulfill newspapers' responsibilities to the public. To the vehement objections of newspaper magnates and editorial-writers upon release of the Report, Kent responded that the tone of the protests attacking his Report clearly showed a lack of professionalism in the newspaper industry.

Chapter Three

THE POLITICS OF FEAR

Environmentalism was a word seldom used prior to the 60's and only then in its more generally accepted dictionary connotation, meaning the conditions surrounding one's life-style. Today, the word is ever before us, as a result of the environmental crusaders. The spectacular emergence of and the subsequent impact and conduct of this cult begs a few questions. Do the environmentalists have a cause worthy of the impact they have made on society? Who *are* these people? Where did they come from? What motivates them? Whom do they serve?

At no time in all the years I worked in the field of environmental control and in its administration, did I ever see credible evidence to justify the hysteria broadcast in the media on behalf of the environmental movement in British Columbia. I attended dozens of public inquiries on environmental issues. At some of these inquiries, I was in the Chair conducting matters, probing for the truth. At others, I presented briefs as a consultant. At no time during all of this was there ever produced authentic evidence to support the claims of the environmental movement, that the world is on the verge of an ecological disaster, as a result of day-to-day pollution. There are, of course, local problems caused by the pressures of our modern way of life, but none that cannot be readily corrected, economic viability permitting — but no widespread, all-encompassing environmental collapse, or doomsday, as so loudly proclaimed.

In addition, it became painfully obvious over those years that the environmental cause was in no way linked to solving the *needs* of society. Those pushing hardest had ulterior motives, self-interest, often political. From my privileged official government position it became very clear that the cause was simply based on supposition; a hypothesis with no foundation; a hypothesis which after many years has never been proven; a hypothesis which the press still pushes; a hypothesis which devious politicans fear to confront, because it might well cost them those much-coveted uncommitted votes.

Unadulterated Nonsense

To better understand the perverse activities of the environmentalists, one simply has to refer to their own efforts. My office was innundated with examples. Take the document entitled, "Fraser River Report", prepared in 1970, under the auspices of half a dozen leading environmental organizations with national and international overtones, including the Sierra Club and SPEC. (In its infancy, the letters stood for Scientific Pollution and Environmental Control, a rather grandiose title for a group motivated by politics and emotions, rather than by scientific realities. Time seems to have alerted the society to their deficiencies, as they now call themselves the Society Promoting Environmental Conservation. Too bad they are not a little more honest by defining their anagram as standing for the Society Promoting Environmental Confrontation.)

The Report, some 50 pages in length, purported to document pollution in the Fraser River. It can be said without fear of contradiction, that it had no redeeming values whatsoever; it was simply unadulterated nonsense, in keeping with the poor taste illustration of a flush toilet on its cover. Why the organizations mentioned allowed their names to be associated with such a document is hard to understand, unless one is to accept the almost indisputable fact that the whole environmental cause did indeed grow out of such irrational beginnings. The main drift of the report relied on innuendoes: the claims were totally unsupported; yet, and this is the sad truth, the press rushed to its aid with such headlines as, "FRASER POLLUTION SOURCES TRACKED" and "FRASER INDUSTRIES RAPPED FOR HIDING POLLUTION FACTS", with uninformed lengthy write-ups.

Though given an air of credibility, this childish and petulant report was technically useless; yet the press took this document and gave its ridiculous recommendations prominence. The recommendations alluded to the complexities of treatment, composting, curtailment of defoliants, establishment of a Biocide Control Board, agricultural research farms, and a Waste Disposal Office. In addition, it recommends that the "construction of new pulp mills at Quesnel and Kamloops, be prohibited." Just where, in heavens name, do the students who prepared the report, or those who condoned its release, get the gall to make such recommendations? But they, and their cause got what they wanted: mileage in the press.

Rachel Carson

On the matter of producing evidence to support environmental hysteria, Rachel Carson perhaps came the closest, but her book *Silent Spring* was an attack on the abusive use of pesticides, a deadly killer if misused or placed in unintelligent hands. This basically was Miss

Carson's message, as she warned against careless use of pesticides in biotic controls: An ounce of common sense is all that is required to recognize the pesticide hazard. Miss Carson probably recognized that an ounce would go unheeded and so she went to work and produced a most forceful story with a devasting attack on human carelessness and indifference. However, *Silent Spring* does not even denounce pesticides *per se;* its author says:

> ". . . this is not to say there is no insect problem and no need of control. I am saying, rather, that control must be geared to realities, not to mythical situations, and that the methods employed must be such that they do not destroy us along with the insects."

and she adds a little later, "It is not my contention that chemical insecticides must never be used. . . ."

It was a contention of mine for many years that *Silent Spring* was the only tangible foundation that the environmentalists had for their hysteria, but, and this cannot be overstressed, *Silent Spring* in no way relates to our day-to-day domestic and industrial waste discharges and developments, which are now the primary object of attack by the environmentalists. There is no foundation at all for the environmental myth that pestilence and death is upon us. To the contrary, world health today is at the highest level it has ever been.

Gods of the Environment

In 1971, when speaking at a Rotary Club luncheon on the subject of putting pollution in perspective, I reminded the audience that in the days when we were less sophisticated and a little more dependent upon faith, a trusting soul seeking help would raise his eyes heavenward and call upon the Divine. Today, we are told we must worship the gods of the environment, or be doomed. And what is this new sophistication? Drawing on personal experience, it is primarily due to a new breed of radical socialist, the environmental ecologist, who is attempting to establish himself in our society alongside traditional professionals. He, more than anyone, seeks a change in the status quo, whether or not it serves the best interests of our society. (Of course, the reader must not confuse these emerging psuedo-experts with those many dedicated biologists, conscientiously seeking answers to life and man's well-being.)

Through the 1960's, biology, ecology and geography students from the University of Victoria frequently visited my office to get background material for papers they were writing on pollution, as part of their courses. No social science curriculum of that era was considered complete without some hocus-pocus about the environment. During conversations, I invariably explored with the students what they saw as their future. None was able to give the type of concise answer you would get from a prospective member of the established professions. It is therefore to be expected that a great deal of agitation can be generated within such academic fields.

Indeed, in my discourse with the students, I could not help feeling that behind the scenes, ecologists at the University were exploiting students in order to build their academic empire. They were, in the first instance, encouraging students into their classes to consolidate their own status with the academic body. Secondly, as a result, the market was being flooded with ecologists who now must find employment in a social structure, which had got by pretty well without them. To change the status quo was a necessity for their personal survival, and so it was that environmental hysteria was unleashed from the campuses in the 1960's. Environmental ideology, based on intangibles and not related to reality became the theme of the day, with the resulting inevitable chaos from trying to change the real world to fit impractical theories.

No Restraints

This emerging cult of psuedo-professionals must be viewed with caution. The recognized professional bodies are bound, or purport to be bound, by a code of ethics, to ensure that those practising in the name of the profession, do so within terms designed to serve the public in a responsible manner. No such restraint exists with respect to the ecologists and environmentalists; thus the mass of radical, contradictory, irresponsible verbiage disseminated by the environmental movement as they concoct causes to further their own ends. If they can brand everything associated with our way of life, with the *status quo*, as 'pollution', as a crime or insult against the environment, and convince society that they secretly, within their ken, have the answer to society's salvation, they are succeeding.

The followers of this new cult profess to be sincere in their beliefs and, as in any religion, are quite sure their dogma is the only one, and everyone else is wrong. In analysing this group, it is well to remember that in spite of their claims of clairvoyance they are ordinary human beings. By far the most perplexing aspect about them is trying to fathom from where they get their gall to assume authority, to give absolute answers for all problems of society. Agreed, faith is a wonderful thing because with it one can surmount all obstacles, including, it seems, commonsense and reason: The politicians, bureaucrats, media and a complacent public are to blame for the runaway environmental nightmare. But perhaps this can now be turned around, for rational people will only be pushed around for so long. Eventually they will strike back when they realize their rights are being eroded.

What are these pseudo-experts after? The Fraser River report, prepared with the aid of the "intellectuals" from the student body and staff of the local universities, recommends that government departments engage "a team of ecologists" to "plot an ecologically sound program for the wise development of the mineral resources" of the land; to oversee exploration practices; to supervise planning of mining activities and conduct various ecological studies.

While the above statements are taken from a report, admittedly of no technical consequence, they do in fact illustrate a rather fantastic hypothesis which has been created by the "intellects" of the world-wide environmental movement, namely, that no government decision affecting our society must be made without their approval. In short, the "intellects" of the environmental movement see themselves as a breed of super-beings and wish to impose their will on all mankind. And the astonishing thing is that they have succeeded, they have been accepted as ecological gods in the minds of their disciples and all to the economic detriment of our society. But, more damning, is the fact that they have been allowed to infiltrate, in large numbers, into government services, a topic fully discussed in a later chapter.

In the Fraser River Report is the statement: "While it is realized that some report contents may cause comment, it has been considered that the student's expressions and attitudes should stand." To be objective in reviewing the attitudes expressed, we must ask ourselves a few blunt questions about the writers of such reports. What do they know of the workings of government, of the political system, of the forces that give inertia to our industrial society? Who are they that they should set themselves up as Solomons with respect to planning pulp mills, mines and other great resource development matters?

That events can and do easily get out of hand, is well illustrated by a news item on an attempted assassination of former U.S. President Ford. The group involved were purported to have in their possession " . . . a death list naming 3000 persons in the war against environmental pollutors", a list inspired, no doubt, by the mass of radical literature now published spreading environmental fear. That such a viperous situation could develop is not hard to comprehend when one notes the role played by all too many prominent, often selfish and misguided citizens, who have aligned themselves with the anarchistic environmentalists.

Most residents of British Columbia in the 60's will recall the name of a renowned conservationist, an author and former University Chancellor who, on occasions, encouraged segments of society to confront those who see progress as an integral and essential part of our social system, *if* such progress necessitates environmental changes. That such advice could be misconstrued, with diabolical intent, is not beyond possibility. But what is worse, these same radicals are today dictating and influencing the environmental laws of the land.

THE ENVIRONMENTAL IMPACT STUDY

Why has the environmental cult been so successful in spreading its politics of fear? In the field of resource management, *the environmental impact study or statement* has been the corrupter. This procedure was devised as an academic tool, purporting to assist those not familiar with what is happening in some specific area of study, to make decisions. In truth, it was devised solely to bypass the voice of experience of the establishment; to brush aside the realistic knowledge of those who had devoted their lives to a particular aspect of resource activity, be it forestry, mining, land-development, agriculture, fisheries, et al.

The environmental impact study is, in effect, the most audacious piece of nonsense yet devised to confound our judgment. It has within its framework, all of the subtleties of a Houdini trick. It claims to present the truth but, in fact, it is an illusion. This piece of gimmickry has received universal acceptance by bureaucrats and politicians alike, who now also use it as a tool with which to kid the public that just and honest decisions are being made, as in the case of the Cowichan estuary study, discussed earlier.

Enormous sums of money have been made available for impact studies through the Federal Governments of both Canada and the United States. The environmental impact study, an academic dream come true, gives authority and money without responsibility. Since recommendations, based on the activist's environmental theme must be negative, against development and damaging to our social structure, the consequences are borne by others.

Garbage In, Garbage Out

Politicians, to their shame, have welcomed the impact study with open arms, as it imputes to give an impartial answer to a controversial issue without anyone's neck being out. It is, in effect, used like the computer. You set up a program, you feed in data and you get an answer, and because it came from the so-called infallible machine, it is supposed to be taken and swallowed without question, like the physician's prescribed pill. But those who understand are well aware that the computer only tells you the answers it is programmed to tell, and it is only as reliable as the data fed to it, and only as honest as those who do the manipulating. Put a bias in the program and you get a bias in your answer. Garbage in, garbage out, is the way the computer programmer puts it.

Environmental Impact Studies start out with a statement as to the objective of the exercise. Here, depending upon who controls the study, lies the first bias. For instance, there is quite a subtle difference between "looking at the environmental *feasibility* of doing so and so" as opposed to "looking at the environmental *consequences* of doing so and so". The first statement more or less is seeking an assurance to go ahead, while the second statement suggests the acceptability of a thumbs down decision by the investigators.

Daisy-Counting Fees

Environmentalists have pressured governments into calling for all sorts of pre-studies before developments proceed. These accomplish little apart from the fact that they provide a fat fee for counting daisies, or, as some put it, for documenting what is there on the pretense that everything must be put back as it was, after the project is completed. How this can be done is hard to perceive as the ecological gods have assured us that once man touches any area, it can never be the same: its pristine attributes are gone forever. So what is the dire need to know what was *there* in the first place?

Surely environmentalists are aware that Mother Nature is more than a little indifferent about the *status quo* when she whips tornadoes around, or shows her force through volcanoes, earthquakes, or great deluges from the heavens. Mother Nature should be told to get her environmental impact studies in order before creating such havoc. After all, the damage from such calamitous disturbances could create an ecological collaspe. In truth, when viewed from afar, man's so-called "impacts" are inconsequential in the out-come of the overall destiny of our planet.

Practical Incident

As a result of personal involvement with impact studies one soon realizes that one can, in effect, get, within reasonable limits, whatever answer is wanted. Here is a practical incident which occurred while I was part of a team doing an environmental impact study for the Federal Government. The study related to a proposed major bridge-versus-tunnel development across Vancouver Harbour. Under discussion was the matter of felling trees to make way for the bridge, or tunnel approaches on the elevated North Shore. One participant expressed, with feeling approaching emotionalism, the need to preserve the trees at all costs, as those living among the trees must surely put a tremendous value on their presence. There were a lot of nodding heads consenting around the table, when another participant interjected with a request to back up a bit. As far as he was concerned, he lived on the North Shore because of the view. He wasn't interested in looking at a screen of trees, he wanted to see the unsurpassed panoramic view out across Vancouver's Harbour, all the way to the mountains of Vancouver Island in the distance, and the glorious sunsets in that direction.

So there you have it in a nutshell: One member of the impact study team evaluates the trees as aesthetically irreplaceable, while another unhesitatingly calls for the woodsman's axe! The findings of such studies are dependent largely upon the terms of reference given at the outset and the personal bias of those on the team.

A statement by an executive director of Greenpeace verifies the devious nature of the impact study. In a December 1980 newspaper article, dealing with the Cowichan Estuary controversy, under the heading "Estuary Study Draws Some Blunt Reactions" he protests:

> "The 1974 task force report has never been discredited by the government and the recommendations it set out were clear . . . The 1980 report indicates *the direct opposite.*"

In the same article, a local politician, taking sides with motherhood, called the 1980 report a "bloody disgrace" simply because it confounded his arbitrary political position. In milder tones he is quoted as saying:

> " . . . it is amazing that the provincial government can spend the taxpayer's money for three years and come up with a wishy-washy report."

It is interesting to observe that the proponents of impact studies only express concern about cost to the taxpayer when the outcome confounds their position.

Honest Denunciation

Perhaps the most honest denunciation of the impact study is in the words of a commonly-used instruction sheet for doing impact studies, which in its concluding remarks points out that the method is a simple way of summarizing which impacts are considered of greatest moment by the people making the assessment. Cogitate on the words, "by the people making the assessment". I shall never forget my inward reaction when I first joined the tunnel-versus-bridge study team. Those who were spearheading the study were, almost without exception, young and inexperienced, predominantly bureaucrats and academics. Some of the hippie type were present. But more astonishingly, not *one* representative from industry or commerce. All the way through this exercise I could not shake a feeling of disbelief that our society had become so defunct in its decision-making process as to put even superficial reliance on the findings of such a group.

Indeed, my disbelief and concern was so real that I recorded my feelings, respecting my participation in the study, by advising in the written report, involving my consulting activities, that I wished to dissociate myself from the final conclusion of the study team. It has been said that it is not so important that justice be done, but that it *appear* to be done. This is the kindest excuse one can give for doing environmental impact studies. Others closely associated with such studies have said "Environmental impact statement studies are window dressing at best". There is little doubt that such studies are condoned by the present day decision-makers, as a hand-out to buy off the environmentalists.

Where Has Common Sense Gone?

Here is what we get for our money. A few years back I attended a seminar dealing with monitoring for environmental protection. One speaker, a renowned oceanographer, presented the findings of an impact study dealing with the status of the mudflats in the delta of the Fraser River. Making the maximum use of colour slides, he showed various aspects of the mudflats, stressing, in touching words, the vital role of every little ripple of sand and its interrelationship with the tiny biological organisms. The essence of his remarks were that the whole interrelationship was so "delicate and fragile" that man could easily and readily create chaos with his intrusion into such areas.

At the end of the seminar, I challenged the speaker: "Where has commonsense gone"? To clarify, I expanded by pointing out that the speaker had ignored the fact that every time there is an onshore storm — of which there are several per month — the beach is ripped to ribbons, that the whole "delicate" structure is brutally assaulted, that the organisms are swept away or buried. I suggested, on the contrary, that it is the very tenacity of nature that makes life return under more placid conditions when each storm subsides and there is nothing even remotely "fragile" about the whole estuary structure. I got no answer.

Delta Life Cycle

The study results which were the subject of the seminar were to be part of the decision-making process relative to the extension of the Vancouver airport, as such extension would encroach upon the mudflats. I pointed out to the speaker that all that would happen, if man extended the runway on to the mudflats, is that portion of the mud would be occupied by the runway. Any surrounding disturbance to the "fragile" environment would, in a short time, be completely re-established, though in truth, inconsequential to the delta life cycle. You see, the same river which built the mudflats keeps extending its own territorial claims by carrying down the river some eleven million tons of silt annually. In time, where mudflats now exist, the river and the sea will have between their combined forces built foreshore swamp areas which in more time will become useable land, just like the whole of the existing delta area on which, today, tens of thousands of people live.

On the matter of foreshore, in her book, *The Edge of the Sea*, Rachel Carson had this to say in her matchless prose:

"Today a little more land may belong to the sea, tomorrow a little less. Always the edge of the sea remains an elusive and indefinable boundary. The shore has a dual nature, changing with the swing of the tides, belonging now to the land, now to the sea. On the ebb tide it knows the harsh extremes of the land world, being exposed to heat and cold, to wind, to rain and the drying sun. Only the most hardy and adaptable can survive in a region so mutable . . . "

Self-Serving Cause

During discussion following the presentation, one biology professor tried to justify the speaker's position by suggesting that any substantial changes to the mudflats could well wipe out the famous Fraser River salmon run, as the fingerlings depended upon the estuary area for survival. Such hypothetical statements are the straws upon which the environmental cause hangs. But more importantly, it is by the use of such unwarranted fear tactics that the environmentalists have promoted their self-serving cause. Nature is much more dynamic and tenacious than portrayed by such environmental advocacy. It is probably true to say that the entire mudflats of the Fraser River could be taken over by man and it would make little difference to the salmon runs in the long haul. There is a dearth of evidence to suggest otherwise, though much public money is being frittered away to research the subject. The reason life has survived on earth so long, is because of the ability of the lower organisms to withstand the holocausts of nature.

The lower forms of life found in estuaries and along coastlines are highly adaptable to the pressures of an ever-changing regime, otherwise they would not be there. In the words of Rachel Carson, "Only the most hardy and adaptable can survive in a region so mutable." If silt is added to a river by man, a howl of consternation goes up by the fishery freaks. Strange, is it not, that the most revered of the salmon rivers of British Columbia, the Fraser, is the siltiest by far? Tut! tut! Mother Nature, how could you? In truth, the greatest threat to our fish is the fishing fleet.

Miracle of the Potholes

Some time ago, there appeared in the *National Geographic* a most enchanting article entitled "Miracle of the Potholes", which illustrates the tenacity of nature and would appear to counter much of the "fragile environment" theme. It is certainly more objective in looking at the facts than the Fraser delta impact study. The article deals with the small potholes, no more than a dozen or so feet across, in the barren, desolate and rocky Utah desert. Abstracted are the following pertinent comments:

>   ". . . how did such life come to occupy this precarious niche, and how can it hope to survive the desiccation ahead? . . .
>   "The stresses on life posed by the pothole are among the most

extreme in the world . . . In shallow pools, the turn from day
to night can bring a 30°F drop in temperatures . . . Sudden
downpours can lower temperatures a degree a minute, at the
same time radically altering the alkalinity and oxygen
content . . . torrential runoff can scour through the pothole
with such force that its small residents are flushed away to
certain death.

"Ultimately the pothole goes dry . . . Estimates of pothole
surface readings range to 150°F. In winter, temperatures in
this mile-high plateau country plunge to below zero . . .

But in the sand the snails still live, and in thousands of eggs
and in the gnats' pupae and larvae, the seeds of a new
generation await only the coming of rain. Then the hole will
fill once more, the water will warm, and the sparkling pool
will teem again with the vigor of the life force as on the first
day of the world."

Brutal Conditions

At the other end of the climatic scale are the polar regions. Like
the desert potholes, the marginal existence of life in these areas is not
as the result of the fragility of the species, but rather of the harshness
of the natural forces. That life is precarious in the far north is not a
result of man's invasion, but a result of brutal climatic conditions where
natural forces can and do wipe out whole areas of species from time
to time. The impact of nature's forces by and far exceed any impact
from resource development projects. It is the very nature of eco-systems
to survive. The basic ingredients to ensure this survival must be
presented by ecologists, not the nauseating doomsday cries of those
who have failed to grasp the almighty forces at work in the miracle
of nature.

Even when confronted with devastating pollution, nature, given
half a chance, fights back. England's famous River Thames, which has
often, with justification, been described as a sewer, has fish returning
to it as a result of a little commonsense remedial action. It is pertinent
to this thesis to note that the Thames basin is only 1/20th the size of
the Fraser basin, yet holds a population six times that of the whole of
British Columbia, equal to half the total population of Canada. It has
been recently reported that Atlantic salmon are making an
unprecedented return to rehabilitated rivers, from where they have been
absent for a century or two as a result of the environmentalist's
"irreversible" interference of man.

There are many rivers and lakes throughout the world which have
become successful commercial fisheries as a result of man's enterprise,
though, at one stage or another, they had been decimated by man's

predatory actions. I know personally of two such cases in the British Isles, one involving a salmon fishery, the other an eel fishery. Both waterways, once threatened for one reason or another, now under the control of commercial companies, have been restocked and managed to the point where a once precarious resource has become a viable enterprise.

Bird Hazard

While on the subject of how man is, in fact, helping nature to carry on, I should point out that one of the issues raised during the Fraser estuary mudflat presentation, was the possible loss of feeding grounds for thousands of wild geese. Just as we can raise livestock and fisheries, we can raise all the geese in the world, if such ever becomes vital to either man's needs or the geeses' survival. That the ecological gods are irrational is evidenced by the fact that they want to maintain a bird sanctuary at the end of an international airport runway. Perhaps, like those who had a "death list" of pollutors, they feel that the loss of an aircraft or two, as a result of bird interference at take-off and landing, is of little consequence.

As recorded a few pages back, impact studies simply reflect those impacts considered of greatest moment *to the people making the assessment.* Here are the consequences: In late 1977 I came across a most astonishing environmental attitude which exemplifies clearly the gist of the theme which is now enveloping society. It was in a draft report prepared by the top environmental resource studies group in Government. The subject of the report was water management of the Coquitlam River. The report, as is now all too common, was being prepared solely to serve political and environmental interests. Here is the quote:

> "The lower reaches of the River have silted up considerably in the past 15 years . . . This condition creates considerable shallows during low flow periods and in turn *makes the migrating fish passing through this reach of the River very vulnerable to birds of prey such as the osprey*.* Consideration should be given to deepening the river channel. There would be some benefit also to flood prevention."

Naive Deductions

Note the soul-wrenching concern for the fish, as opposed to the casual treatment of flood alleviation, a matter of so much concern to Government today that there is special flood-control legislation covering the area in question. How is it possible for so-called highly trained professionals to make such naive deductions? The answer is simple, and again I quote from the same report:

> "This report takes the attitude that with today's standards

*Emphasis by Author

of environmental concern, the silt loading to the river simply must be minimized.''

Note the brazen admission that the report is to serve the interests of environmentalism, and be damned with the facts. Incidentally, if the river were deepened solely in the interests of the fish, the osprey would simply seek out shallow pools elsewhere along the river to get their food. In early February, 1981, it was noted in the Squamish area of British Columbia that the normally large eagle population which frequents the area was absent, as a result of low fish stocks following severe floods which had wreaked havoc upon the fish population. There were no eagles dying of starvation; they had simply moved on to more fruitful hunting grounds.

While one may take a "so-what?" position to such attitudes of environmentalism, the matter cannot be so lightly dismissed, for there are some very disconcerting and far-reaching consequences to be considered. In the case in point, in February, 1981, a gravel removal firm was fined $190,000 under the Federal Fisheries Act for causing silt pollution in the Coquitlam River. In sentencing the company, the judge said that the deposits *may* have done serious damage to the river, the food chain and the reproductive processes and environment of fish. The learned judge would not, we hope, consider himself qualified to make such an assessment of the situation on the basis of his own training. On whom then does he rely?

Decisions Influenced

It is scandalous to contemplate that such crucial decisions are being influenced in no small way, to the detriment of society, by the self-serving attitudes of the environmental cult which, through federal bureaucrats, now pervade even the court room. Before passing sentence, it might be well to contemplate what happens every time there is one of those all too frequent deluges which scours untold tons of mud, silt and debris into the waterways, which rips up the river bed and dumps it elsewhere with contempt for man and fish. Such an event, resulting in extensive property damage, happened in the Coquitlam basin a short time after the court decision. The destructive power of nature on the rampage was horrifyingly apparent to all through the 1982/83 floods in the Lions Bay area of British Columbia, where eleven lives were lost as flood waters tore creek beds to shreds. That the "fragile" ecology of the streams had been decimated by Mother Nature in one of her tantrums needs no qualification.

Even fishery officials are apprehensive about the intervention of the courts. In explaining the administration of the Fisheries Act, a Fisheries official puts his concerns this way in a letter from the Ministry of Fisheries and Oceans of the Government of Canada: " . . . once

the provisions of the statute are enacted the courts of the land make
the ultimate and final decisions. The decision-making process, including
the political level, are then removed and a Provincial Court Judge
decides on what may be a very complex technical issue. This does not
always serve in the best interests of any of the parties involved."

Opposed to Plough

I have heard it presented that the impact study, at best, should
be directed towards the possible impacts of new technology in those
areas where history can be of no help. Even here, commonsense must
prevail. If we were today to discover the plough, there would be many
opposed to its use. They could develop an impregnable argument against
it. The ecologist's scenario would be quite frightening — stripping
nature's precious cloak of vegetation, ripping up the surface of the earth
caringly fostered by the forces of evolution, upturning of the soil, the
burying of all surface life, the violation of the habitat of the worms
and other soil organisms, and so the nausea would go, ending with an
emotional declaration that, in time, we would be left with a "biological
desert". Unaware of the awful scenario, the farmer, through the use
of the plough, sustains a population which could not otherwise exist.

Fear of the Improbable

Environmentalists have cunningly and effectively used "fear"
against society - fear of what may never happen - fear of the improbable.
Taken from the Sierra Club Handbook for Activists are the following
fear inducing expressions: "The ecology of the earth's life-support
system is disintegrating."; "Environmental violence far exceeds that
of street crime"; " . . . frightening effects on the world weather
system."; "What makes these nightmares really big is that no one can
know . . . if they'll ever come true."

Just about every environmental issue contains a plot of fear about
some "unique" situation. Just as the word "environment" entered our
every-day vocabulary in the 60's, so did the words scenario and unique.
Environmental scenarios, purely figments of the imagination, are used
at every occasion to intimidate with portrayals of pending horror. They,
invariably, relate to what is claimed to be "unique" situations. Every
pond, marsh, woodland, valley, mountain peak, and what-have-you,
are all declared inviolate on the basis of their "uniqueness."

Certainly, no one with the semblance of a soul within his breast,
would dare endanger something that is "unique". But what does this
mean in environmental terms? In a way, everything in existence is
unique. You and I, as individuals, are unique, but are we not, in reality,
all out of a common mould? The deaths of millions of our species,
in no way endangers the survival of the human race. And so it is with
the great mass of so-called "unique" eco-systems as decreed by the

*Emphasis by author.

environmental cult to confound our logic. The following shows well how it works:

Scenarios Of Fear

Imagine, if the automobile was invented today, the fearful case the environmentalists would have against its use. Could society allow the establishment of a form of transport predicted to kill and maim tens of thousands of people each year, which would require millions of miles of supposedly environmentally damaging roads, which would pollute our city centres on a few days each year (there are, of course, those that would claim that we would all be instantly asphyxiated) and so on?

If an environmental impact statement had been required to be filed before the automobile was put into service, there is no doubt that Henry Ford would never have got started. If you will reflect on this, you will perhaps realize how ridiculous is the environmental impact statement and other such nonsense with which we are polluting our present-day decision-making. In effect, the real priorities open to society must be decided on practical issues. We must be wary of those who serve only themselves and in doing so would undermine the very structure of our present day society with their *scenarios of fear.*

Chapter Four

POLITICAL EXPEDIENCY

Environmentalists, with their false doctrines, have warped the very essence of our political, bureaucratic and public conscience. This is readily and outwardly portrayed by the stampede of governments to supplant the names of long-standing and well-known departments of government with new titles incorporating the word "Environment" as an umbrella under which to hide their dismal lack of understanding of what is happening, or perhaps, more realistically, to pretend they are "with it".

The Federal Government was the first to participate in the masquerade. It look long-established departments with well-known names and reputations (Fisheries, Forestry and others) and placed them under a newly-formed Ministry of the Environment, to later bear the grandiose title of Environment Canada. (Due to philosophical incompatibilities, some of the recruited agencies were later allowed to re-establish their independence.) Provincial Governments, not to be outdone, followed suit. This allowed the governments, as a sop to environmentalism, to recruit masses of ecologists, environmentalists and social scientists, whose attitudes have been fundamental in bringing about a crippling increase in bureaucratic red tape, to frustrate the economic and traditional growth of the nation.

Inept Political Attitudes

The finger of accusation has been pointed at the media. This same finger now points at the politicians. There is little doubt that the environmental hysteria, which took hold in the sixties and is now strangling the rational development of the natural resources of this land, resulted from ignorance and inept political attitudes.

In a brief presented publicly at an Inquiry looking into environmental matters in 1970, I summarized thoughts and concerns gleaned over the years as head of pollution control in British Columbia:

"In British Columbia we are most fortunate to have on the statute books an excellent format for controlling pollution . . . No piece of legislation is perfect and it has never been claimed that the present legislation is so. But the tragedy which has unfolded over the years with respect to pollution control in this Province has been a reluctance to accept, respect and support the legislation by those who are clamouring most for controls."

To better understand the situation, let us step behind the scenes to observe the unadulterated politicizing power-plays that were being made under the guise of the environmental cause. The hypocrisy was unbelievable. I was to find out that it was just not possible to run a rational commonsense administration under the circumstances.

In the late 1960's, and it still applies, it was very evident that the easiest way to get one's name in the headlines was to spout off on environmental issues. The more irrational the verbiage, the better the press liked it, and the bigger the resulting headlines.

Irrational Events

In mid-1968, a series of events took place which had a very direct and disastrous bearing on the administration of pollution control. The matter indeed was so sensitive that I was at one stage suspended for 24 hours because I stood in the way of arbitrary and political actions to help save the face of the Cabinet of the day. The irony of this affair was that it occurred shortly after the "House" had been assured that there was no political interference with the administration of pollution control.

The episode occurred at the time the provincial government was preparing to make its own film to tell the environmental story in British Columbia, as the media had failed to be honest in its handling of the subject. The Minister of Health of that time seized the opportunity to play *the White Knight*.

He decided, with little regard for the consequences, that he, through the use of his Department, would take the applause for development of pollution control and to hang with his colleagues. And so the film was produced to serve his cause. And what a cause it was: It split the Cabinet and was, without doubt, part of the turmoil that started the collapse of a twenty year regime which ended in 1972 with the defeat of the Social Credit Government at an election, in which the same Minister presided over the campaign strategy.

To understand the irrationality of the events bear in mind that, at the time, Pollution Control was under the jurisdiction of the now-named Ministry of Environment, not under the Health Ministry. The jurisdiction had, just two years earlier, been transferred from Health.

There was much wrangling over the intent and purpose of the film which, in the final analysis, became nothing more than a grandiose piece of propaganda to further the cause of the Minister of Health. To make the film, the script writers were anxious to document some factual pollution. I suggested that one of the so-called "outfalls" in the Victoria area be used. In due course, the Minister of Health and others, including the Minister rightfully in charge of Pollution Control, were invited to be filmed on site, purportedly inspecting with concern the outflow of sewage.

War On Outfalls

Suddenly, in the political power play for the limelight the Minister of Health, without consultation or regard for the jurisdictional rights of his colleague, who was in charge of Pollution Control, issued an edict that no further untreated sewage be discharged anywhere, even into the marine waters of the Straits of Georgia. He achieved what he wanted — massive headlines: "WAR DECLARED ON OUTFALLS", cried the media. The mileage was there and he used it without regard for the confusion to follow. The press loved it: they fuelled the rift between Ministers by supporting him; the environmentalists hailed him, despite the fact that his position was purely arbitary, taken without prior consultation with any of the accredited experts within the Pollution Control Branch, or even within his own department. The position taken was without scientific foundation.

Thus started one of the most vicious internal powerplays over environmental issues seen in this province. Various Cabinet Ministers were jockeying for whatever advantages the issue offered. It was given to me in good authority that the rift within the Cabinet was bitter and that blows were threatened. I even heard a whisper that some were thrown and the combatants were held back by colleagues. This turmoil raged on for some six months, during which time the various applications for permits affected by the policy struggle were held in abeyance. I had been discretely requested, through the Chairman of the Board, to use whatever bureaucratic practices were available to delay processing of applications for permits in the affected area until the Cabinet resolved its internal conflict and made its policy known.

Then, in mid-January 1969, after a period of several months, the Cabinet announced that the matter had been resolved, that the jurisdiction was with the Pollution Control Act and that the Minister of Health was to back off. "HEALTH MINISTER LOSES FIGHT ON POLLUTION STANDARDS" went the headlines. During the next few weeks, processing of certain very important pollution control permit applications were re-activated. The one of significance to this story being the extension of the Macaulay Point outfall in Victoria, over which there had been much nonsensical public and political debate as to whether extension of the outfall for a distance of almost one mile out to sea would be adequate.

Matter Not Closed

In spite of the Cabinet concensus, the Minister of Health refused to publicly concur with the Cabinet's decision that such matters in the final analysis came under the purview of the Pollution Control Act. He still let it be known to his colleagues, as well as the press, the matter was not yet closed. It was great publicity and on the side of the media, too. A divided Cabinet, intimidated by environmental hysteria, chose to let him get away with it.

In one of my weekly meetings with the Chairman of the Pollution Control Board, I informed him I was about to issue a rather important discharge permit for the Macaulay Point outfall as it was technically sound and met all of the requirements of the legislation. The Board Chairman, with some wisdom, cautioned all was not well within the Cabinet, that they were trying to come up with some face-saving gimmick for the Minister of Health who might find himself publicly ridiculed for backing down on his stand, particularly as he had, at one stage, openly called for the support of the environmentalists:

"If the people who are opposed to pollution are looking for an ally and a proponent, they've got one in me. I'm prepared to stand and be counted right now."

Needless to say, at the time, chaos was rifer than usual within the ranks of the Health Branch on issues affecting the pollution control legislation. One incident has a bearing on this episode: On January 31, 1969, I dispatched to the Chairman of the Board an inter-office memo dealing with the deplorable state of the administrative relationship between the Health agency and the Pollution Control Branch, with a request that the matter be laid before my Minister, that is, the Minister in charge of Pollution Control. I sent a copy to the Deputy Minister with a footnote which read:

"Since it is self-evident that the Government has lost its way in this whole affair, I would think the least they could do would be to back the technical position, until they have decided on which arbitrary position they want to condone."

Suspension Threat

About this time, I advised the Chairman of the Board that I had personally reviewed, with my staff, in great detail, every aspect of the proposal to use a 4,800-foot long outfall at Macaulay Point and unless instructed not to do so, a permit would be issued within the next few days as further delay was not warranted and would make us look somewhat ridiculous in the eyes of the applicant, who had now been waiting close to a year for a decision. At the time I felt the Chairman appeared to understand my dilemma.

On February 21, 1969 I duly signed and dispatched a Provisional Permit to the Regional District of the Capital of British Columbia. As a courtesy, I advised the Chairman of my action.

Around noon on February 22, which was a Saturday, I received a call at home from the Deputy Minister. He sounded more caustic than usual while advising me that he wanted the permit recalled to accommodate certain political manoeuvres deemed necessary to save face, as issues within the Cabinet were still not resolved. I was, in short, advised that I either phone the Secretary of the Regional District and pick up the permit, or be suspended. As the permit was in order, I could think of no valid reason to recall it. I advised the Deputy Minister that I would have to have time to think the matter over, whereupon he advised me that I was forthwith suspended. Without further ado, I phoned my lawyer and met with him the following day, Sunday. That afternoon I received a second call from the Deputy Minister advising me that as a result of numerous phone calls, the permit was to be returned to my office on Monday morning and that I was to take receipt of same as the suspension was being lifted.

On Monday morning, February 24, 1969 the Secretary of the Regional District arrived at my office and sheepishly handed me the envelope and contents which had been dispatched from my office to him the previous Friday. His passing explanation was to the effect that he had been asked "politically" to return same. (Incidently, he later became a deputy minister.)

I forthwith drafted a letter to my Minister requesting an audience and an explanation as to the intolerable interference which had occurred and asked for a meeting at which the Deputy Minister would be present. The meeting duly took place. During the discussion which followed it was all too obvious that political expediency was solely the cause of the highly irregular actions. I was sincerely exhorted not to make a hasty decision as to my future.

Priority Importance

It took a full month of internal exchanges to reach what appeared to be a resolution of the internal problems. Three Cabinet Ministers, respectively representing Health, Pollution Control and Municipal Affairs were appointed to sit on the Pollution Control Board. In a statement released by the Board on March 14, 1969 the following was stated:

> " . . . the Ministers . . . would be serving, not in their capacity as Ministers of the Crown, but in the capacity of co-ordinators to help bring about a full understanding between

all levels of thought on pollution control as the public presents them to various government departments.

"The Chairman said the meeting recognized that pollution control is assuming priority importance in the public mind, *even though many members of the public find it difficult to specifically define the nature of their concern.*

"It was considered vital that the board be able to express itself at the public level and help keep the public advised of the efforts being made to understand and resolve the entire matter of pollution control in the public interest."

The statement went on to enunciate a so-called "declaration of policy" on behalf of the Government for the control of waste discharges. It is most significant to observe that the policies declared were solely arbitrary and political in origin. At no time had the technical competence within the bureaucracy been consulted. It is also highly significant to note that while the Minister of Health had been appointed to the Board, he was not present at the meeting when the policy was approved, though he, more than anyone, was instrumental for the change. *Nor did he ever attend a single meeting over the ensuing months,* a most extraordinary example of irrational behaviour.

Sop to Minister

As far as the controversial Macaulay Point discharge was concerned, the new edict, issued as a sop to the Minister of Health, proclaimed that his department was to set standards to protect public health and these were to be incorporated in any permits issued. The irony of the situation was that all known health precautions were already being incorporated into the permits. After all, just two years earlier the Pollution Control Act had been administered solely by public health staff, under my guidance as Director of Public Health Engineering. In addition, the application to discharge had been submitted to the Health Branch for review and had been cleared. This whole farce was nothing more than a nauseating face-saving exercise.

Following the release of further policy declarations, the Macaulay Point permit was reissued in the same form, with but one addition: One of the clauses in the original permit read:

"The Permittee shall not fail to provide treatment, or other works, should there be presented documented evidence that a hazard to health can be attributed to the method of disposal . . ."

The new version read the same except that the words, "in the opinion of the Health Branch", were appropriately inserted. On the same date that the permit was issued the Chairman of the Board released the following statement to the press:

" . . . a Pollution Control Permit has been issued to the Regional District of the Capital of British Columbia authorizing discharge of sewage effluent at Macaulay Point . . . The Permit sets out among other things that treatment will be required should there be in the opinion of the Health Branch . . . and the Pollution Control Branch . . . a hazard to health attributed to the method of disposal authorized . . . "

Thus was the fatuous exercise of face-saving completed. Homage had been paid to the environmentalists. The damage to the morale of the Branch administration was of no consequence. The humbug of the whole affair, the futility and lack of political fortitude, had no small bearing on my decision to resign some time later.

A Buttle Lake Committee

What I have described is not an isolated instance. Here, briefly, is one more of many where political expediency necessitated the suppression of the truth about the blatant distortions of environmental realities. This incident also illustrates rather well the truth that environmental issues are distorted and deliberately warped to suit the specific ends of those creating the nonsense. However, it is recounted with some reluctance as it involved the highly-respected medical profession, or to be more accurate, involved the activities of an Environmental Health Committee of the British Columbia Medical Association. Perhaps the incident will serve best to remind us that doctors are only human beings, with all the inherent weaknesses of the species.

While I have every respect for the knowledge of doctors practising within their field of competence, I have, from first-hand experience, learned to be extremely skeptical of their capabilities to apply commonsense in areas of competence covered by others. I found this to be all too true when I was with the Health Department, where my duties included acting as consultant on environmental matters to medical health officers throughout the Province.

One day in 1967, I was more than a little concerned when I received a directive from my Deputy Minister to participate in the investigations of a Committee set up by the Medical Association to look into environmental matters relating to the discharge of mine tailings into Buttle Lake on Vancouver Island. This subject was, and still remains, a highly controversial issue.

In 1966, Pollution Control Permits were issued by the Board to a mining company to discharge tailings from its concentrator into the head waters of Buttle Lake. These permits were appealed by the Greater Campbell River Water Board. The Court of Appeal judgment was handed down on January 16, 1967, ordering that the permits be quashed.

After the initial review of the judgment, it was the consensus of those involved within Government that an appeal against the decision should be taken to the Supreme Court of Canada. There were many technical justifications for such action and on the surface a favourable decision could be anticipated. However, the political machine of the day decided that to win the appeal could well be a hollow victory. The elected representative from the area was a Cabinet Minister. It was deemed inadvisable, by the political pundits, to take a course of action which, if successful, would in effect mean that the Government had defeated the People.

Second Kick at Cat

It was therefore decided to abandon the appeal and rewrite the Pollution Control Act forthwith. The Deputy Minister, a departmental solicitor, and myself were entrusted with this task. As a result, in March of that same year the Pollution Control Act 1967 was promulgated as law. Among many changes, the two most significant were the transfer of the responsibility for issuance of permits from the Board to the Director of Pollution Control, a newly-established position to which the writer was appointed. This change would allow the Board to act as an Appeal body, or tribunal, in matters under dispute, or as the matter was put to me at the time, "it would allow a second kick at the cat."

In May 1967, the Permit to allow discharge of tailings to Buttle Lake was reissued by the author in substantially the same form as the earlier one, with the addition of a clause containing legal jargon respecting the rights of objectors.

The above facts explain my deep concern when advised of the proposed meddling of a self-appointed medical *ad hoc* committee and a request for my participation. Such a committee could serve no useful purpose. All of the expertise needed in health matters was already available within Government and had indeed been utilized in both issuing and reissuing the permit. With a long-established knowledge of how such environmental committees worked, how poorly informed they are, and the insensitive and irresponsible manner in which so-called factual findings are handled, I implored my Deputy Minister to have me excused from participation. I pointed out how sensitive the whole situation was and that I was too well-informed on the whole subject to allow my name to be associated with an investigation over which I would have no control as to the findings. I also reminded him of much of the nonsense which was going on within the ranks of the Health Department.

The Deputy Minister assured me that he understood that the committee was to be very objective in its approach and only wanted to find the truth. It was felt that my attendance in this regard would help. The tune sounded so familiar. (What the Deputy Minister failed to advise me of was that the head of the *ad hoc* committee was a neurologist, who at the time was treating the Deputy Minister for a serious back ailment, all of which would suggest that the Deputy Minister was not being too objective about my concerns.) Be that as it may, I was duly prevailed upon to participate with the committee, but on the clear understanding that I must have an assurance from the committee that I would be given the right to veto the findings and the use of my name, if I felt they were not representative of the facts.

Position Stated

I met with the committee in one of the member's homes. There was a short informal exchange on general matters, followed by the Buttle Lake issue. At the outset of the Buttle Lake part of the meeting, I stated my position. The terms for my participation were that I was prepared to help the committee with factual information so that it could form rational conclusions for publication.

I made it quite clear I could only participate if the committee could assure me of the right to veto information which I personally deemed not representative of the situation as I knew it. After all, I could find myself in a most untenable position: I had issued the permits and by doing so had assured the objectors there was no hazard to health. I had also, during the appeals, been subpoenaed as a witness and testified before the courts that in my considered professional opinion the possibility of the mining operation affecting the Cambell River drinking-water supply could be dismissed. How could I possibly be party to a report which might cast aspersions? My credibility could be at stake.

All of this I had earlier explained to the Deputy Minister. It had been rejected, as he was most emphatic that the committee was only interested in the facts and as the facts spoke for themselves what had we to lose? I had been pessimistic, and as it turned out, not without reason. The Committee heard me out but they were adamant that I could not be offered any special voice in the deliberations. I politely asked to be excused and withdrew.

Now let us look at the report of the Committee, a most misleading and mischievious document: Under the report subject title, "The Buttle Lake System", one finds at the outset the statement:

"... the first meeting of the Committee was held with Mr. Keenan who represented the Pollution Control Board ... "

I was incensed. The very thing I had done all in my power to avoid had happened. Here was the diabolical inference that I was party to the findings of the Committee, that they had got their facts from me, that they had been wised up and now knew the truth and so could make judgment.

Little Pollution in Comparison

In the second paragraph of the report is a statement portraying my actual input to the Committee. It deals with general statements that I had made prior to giving the Committee my terms of participation, as just explained:

> "Mr. Keenan spoke to the Committee concerning pollution problems in general as related to British Columbia. He stated this Province had very little in the way of pollution in comparison with other Provinces . . . "

My total contribution to the Committee was general in nature and at no time were there any specific remarks made relative to the Buttle Lake system. Why then the unforgivable inference that the matter had been discussed with me? It was, I submit, that their facts were so meager that to make recommendations, with any weight, they had to infer that they had had intimate discussions with the one person who knew all the facts.

Now a brief look at the recommendations. The first one stated:

> "The Committee believes that while no health hazard may result from the proposed method of disposing of mine mill tailings, nevertheless, it believes that there is sufficient doubt about this . . . "

The doubt raised was totally without foundation. There was not one iota of evidence to support the supposition. Indeed, all of the evidence clearly and positively indicated that no possible health hazard could arise. The application had been reviewed in detail by the Health Branch.

I had testified under oath before the Courts that in my considered opinion the operation would not materially affect the quality of the Campbell River drinking water abstracted from the lake system some 12 miles away. During the years which have subsequently elapsed, this has proven to be a reasonable assessment of the situation. However, in keeping with environmental hysteria, the case of the committee was based on surmise.

Recommendation two said:

> "The Committee questions whether the Board considered all evidence available before issuing the second permit in the Buttle Lake matter."

The statement is both false and absurd. The authority to issue the second permit no longer rested with the Board, but with the Director of Pollution Control. My signature was on the permit. As mentioned earlier, the legislation had been changed because politicians intimidated by the media and electorate chose it to be that way. The Cabinet, with one worthy exception, my Minister, preferred to go along with surmise, rather than stand by the facts.

The Minister in charge of Pollution Control had personally been displaying tremendous fortitude in the face of the onslaught from his colleagues in the Cabinet, the environmentalists and their cohorts, such as the committee under discussion. He had, in the midst of the Buttle Lake affair, when countermanding the unrelentless pressures from the environmentalists, publicly said:

> "All I can say is that I honestly think from the standpoint of experience, knowledge and my understanding of the problem that Keenan is without doubt one of the top men in Canada."

While honesty prompts me to disclaim the ranking as one of the top men in Canada, I do in all modesty accept the fact that because of the mass of information before me, it was not too difficult to deduce the truth. At the time, in a memorandum to the Executive Council of the Cabinet, it was stated:

> "It should be noted that all of the objections were based on surmise, not one piece of factual technological evidence was submitted or quoted."

A Number One Issue

Now back to the question raised by the *ad hoc* committee as to whether all evidence had been considered before issuing the permit: For the best part of a year the matter had been a number one issue with myself as well as with the Board and several departments within Government. The matter had been to court. Testimony had been prepared. Every iota of information was valued. Special consultants had been called in; and the *ad hoc* Committee of learned gentlemen asked *whether all available evidence was considered before issuing the second permit.*

As we move on, we shall see what the Committee really had in mind. As postulated earlier, environmental issues are used for ulterior motives, and this case was no exception. In recommendation four, the Committee said:

> " . . . that an independent University biologist of recognized standing be appointed to the Board and by the same token, an eminent independent counsel . . . "

It is interesting to note that on the same date that I met with the Committee there was present and participating in the discourse an independent University biologist and an eminent independent counsellor. That the committee got carried away on its self-serving spree, is evidenced by recommendation five:

"It is recommended that all pollution control be more properly placed under the Department of Public Health . . . "

Was the Committee not cognizant of the elementary fact that health is but one of many aspects of environmental control and that pollution control had, ironically, up until two years earlier been administered solely by staff from the Health Branch? Thus the approach suggested had been tried but found wanting for many reasons, some already stated, some which shall appear later. Of course, as one would expect, the Health Department too had a representative at the Committee meeting.

Medics Discredited

When I started to recount this episode it was to illustrate what happens in the interests of political expediency. Now that the background has been developed, I can proceed. In November 1967, I wrote a letter to the B.C. Medical Association complaining bitterly respecting the findings of the Committee and in particular with the inferences to my participation. I made it quite clear that I considered the report irresponsible and a discredit to the medical profession. I sought an opportunity to set the facts straight with the committee chairman. However, the matter instead was presented to my Minister, a contemptible course of action, as it leaves a recipient in my position, a public servant, with no recourse but to listen, which I dutifully did.

The Minister, while expressing sympathy to me on the one hand, came down hard with the other. He said he recognized that I had been quite properly disturbed by the report. He also assured me that I was not alone in my concern respecting the activities of the said Committee. Their report incidentally was rejected by the Medical Association, probably on account of the confrontation of the hypocrisy being perpetrated. But I was told in no uncertain terms not to have any further contact with the Medical Association as the Government and the Association were attempting to reach agreement on more vital issues respecting medical services and that my personal attitudes respecting the competence of doctors in the field of pollution control might create unnecessary animosity between the Medical Association and the Government.

To round off this chapter, a few anecdotes on politicking are offered. One day a press report carried the headline, "POLLUTION CONTROL BOSS HIT". An elected member of the Government at a political rally, while purporting to defend the Government's regulations on pollution control, said that the regulations were just fine, it was lack of enforcement by the Branch that was the problem. He obviously wasn't aware of the political humbug just recounted. That same ingrate went so far as to say "Keenan's quitting, thank God for that", as I had just then announced my resignation from the service. A letter from my solicitor promptly shut him up.

Perverse Nonsense

The facts behind the outburst are of interest as they typically illustrate the insidious, perverse nonsense fostered and perpetrated by politicians using the cloak of environmental concern. A few weeks prior to the events just described, the politician in question had phoned my office to discuss alleged pollution coming from the main treatment plant for Vancouver. The discussion was initiated with expressed concern about the odours, or stench, periodically coming from the foreshore area near the outlet from the plant. As this was an age-old complaint — fostered by local environmentalists to further their cause — I had the answer ready: — I had on numerous occasions looked into similar charges. The primary source of the odours resulted from decaying algae on the extensive gooey mud flats created by the Fraser River. In all probability the location of the outfall contributed indirectly, in a small way, through enhancement of algal growths, a common natural cause of odours. At certain times of the year the rotten egg smell of hydrogen sulphide gases from decomposing algae can be substantial. I have investigated many such complaints in many other areas well-removed from outfalls, with the conclusion that Mother Nature was being her troublesome self.

I recall the M.L.A. talking emotionally about the treatment plant interferring with the recreational potential of the area. I recall too, the curt response when I explained that the area was nothing more than tidal mud flats created by millions of tons of slimy silt brought down by the Fraser River. These are the mud flats to which reference was made earlier when discussing the extension of the Vancouver airport. Those who claim that the area has prime recreational potential are suffering from some sort of delusion.

Matter Had to be Dropped

When the press report appeared, I of course, raised the matter with my Minister, who assured me that he and his Cabinet colleagues were having just as much trouble with the member in question, in trying to get him to take a more rational position on environmental matters. Again the matter had to be dropped; there was just no chance that the body politic would come out from behind the environmental curtain.

About a dozen years after the above incident there appeared an interesting headline in the Times-Colonist: "A Treasure Found Amid Sludge". The article which followed stated: "Sitting amid sewage sludge, breathing sewage fumes and hearing sewage noises, a group of two dozen excited people awaited the arrival of a . . . rare sandpiper blown in from Siberia." The rare and unusual visitor was discovered at the Vancouver sewage treatment plant. When interviewed, the bird watchers explained that the area " . . . is a paradise for shore birds that feed on the larvae of flies breeding in the sludge . . . (the bird watchers) visit the area almost daily in a quest to earn a record for spotting the most species of birds." One watcher said " . . . they like the location and the smell doesn't bother them. I think we've all lost our sense of smell out here."

Treatment plants, like a farmyard, have characteristic odours, which are all part and parcel of our environment. Occasionally then, it would appear that the media can get things into some honest perspective, though in this case, while trying hard to stay with the facts, the reporter got carried away with his scenario " . . . breathing sewage fumes and hearing sewage noises . . . " Sewage noises???

Hydro Get-Togethers

Perhaps the following brief incident puts much politicking into perspective. In the mid-1960's, at the time when the Arrow Lakes dam was to be constructed on the Columbia River for the purpose of developing hydro-power energy, I was requested to meet with a number of the local municipal politicians in the Columbia Valley to discuss measures to protect the water supplies of downstream communities during the period of construction. B.C. Hydro was also represented at the meeting. Indeed, it was the Hydro representative who had arranged the various get-togethers.

One particular discussion took place with the Mayor of one of the communities. He, the Hydro representative and myself, were in a three-way discussion around a table. From the outset I was at a loss to understand some of the logic being put forward by the Mayor. He certainly was not speaking within the terms of reference for the meeting, as I understood it. He was making a very forceful pitch to the effect that the people who lived in the Columbia Valley were the rightful heirs to a substantial portion of the monies which the British Columbia Government had negotiated and obtained from the United States to build the dam.

Eventually I interrupted and said something to the effect that I couldn't follow his logic. He looked me straight in the eye and said, "Logic has nothing to do with it; I'm talking *politics.*"

Instant Experts

Much environmental trouble arises because politicians often present themselves as instant experts. In the late 60's, I was invited to speak to a public gathering in the town of Quesnel on the subject of pollution control. As chance would have it, the federal government called an election just prior to the scheduled meeting. The federal representative of the area, the Minister of Justice, arrived in town that afternoon. As no politician would ever pass up the chance of a ready-made public gathering, no matter how humble, he turned up and as a courtesy was invited to share the platform. I presented my topic in a much abbreviated form to allow the distinguished visitor use of the platform for his forthcoming political campaign. While I expected him to address himself to the political situation, to my surprise the Honourable gentleman pursued the pollution topic.

Without ado, he disagreed with the expert opinion that had preceeded his by giving credence to many of the well-known environmental cliches, no doubt for the purpose of vote-gathering. When the meeting ended and at a discreet moment, in a brief undertone discussion, I attempted to explain some of the misconceptions in his statements. Need I say he was not the least interested, preferring the more popular environmental theme. The damage done when such prominent people speak as experts, is inestimable. Little wonder all is not well with society.

Chapter Five

VENDETTA AT BUTTLE LAKE

The political system, through constant attack from the media, has become so sensitive of its defects that it no longer functions objectively. This is well-illustrated by the Buttle Lake episode to which reference has been made in the previous chapter.

Prior to 1966, a mining company had been given all assurances necessary to operate an underground mine on the edge of Buttle Lake within Strathcona Provincial Park, on Vancouver Island. Initially, the main issue at stake was not pollution but the principle of mining within a public park. The pollution aspect was pushed when the park purists failed to get their way with the Government. The whole matter was a political issue, purely and simply, and should have been treated as such but the elected leaders of the day lacked the spunk to take a stand. Instead, as in all too many such political issues, pollution was made the whipping boy.

In June 1966 an Order-in-Council was rushed through placing Strathcona Park under the jurisdiction of the Pollution Control Act, a move worthy of a Pontius Pilate. That the mine *per se,* was to go into production was *"a fait accompli"*, decided by others.

After lengthy deliberations as to the various alternatives available, permits were issued permitting discharge of the tailings into the lake, under controlled conditions, as it had been deduced by those involved that this method of handling the tailings would create the least disturbance to the area. Since there had been close to one hundred objectors to the application to discharge tailings to the lake, including several environmental groups, a Water Board and a Town Council, it follows that all hell broke loose when the permit was issued and the protesters were advised their objections had been dismissed.

Environmental Band-wagon

To the vexation of those who jumped on the environmental band-wagon, their case was indeed a tenuous one. While many protests were lodged, none was supported by facts. All spoke vaguely of environmental disaster. Here is how one university intellect summarized it on the basis of two years' study:

> " . . . .the mining action may have unforeseeable and immeasurable consequences. Has it occurred to the parties involved that the Buttle Lake system contains what is very probably some of the best quality water in the world? Its price per gallon in the year 2000 is difficult to estimate, but I would place it at a figure much above that of the copper at the same time."

Such unadulterated drivel was, in general, the case of the anti-mining proponents. The objectors had demanded a public hearing. It was obvious from a scrutiny of the objections obtained that there was no substance to the protests. In a memorandum to the Deputy Provincial Secretary, for use of the Cabinet, I said:

> "It should be noted that all of the objections submitted were based on surmise, not one piece of factual technological evidence was submitted, or quoted,"

The press at the time quoted me as having said:

> "On the basis of all the technical evidence, it seemed superfluous to hold a hearing."

And so it was that no hearing was held.

At the time, in an attempt to make a case, the objectors retained the British Columbia Research Council to review the facts on their behalf. While the results produced by the Research Council are in most cases impeccable, an occasional fiasco may occur. With regard to Buttle Lake, everything else had gone wrong and so Murphy's Law was to be proven true. I was personally looking forward to the findings of the Research Council as I had worked closely with the Council on other projects and had considerable regard for their prowess, particularly in technical matters.

Report Recalled

When copies of the report arrived, I gave one to a staff engineer who had been responsible for the day-to-day matters of the Buttle Lake permit application. With a feeling of anticipation, I read my copy of the report. I was aghast. I couldn't believe it. I reread it and then consulted with my staff engineer. His conclusions were the same as mine: the report was erroneous, the facts were not correct, it was anything but scientific. The conclusions were simply surmise. Emotionalism had taken over.

I immediately telephoned the head of the Research Council, expressed my concerns and asked if the report had been checked and approved for release. The reply was somewhat non-committal: There was a promise to look into the matter immediately. I couldn't help feeling that my inquiry must have sounded a little impertinent.

A few hours later I received a call from the head of the Research Council who expressed deep concern over the report. He advised that the report was to be recalled as it had not been checked through the normal channels. It was indicated that the writer of the report had taken certain liberties in his work.

Two or three days later a revamped report was hurriedly released. While the more obvious errors had been deleted, much of the main context or philosophy remained. This was unfortunate, but in a way unavoidable if the Research Council was to meet its deadline. It would have been most embarrassing for the Research Council to have to abort the whole effort. It was too late to start again. And so it was that after a hasty rewrite of the original report, a second edition was released. Under the circumstances, it is not too difficult to recognize that the final report was far from being a factual, unemotional research document, up to the usual standards of the Council.

Full of Innuendoes

I had, at the time, written the following comments in a memorandum to the Chairman of the Pollution Control Board to accompany a copy of the report which I forwarded for his information. My memorandum said:

> " . . . the British Columbia Research Council report presents no new evidence which was not considered by the Board and/or by the technical staff of the Pollution-control Branch. That minor areas of doubt exist with respect to operation has been recognized by the Board and has been adequately covered in the special conditions of the permits issued, wherein the Board has reserved the right to re-enter the permits and re-establish new conditions to meet any contingency which may arise . . . The report is full of innuendoes . . . A deplorable state of emotionalism has been allowed to creep in and undermine the factual, materialistic approach one associates with research . . . "

Of course, the Vancouver press had another field day. Under the heading "THE FINAL INDICTMENT" an editorial said:

> "The B.C. Research Council report spelling out the real dangers of Buttle Lake mining pollution is at once an indictment of badlands capitalism and a blessed lesson in comparative ethics.

"It took courage for the council to tear Western Mines' technical arguments to shreds and to show up the provincial government as an incompetent protector of our natural resources . . . .

"In the crisp, unemotional, scientific jargon of the biologist, this report contains all the information anyone should ever need to stamp the combination of careless promoter and accommodating government as a threat to the province's good . . .

"What is most terrible of all is that the B.C. Pollution Control Board, the protective agency of the provincial government, was the eager handmaiden in this lamentable affair. It not only accepted the promoters' fast-talk without challenge; it went out of its way, by sneaking out of a pollution board hearing, to make sure that no challenge could exist . . . "

Vendetta Against Government

How is that for a seething indictment, based on a very dubious piece of scientific work? There was little doubt that the press was being callously vindictive. Admittedly, the editor was unaware of the weaknesses of the document which he used to support his vendetta against the Government. Be that as it may, the truth of the matter is that the facts, as presented in the patched-up report, were misrepresented and grossly exaggerated in the press report, so much so that the now highly-embarrassed Research Council had to react publicly. The following statement was issued by the Research Council on the day after the quoted editorial remarks:

"The British Columbia Research Council wishes to refute the misleading publicity arising from its report to the Campbell River Water District. Some media misrepresented the intention of the report . . . .

"The principles upon which the tailings disposal system is based are considered to be sound and the Council believes that a well-designed system based on these principles would maintain chemical contamination and turbidity well under control so that the purity of the waters in and passing from Buttle Lake would not be impaired insofar as human health and fish life are concerned."

Needless to say, an arrogant press, hell-bent on destroying the Government, ignored the reprimand. There were further exchanges over the succeeding days, weeks and months, all of which provided controversy and those all important headlines. The media always having the last say by virtue of sole control over what is to be published, or broadcast, continued to create the illusion of being right. In the episode recounted, the truth had not come out. The public, who are forever being exhorted to take a position, could only form opinions on the basis of distorted reporting.

In all fairness, in this case, it was one particular leading newspaper that was spearheading the attack on the Government. Another paper, of lesser circulation, *The Columbian,* published a fine and succinct editorial under the headline "COSTLY CROCODILE TEARS". In part it said:

> " . . . The blatant bias exhibited by a Vancouver daily against this development — an attitude obviously politically motivated — forces us to break silence.
>
> "It's time someone considered the economics of this development and brushed aside the crocodile tears encouraged by political strategists dedicated to embarrassment of the B.C. Pollution Control Board and the provincial government with little regard to the welfare of British Columbia.
>
> "True, this new mining operation happens to be located in a provincial park and there are those who would condemn it on this basis alone. But it is also true that of the 560,000 acres in the park, the mine operation and townsite involves the clearance of only 200 acres at the most . . .
>
> "It is also a fact that the company has contributed some $2 million toward a first class access road the length of this lake which has previously been a recreational mecca accessible only to the wealthy sportsman equipped with aircraft or launch . . .
>
> "If the pristine attitude adopted by pseudo-conservationists is permitted to dominate in this issue, this wealth of ore will remain in the ground and revenue amounting to something like $10 million annually will be denied this province . . . "

Still Hope for Media

Editorials like the preceding confound some of my charges against the media — which goes to prove that there's still hope. At no time throughout the Buttle Lake affair had commonsense prevailed. As I recounted earlier, this fiasco resulted in the rewriting of the pollution control legislation and the production of much environmental nonsense. The servants of the people were accused of collusion and the environmental parasites won another victory in the press.

And now, a couple of decades later, what is the situation? The media unabashedly continue to use the Buttle Lake issue to foster and bolster the cause of the environmental anarchists through hysterical reporting. *The Daily Colonist* of May 31, 1980, displayed the following in bold print, right across the top of the front page: "Buttle Lake could be dead within a decade". The article stated: "Buttle Lake is fast approaching the day when it will no longer support aquatic life. Unless trends can be reversed the lake has 10 years to live." All very dramatic, but the bottom line is: Would the reporter be prepared to place a bet on the Lake's demise?

Past Involvement

Because of the writer's past official involvement with the Buttle Lake issue, I felt obliged to pursue the report of pending disaster. The reporter had purported to be quoting the author of a February, 1980 "Preliminary Review" report on Buttle Lake water quality. The response from the report's author was, and I quote: "The *(Colonist)* article was based on the reporter's reading of my report, not on an interview. I am sure you will not find either the words 'dead' or 'dying' in my report." Believe it, or not, he is correct. In fact, the report states that: "The quality of the water leaving Buttle Lake was better than the acceptable limits for Canadian Drinking Water Standards." The reader should be fully aware while considering this statement that the Standards quoted **are among the most stringent in the world,** not, mark you, because they are needed, but rather because such stringent standards are readily attainable in the Canadian environment due to abundant water resources and a limited pollution base.

What the report established, in effect, was that there had been a *measurable* change in water quality, measurable meaning just that — it can be measured using today's highly sophisticated and sensitive techniques. The report does not establish if the change is detrimental, of no consequence, or beneficial, as the case might well be. It is known that waters deficient in minerals, just as with soils, can be poor supporters of biological processes. The pharmaceutical business thrives on the knowlege that the human body can often benefit from the addition of minerals, over and above those supplied by our daily diet — vitamin C, Geritol, et al. It is possible, quite probable in fact, that the total minerals being added to the lake could be just as much beneficial as detrimental.

Philosophy Wrong

On May 30, 1981, there appeared in the press a statement that Western Mines was to be prosecuted under the Federal Fisheries Act for an alleged violation of their discharge permit. Specifically, a spokesman for the Federal Fisheries explained that a matter of some concern was an increase in the amount of dissolved zinc. Since zinc is one of the elements being discharged, it should not be surprising to find an increase. The question, of course, must be, is the increase harmful and to whom or what? Five days later the press carried another report to the effect that a Washington State fish company admitted that " . . . its (feed) product caused blindness in about one million chinook fingerlings in British Columbia hatcheries and about 20 million in Washington hatcheries." The article went on to explain " . . . the blindness was caused by a lack of zinc in the feed . . . To correct the situation we started adding additional zinc."

The foregoing must not be taken at face value, an artifice used by the environmental cult to win converts when a situation can be misrepresented to their advantage. Zinc, like other heavy metals, can be in different forms, with varying degrees of toxicity. With respect to drinking water standards, the technical literature points out that " . . . zinc has no known adverse physiological effects upon man except at very high concentrations (hundreds of times greater than the Buttle Lake concentrations) . . . zinc is an essential and beneficial element in human nutrition." What this brief technical side-trip shows is that the line between what is, or is not harmful, requires the application of a lot of commonsense.

To press charges under the Fisheries Act on the basis of an increase in levels of elements which occur naturally and beneficially in the waters of the lake, which is low in mineral content, is incomprehensible. As brought out forcefully in a later chapter, the philosophy used by the regulatory agencies in setting effluent criteria is wrong. Simply stated, it is not possible to mine without some changes in the environment. If society is to continue its enhancement of our life-style, controls must equate the economic and social returns against environmental losses, *if any*.

When an industry is created, be it a pulpmill, a mine, or whatever, part of the natural land environment must be sacrificed, or traded-off, to facilitate the realities of location and operation. It follows just as logically that part of the water environment must equally well be yielded in the interests of economic reality. Water covers close to three-quarters of the surface of the planet. It is well to reflect that only a small portion of the land area is habitable or suitable for man, the greater portion being mountains, deserts, jungles and arid or frozen wasteland. As a consequence, greater use must be made of our water space if we are to preserve and make the best use of our more precious land areas. In short, society must recognize that portion of the extensive water areas which envelope the globe, must be traded off for use in the natural and essential process of dispersing, dissipating and assimilating wastes. The fraction of the water so needed is infinitesimal compared with what is available.

Self-education Report

Again, in late 1982, a media "expert" churned out an article under the heading, "Westmin Mine Threatening Life in Lake". The article, of course, had all the nebulous ingredients and innuendoes to produce a state of fear, and I quote, " . . . threatening aquatic life in the watershed . . . the fish may be in danger . . . although statistically valid (the data) suggests that fishing in Buttle Lake has become poorer . . ."

Not to be outdone, an editorial column in the same paper was headed, "Buttle Lake Dying by Inches". The substance of the column was that the mining operation was "poisoning the water". The item also included the usual attack on the ever-ready whipping boy — the Government, in the words: "Despite the mounting evidence, the province continues to snooze like Rip Van Winkle. Only when the water supply for Campbell River becomes downright dangerous will the government leap to the defence of that community's citizens, undoubtedly making suitable sounds of outrage in the process."

And the facts? The report that stimulated the outcry consists of three volumes totalling 960 pages, all paid for by the taxpayer, in what amounts to the self-education of the authors, who, while being employees of the government had the effrontery to preface the report with the words, "The views expressed in this document are those of the authors and do not necessarily reflect the policies or position of the Waste Management Branch." Just what were they hired for, Mr. Minister?

The report, therefore, ends up being but one more statement without credibility to add to the mountain of such documents already in existence. In keeping with the environmental attitude, the report neither deals with the economic realities of society nor the truths of nature.

It pursues the all too obvious theme — more handouts for environmental parasites. It discloses that no less than eight research or investigative contracts were let to Universities and so-called consultants. One would be naive to believe that the recipients of such funds would ever be so audacious as to reach a conclusion that might terminate such a lucrative livelihood.

The report, in essence, condones the widespread ridiculous attitude that industry must operate without upsetting the surrounding environment. If the same approach were applied to our civilization, then cities and everything pertaining to our way of life must surely be abandoned. How happy would be the Indians! This hypocritical persecution of industry must be seen for what it is.

Fish Still There

The main drive of the report is that fish habitat must be maintained, come what may. And what of the economic realities? The mine, at its 1980 level of operation provided jobs for over 300 permanent employees and possibly another 100 or more on a secondary basis. And of fishing? In truth, all the fish caught in the lake over any year would not provide the economic support for a single person. In any event, the fish are still there.

And another truth: Believe it or not, the lake falls into the scientific classification "oligotrophic", that is, it is naturally low in biological life and the supporting food chain. In addition, the use of the lake as a hydro-electric storage reservoir, subject to annual drawdown, is another complicating factor that has been ignored by the anti-mining fanatics. The report claims that " . . . fishing in Buttle Lake has become progressively poorer." There is little room for argument that, in view of the low natural productivity of the lake, the decline in fish is more likely to stem from the pressure of fishermen, rather than from the mine.

Of course, the mining operation is made to look guilty. The report states that it has a " . . . history of non-compliance" with the conditions of the discharge permit. The irrationality of condemning on the basis of discharge criteria, and the fallacies of such criteria are fully addressed in the chapter on the Public Inquiries` Farce, where it is established that the present philosophy towards standard setting is wrong.

At this juncture, however, for the benefit of the reader, a few of the flaws of the report should be mentioned. It states, " . . . a serious deterioration of water quality is emerging." In the facts column one discovers such statements as " . . . the water quality continues to meet public drinking water standards" and " . . . that consumption of Buttle Lake fish does not present a health hazard." As expected, such assurances are not acceptable to the proponents of "fear", for they go on to proclaim " . . . some fish did show levels for possible concern." The report does not define what is "possible concern". It may be in the same category as another warning that " . . . Trumpter Swans, an endangered species, overwinter on the lake." How they are threatened is not explained, but never mind, it is all wonderful motherhood stuff so no explanation is necessary unless you are an environmental heretic.

To put the Buttle Lake espisode into perspective for the moment, until later chapters are read, we must not forget that the changes which occur at a mining site are, in geological terms, insignificant when reviewed against the awesome transformations that nature has done and will continue to do to our planet. At the time of writing there is a Reuter report that 16 million birds have suddenly disappeared from Christmas Island.

Speculation is that a drastic change in ocean conditions may be responsible. A similar freak occurence took place some years ago with respect to anchovy off the coast of Chile. Such are the vagaries of nature. What we must be concerned about in evaluating resources, is not the so-called delicate and questionable value of an eco-system, but rather the realities and benefits of "trade-offs", which must be made so that our society can maintain the position of well-being that has been achieved through industrialization.

Chapter Six

PUBLIC ATTITUDES AND HYPOCRISY

In the midst of Victoria, the capital of British Columbia, there is a pretty body of water called The Gorge. The upper reaches of The Gorge, known as Portage Inlet, has a small peninsula named Christie Point reaching out into the inlet for a distance of about one-third of a mile. Back in 1959, when I first became aware of this attractive piece of land, there was a mild controversy developing as to its destiny.

As is usual with attractive water front property, developers were showing interest. Also, since the peninsula had such an extremely attractive setting, it had been suggested by some, implying to be civic-minded, that it should be acquired as a park. The owners of the property were not opposed to this idea. The Parks Branch of the Provincial Government had an evaluation run on the land but found that it did not qualify as a park under their guidelines. It was determined to be too small, the wrong shape and not properly located, plus all the other reasons which a Department of Government finds when it wants to wash its hands of a problem. As a result, developers decided to push their interests. It was at this point that I became officially involved with the matter.

Subdivide for homes

It was decided initially to subdivide the land for private homes, using ground disposal for the sanitary wastes. A segment of the public which surrounded Portage Inlet became incensed with the proposal. They made their views known and the media took up their cause, as it made good copy. The point at issue was alleged to be the pollution of the Gorge, by seepage from proposed septic tanks.

At that time, I was responsible for assessing, under the Health Act, the suitability of the proposal. As well as the developers' plans, several bulky petitions arrived on my desk. This was my first introduction to petitions. My engineering training took over and I found myself objectively reviewing the hundreds of signatures. I found to my surprise (being naive at that time) that a great many of the signatures appeared to have similar characteristics. Quite often three or four names of one family appeared in identical handwriting, obviously written by the same person. Many cases were evident of names of different people in a common hand. As the petition had been gathered by several different parties, the same names appeared several times in different places. I recall while visiting a downtown Victoria department store, nowhere near Christie Point, being solicited for my signature. Naturally then, the review of the addresses on the petition showed that many of the signatories did not live anywhere near the Gorge.

All in all, about one third to one half of the signatures were obviously not valid. While this analysis was purely academic, there were still enough genuine names left to make it evident that a fairly large group of people purported to be concerned, particularly those living around Portage Inlet. The petition, and this is very important, was specifically concerned with possible pollution of the Inlet waters from the proposed development.

Counter Offer

From an inspection of the site, there was little doubt that much of the effluent, if discharged to the ground, would eventually reach the inlet, as a result of rock outcrops, unsuitable soil, the general shape of the peninsula and other factors. Thus, on a strictly technical basis, to the delight of the objectors, the developers were advised that the site was not suitable for use of the conventional septic tank system. The developers countered with an offer to put in much more sophisticated treatment systems, using filter beds, carefully selecting the sites, etc. None of the alternatives offered were deemed entirely satisfactory. In any event, as the cost was going to be high, the proposal to subdivide for homes was dropped.

In time, as always happens, a new developer became interested, this time proposing apartments, as this would improve the economics to meet treatment costs. It was now proposed to collect the sewage and pump it to a municipal sewer, a little over a mile away. This scheme was approved, as it met all public health and other Government requirements. *It was then that I got my eyes opened.* The objectors turned hostile, several came in to see me, others phoned, many wrote, all were outraged that the peninsula was to be developed, and not with homes, as first proposed, but with "objectionable" apartments, which in the end, to better suit site requirements, ended up as townhouses.

The opponents assured me in no uncertain terms that they were opposed to any development on Christie Point. In fact, they made it quite clear that the objections based on pollution were not so much a concern for pollution, but a desire to block any development, of any kind, on the Point. Those whose houses overlooked the area were most upset that they would now have to look across the water at fellow-dwellers, and made it quite clear that this was why they got on the anti-pollution bandwagon. I felt little sympathy for such hypocrisy and made it quite clear that if they wanted to block development on the Point, that is what the petition should have been about and should have been taken through appropriate political channels.

Vindictive Attitudes

While the Christie Point development is quite attractive and no doubt greatly enjoyed by those who live there, there is little doubt that the public interest would have been better served by using the area as a recreational park. The subtlety in this issue, which I soon learned to detect in practically all environment outcries, was that pollution *per se* was not in truth the issue. There were and are, all too often, deeper issues concealed, which upon examination invariably relate to selfish, envious and occasionally vindictive attitudes.

Over the years which followed. I was to note, almost without exception, that every protest submitted on the basis of alleged pollution had an ulterior motive. Certainly all displayed a degree of unbelievable selfishness. Many years later, when holding hearings on the Gulf Islands in the Straits of Georgia with respect to waste discharge from proposed subdivisions, I was again shocked at the selfish and irrational attitudes of many of the Islanders attending public hearings which I chaired in 1968. It had now become so obvious that objectors had other motives than those of pollution that my opening and closing remarks at the public hearings on Salt Spring Island in 1968 are not only pertinent but illustrate a disconcerting trend in public attitudes:

> "The purpose of this meeting is to look at the *facts* and to determine if pollution is a probability.
>
> "The Pollution Control Act is not to control development. The size, location or type of development is of no concern to those that administer the Act. Indeed, for us to attempt to control development by use of the Pollution Control Act, would be an intolerable bureaucratic interference . . .
>
> "Albeit, in some cases, because of the nature of the waste to be discharged, development, in fact, may be curtailed or prohibited if an acceptable method of disposal is not found.
>
> "My purpose is to allow you an opportunity to lay before me

your facts, which I may take into account in arriving at a technical decision as to whether or not this proposal is sound . . ."

Hostile Reception

There followed a long, hostile hearing. Those participating made it quite clear that "outsiders" were not welcome. Attempts were made to intimidate me, as chairman of the hearing. A loud speaker system had been erected outside the hall to transmit the proceedings to those who preferred to stay outside in the sun and guzzle beer. There were many people in the hall displaying placards and banners with intimidating captions. Before proceedings got underway I ordered the removal of the speaker system and the offending banners. The press too, of course, had played its role of inciting the public.

As it happened, in the interests of proper administration, a second hearing was needed some three months later. It too followed the same hostile pattern. Participants made it quite obvious they were not interested in having developers opening up subdivisions for "outsiders". My closing remarks at the second inquiry were:

" . . . it is my duty to now evaluate this application and to arrive at a decision based on the technical facts, as to whether or not the proposal will cause pollution . . . may I make it quite clear that the Pollution Control Act is to control pollution, not development.

"To reassure you that an unbiased decision will be made, I offer the following. On Monday I dispatched a letter to an applicant advising that his application had been refused. It is of academic interest to point out that there were no objections at all to the application. But none-the-less, because it was technically unsound, it was rejected.

"I might also add that an application by the District of Central Saanich was rejected last year, even though a high degree of treatment was offered. The point of discharge was unsatisfactory. I simply mention these instances to assure you that my decisions are not arbitrary, but related to the facts."

In due course, a discharge permit was issued. A review of resulting press reports is quite revealing. First the headlines, "ISLANDERS BOIL OVER APPROVAL GIVEN OUTFALL", "CONFLICT OF INTEREST AT HEARINGS, SAYS M.L.A." (who, by the way, was not present, and although a member of Government, was so irresponsible as to choose to undermine the administration for the sake of a few selfish votes). "SALT SPRING DECLARES WAR ON POLLUTION", "FURIOUS ISLANDERS FIGHT SUBDIVISION". No one can deny that it's great copy for the media. Now let's look at some of the remarks made by objectors.

> " . . . Government's own pollution watchdog sets precedent which will endanger the beaches, sea life and health of residents of all Gulf Islands unless he is overruled."

or this:

> " . . . an appeal will be made to Keenan's superiors and if it is not successful then the matter will be taken to the Provincial Cabinet . . . the whole Island's population is bitterly angry over Keenan's action in issuing a permit . . . If this is allowed to stand, it will destroy the Gulf Islands — there are so many new subdivisions proposed."

Emotionalism and Hysteria

I believe the remarks made by me were very appropriate in view of the facts as presented at the hearing. The press reports certainly confirm the presence of emotionalism and hysteria which callous, insensitive reporters were all too willing to whip up into a raging inferno to make copy. The anti-everything elements were out in force. But the issue was not pollution; the measures taken to prevent same were more than adequate. The developer was in fact prepared to put in whatever would meet all requirements.

The public hearing had been called to assure the local populace that proper care was being taken to prevent pollution, which might in anyway impair the usefulness of the receiving waters. But the local people were not prepared to be rational. Furtive politicians representing the area were too intimidated to support the facts. The local elected representative of the Legislature had on more than one occasion called my office. It was all too evident that he was not prepared to present facts to his constituents; he was only interested in going along and could not understand why I too could not acquiesce to this form of anarchy, which politicians have allowed to warp decision-making.

In truth, subdivision development was the real issue and shortly after the issuance of the permit, which was appealed, but unsuccessfully, the Government put a land freeze on Gulf Island development. But at the time, pollution was the whipping boy. I was accused of being arrogant and highhanded, because I refused to knuckle under. In other words, to find favour with the Islanders, all I had to do was adopt a little of the hypocrisy that is all too prevalent in the political system.

Perhaps the reason for the hostile front resulted from the fact that I had conducted an earlier hearing on another of the Gulf Islands, which when it was over, the objectors treated us all to tea and cakes, a most gracious gesture. Unfortunately, for the objectors, that permit too was granted. So having seen kindness fail, the second group perhaps decided to follow the militant route.

Hatred and Venom

It is sad to concede that militancy now seems to be an integral part of the decision-making process. The news media constantly offers examples of how vitriolic, selfish and capricious members of the public can be when demanding their so-called democratic rights. In one news report, the Mayor of a local Victoria-area municipality claimed he was shaken by the hatred and venom directed against him following approval of a housing development.

He is quoted as saying, "There were many filthy, foul-mouthed remarks directed at me . . . I couldn't believe it, it was a shattering experience." Personally, I am all too familiar with the scene. The protestors who pack meetings, demand their "democratic" right to be heard. But woe-be-tide the decision-maker when he exercises his democratic right and votes against them. It is ironical, of course, that the Mayor in this instance attained office through a platform opposing a development issue in another area of the municipality. Obviously, to each the system is only democratic when it agrees with his own bias.

Destroy Quality of Life

At a seminar in Victoria on the subject of growth and jobs, the position taken by one speaker, a lawyer and a former Liberal Member of Parliament who pushes the environmental cause at every opportunity, was that we should attempt to discourage growth in the Victoria area as more people will simply destroy the quality of life which we few already enjoy. True, indeed, but the bottom line has to be that most of us making up this unique middle class drop-out society came from somewhere else and by so doing have already made a contribution to the inevitable outcome. If growth is to be limited then the only equitable solution would be to set up a transfer system whereby it is only permissible to reside in the area for a limited period of time, then move out to allow others to enjoy the amenities for their allotted term. Such regimentation of life-style choices would certainly meet the goals of socialism, a spectre ever before us as increased population continues to limit our choices and individualism.

Every now and then the media confounds our feelings towards it with an astute article. The Editorial in *The Daily Colonist* of November 10, 1978 puts this whole matter into a perspective that I cannot equal:

> "There is an ugly selfish trend apparent in Greater Victoria these days when people gather together at public hearings to "protect" their neighbourhood.
>
> "Nothing is more understandable than each of us wanting to guard our homes. After all, the house we live in and the land around it we tend, that's our personal world, the place where we spend much of our lives, the biggest investment most of

us will ever make. Not just in money either — in blood, sweat and tears, in hard work, sometimes over many years, making it just the way we want it to be.

"But when some neighbours speak so passionately in defence of their corner of the world at public meetings nowadays, it has become increasingly obvious what they want is to shut out anyone else.

"One of them put it frankly the other day saying he believes every time someone new moves into the community it lowers the standard of living, however slightly, for all of us.

"It leaves one wondering where he would be, indeed where many of us would be, if that attitude had prevailed when we decided to move here."

As I said earlier when criticizing the media, it is by far the mightiest weapon we have for social justice *when responsibly used.*

Fish and Game Club Nonsense

To illustrate the general public-wide nonsense going on and being condoned, let us look at but a few examples from the hundreds of letters which were on file. The first comes from a Fish and Game Association Club:

" . . . The members of this association view with grave concern the Municipality's application for a sewer outlet into Somenos Creek. We wish to draw to your attention that should this application be granted that Somenos Creek will have in one mile, three sewage disposal systems on a stream, that at one time was the principle spawning ground for the native cut-throat trout . . . We feel that the members of your board would be well advised to recommend to the Municipality that a one sewer system be instigated in this district, with the discharge at the mouth of this Creek to take advantage of maximum dispersal in the Cowichan River which has a controlled minimum flow."

So what is wrong with this you ask? Nothing, absolutely nothing. Indeed the letter shows what would appear to be a great deal of commonsense. After review of all the facts it was decided the objection should stand, as the logic was sound. A letter was despatched to the Municipality in question, ordering them to consider discharge to the Cowichan River. The advice was taken. Six months later a new application, adopting the proposal outlined, was submitted by the Municipality to be followed immediately by a letter from the *same* Fish and Game Association group which read:

"The members of this Association wish to oppose the application by the Municipality to discharge sewage into the

Cowichan River. Clean, fresh water is not ours to do with as we wish, it is inherited, and we are obligated to pass it on to future generations."

I will leave the matter with the reader to rationalize. Needless to say, a permit was issued.

Union Protest

In order to show that the environmental nonsense is not restricted to any particular segment of the population, I am offering examples from as wide a variety of sources as possible. Here's one from a Workers' Union. An application seeking a permit to discharge was advertised in the press. It said, in part:

" . . . the type of treatment to be applied is primary and secondary treatment . . . "

The letter of objection from the Union said:

"It is our contention that any additional raw sewage dumped . . . will rob the Kootenay River of vital oxygen and render it useless . . ."

The charge that the Kootenay River would be robbed of oxygen to the point of making it useless is, speaking technically, utter nonsense, as the river in question is large and the quantity of effluent small. However, the point of interest to this story is that the application was for highly-treated effluent, not raw sewage as referred to in the objection. That emotionalism was rampant with those who wrote the letter, is all too obvious. Perhaps, in a way, this also illustrates what is wrong on the labour scene, if unions are taking such arbitrary and illogical stands. In addition to the union protest, the local Wildlife Association objected with the words:

"We wish to add our protest, with those of others to the application to dump raw sewage. . . "

Note again the erroneous assertion; no acknowledgement of the treatment which was advertised.

Both parties were contacted to clarify that the effluent was to receive *secondary* treatment, and in the light of this, were they prepared to withdraw their objections? Neither party agreed to withdraw one word, in spite of their ridiculous positions. The objections were simply overruled and a permit issued. It is hypocrisy of this nature that has brought about the adoption of totally unrealistic, arbitrary and economically untenable pollution control discharge objectives and environmental attitudes in this Province. And what is worse, these hypocritical philosophies are being condoned by our courts, to the detriment of society.

Some time ago I received through the mail, a brochure advising of a new book entitled *Environmental Assessment Law in Canada*.

While it is inevitable, it is indeed dismal to observe that the legal profession will be more than pleased to utilize to their monetary advantage the hypocritical nature of environmentalism as an outlet for their oblique double-talk. I recall one environmental lawyer on a public panel on which I sat talking nonsense about the legal rights of fish. He never did get around to telling us how they could protect themselves from those vicious, barbed, cunningly disguised hooks which fishermen drag through the water.

Before closing out this chapter, let us look at a couple of the more general types of protest which come in from the man in the street, that person who relies on the media to keep him informed; poor trusting soul. Masses of objections were received routinely from people who knew nothing of what a particular application was about. Here is a quote from a typical letter from someone who lived over 300 miles from the point of discharge to which the person was protesting:

"As a British Columbian, I object. I am not acquainted with the developer, nor the exact location of the subdivision, but the request is an abomination."

Perhaps this quote from another objector has the answer to our problems:

"I say it is time to halt this method of getting rid of waste by dirtying up our rivers. The world is crying for fertilizers, China is famine ridden, India is cow-ridden, let's ship our shit there instead of pouring it into our streams and rivers."

Incidentally, maybe the writer last-quoted knows more than I am giving him credit for. In certain parts of rural India, they have developed a very practical method of disposing of human excreta. Outhouses are located in such a way that the waste material drops into pig-feeding troughs, where it is quickly "recycled" as food for the piggies which are kept by those who can afford them. In China, too, human excreta is treasured in rural areas as a source of energy for cooking and heat, as well as being used widely as a fertilizer.

People shun reality, preferring to be hypocritical. I recall well shocking a gathering of the learned members of the Union Boards of Health that I was addressing at a conference in Penticton, with the Minister of Health sitting beside me at the head table. In presenting the subject of my talk, "Pollution in Perspective", I posed the reality of discharging treated waste to rivers, as they are, in effect, nature's sewers. There were audible gasps of disbelief and protest from the audience as I continued to point out that rivers are nature's way of getting rid of the excess waters which fall on the good earth. When I sat down after completing the forty minute address, the Minister leaned over and whispered, "Good for you, I daren't say what you just did." Such is the way of politics.

Chapter Seven

BUREAUCRACY

Part I: THE PROVINCIAL SCENE

The Public Service " . . . is too large and growing too fast. There are many on the staff who are being paid more than they are worth. And many employees are grossly under-employed." This damning statement is attributed to John Starnes, a retired executive of the External Affairs Department, who headed a Federal Treasury Board task force on expenditures in the public service. "The general attitude" according to Starne's investigations and his long-time association with the public service, "is one of weary, sometimes cynical acceptance of a system of public administration grown too complex and too large to control. . . and suffering from a drift at all levels." This drift is all too evident in the bureaucratic administration of environmentalism.

In the mid 1970's the Provincial Government received a request from an agency of Environment Canada to participate in an all-out study of environmental issues pertaining to the Yukon River, which rises in northern British Columbia and flows northward through the Territory of Yukon and the State of Alaska into the Bering Sea. No official reason was given for the study. The Provincial representative appointed to participate was unable to attend the initial meeting in Vancouver. The author was delegated to go instead.

There was present at that first meeting some ten senior representatives of various bureaucratic agencies. As the meeting was preparing to get underway, I asked the chairman by what authority we had been called together. There was a brief silence as people around the table glanced furtively at one another. After an interminably long pause, someone mumbled that they couldn't understand my question, as I was obviously present as a result of the authority of the Provincial Government. I rebutted that I was present only as an observer to find out what was going on and to decipher by what authority the meeting was called. Only the first part of the statement was true as far as my department was concerned; the request for the authority was of my own initiative, being all too cognizant of how bureaucrats operate.

Creating Work

The chairman eventually, and with some hesitation and embarrassment, explained that the meeting had been initiated as a first step in preparing a memorandum to seek federal departmental authority for the study, as there was a need in the minds of those at the table that such should be done. I responded, a little heatedly, that it looked to me that a bunch of bureaucrats were simply trying to create work for themselves. With sheepish grins, several at the table nodded their heads, while the chairman suggested that the matter could be put that way, if I so wished.

Upon returning to my office in Victoria, I immediately drafted a memorandum stating the facts as presented and pointedly asked what was the Provincial position. No response was obtained. I never attended another meeting as I had, in the first instance, only been a substitute. The study was initiated and completed at great expense, including visits to the area by numerous bureaucrats all the way from Ottawa, some 4,000 miles to the east. What purpose the study served other than feeding public servant egos, or to what use it has, or can be put, defies rational explanation, as no public or political terms of reference had been prescribed.

While the above is more of a federal bureaucratic matter, it has been introduced here as it establishes, rather well, the true nature of the bureaucratic scene in environmental issues and should assist the reader to better understand the vagaries involved. Professor C. Northcote Parkinson many years ago gave us an astute insight into the flaws of the bureaucracy in his amusing and delightful book, *Parkinson's Law*. He explained, "Politicians and taxpayers have assumed that a rising total in the number of civil servants must reflect a growing volume of work to be done", a proposition he effectively made look ridiculous.

Two Headed Monster

Environmental management first emerged in British Columbia as a pollution control entity under the Health Department. This was quite understandable. The need for public health legislation had come to the fore towards the close of the last century. Such legislation invariably covered the discharge of domestic wastes, well-known for its dreaded capabilities of spreading communicable diseases. Engineers, with specialized training in environmental and public health issues, were on staff. Thus in the mid-1950's when it was first decided in British Columbia to legislate pollution control as a specific entity, the day-to-day administration of the technical aspects of the legislation was placed in the hands of the Health Department.

Unfortunately, the administration of environmental issues within the structure of the Health Department left much to be desired. In keeping with so many of our bureaucracies, they had to live with the unavoidable conflict of the mythical two-headed monster. On the one hand, there is the centralized organization purporting to have the final authority, while on the other hand there are established local health entities, under medical health officers, to carry out the administration of the legislation in the field. Because of the inherent nature of administrators, autonomy inevitably becomes an issue, giving rise to much conflict.

Predictions of Sleeping Sickness

In the mid-1960's a letter from a medical doctor appeared in the press under the headline "POLLUTION IN THE PROVINCE". It went:

> "I have a photostat from the Minnesota Emergency Conservation Committee, which is a seething indictment. . . on the overall degree of air, water and soil pollution which exists in British Columbia. . . and mainly on account of our 'stink mills' — horrible 'crimes against humanity' — and the filthy state of the major rivers, lakes and tidal estuaries. It is indeed a sad reflection on the lack of moral fibre and intestinal fortitude of the provincial health branch, which, obviously, is both incompetent and impotent, and which must share the responsibility for the continuation of the escalating pollution problem, particularly for the epidemics of 'sleeping sickness' which could strike this province in 1966.
>
> "This prediction follows on my warning to the deputy minister of health and his aides in 1963-4, when I was a medical health officer in the Province. But my advice was rejected on the grounds that I was not a sanitary engineer. Yet, sanitary — or any other — engineers are not versed in microbiology and thus are not capable of passing an opinion properly in the matter of what really is a biomedical problem in sanitation.
>
> "Therefore, in the interest of the public health, this matter should be brought to the attention of the general public who are the unfortunate victims of gross bureaucractic mis-administration and selfish interests!"

The letter was signed by a medical doctor, M.D., D.P.H., whose name need not concern us. While the writer of the letter claimed to be a former medical Health Officer, he failed to point out that he had been dismissed from Government Service, his judgment on environmental matters being not the least of the reasons for dismissal. His predictions of sleeping sickness in 1966 was a false alarm; no epidemic occurred, nor did his other doomsday horrors.

The doctor stated that his advice on sanitary engineering matters had been rejected on the grounds that he was not a sanitary engineer. At the time of the events I was, as Director of Public Health Engineering, in charge of sanitary engineering matters in the region under his control as Medical Health Officer. I recall distinctly a meeting in my office in Victoria. He had been called to central office at the Deputy Minister's request as a result of grave concern arising from his actions as Medical Health Officer. He met first with myself to discuss sanitary engineering matters, later with the Deputy Minister and (I believe) finally with the Minister.

Pleasantly Surprised

With regard to the meeting in my office, I was pleasantly surprised to find that we appeared to reach a quick understanding as to what the score was and who made the decisions in sanitary engineering matters. When I reported this later to my seniors in the hierarchy, I was told to be cautious, as other meetings had not gone too well. I certainly recall some shocked faces and hushed comments in the department after the meeting with the Deputy Minister. Apparently there was some confusion as to who was chastizing whom. My hopes that agreement had been reached were indeed short lived. No sooner had the doctor returned to his fold than all hell broke loose. It was soon obvious that sanitary engineering matters were to be decided on his whim, rather than by the application of the scientific knowledge within the department.

The reader can be forgiven if he cannot understand why authorative action was not taken forthwith. Those in central office were certainly unanimous that the offending health officer should be discharged, but they were only one voice in the issue. The other head of the monster, the local councils and health boards, jealous of their autonomy, would not agree, though, eventually, when the situation became chaotic, they concurred with the wishes of central office.

Ulterior Motives

From an environmental stand-point, many aspects of the doctor's letter are most enlightening. They show the nonsense which allowed environmentalism to gain a voice in the decision-making process. First let us consider the Minnesota Emergency Conservation Committee referred to in the letter. It's a very imposing title. Since I have always sought the facts and made my case accordingly, I wrote to the Department of Health in the State of Minnesota. I was advised by them that the M.E.C.C. was an *ad hoc* group composed of a Chairman and a Secretary. The letter went on to say:

"We presume there may be others of this organization, although we know of none. They are a private organization with no connection whatsoever with any subdivision of government in the State of Minnesota. Their news releases tend to be hypercritical of government units. As you can conclude from this information, they (four names including the doctor's) are a part of a small group which is strongly opposed to the construction and use of sewage stabilization ponds. Each, we suppose, has his own reasons for such opposition, not all of which, we suspect, are included in the news releases."

Note the inference in the last sentence, that ulterior motives may be present, a proposition put earlier based on my own personal deductions from hundreds of meetings with those purporting to be environmentally concerned. There was much more all discounting the claims made by the doctor and his cohorts. The predictions that "epidemics of sleeping sickness" were about to strike the Province were ill-founded. At the time, to ascertain the position, I contacted my counterparts in other western Canadian provinces and in various States across the border, where lagoons were used extensively. The replies left no doubt that the charges were indeed environmental hysteria.

Financial Post's Devastating Article

When this whole farce was at its height, *The Financial Post* wrote a devastating article attacking the use of sewage lagoons under the heading "LOW COST SEWAGE DISPOSAL POOLS — UNDER FIRE AS DISEASE SPREADERS". Shortly thereafter, I received a call from a reporter of the *"Post"* who asked if I had seen the article and did I wish to comment, as he would be pleased to interview me. I made it very clear that the damage had been done and I expressed concern that a paper of the calibre of the *"Post"* had not checked its facts first.

For once, the media had a scapegoat. The reporter pointed out that his information had come from an article published in the *Canadian Medical Association Journal*. What better authority could he have? The article to which he referred had been submitted to the *C.M.A. Journal* and had been published as a "View Point". It was by none other than the good doctor of our story. Unfortunately, when the article had been published no disclaimer by the *Medical Journal* as to its authenticity had been included. The fact that the article, without scientific foundation, had been published in a leading medical journal had caused considerable concern to everyone involved. It was not based on facts, or on the extensive experience gleaned from the use of sewage lagoons over many years in many countries.

The type of incident just recounted was by no means an isolated occurrence. There were others. I recall well one Health Officer who exploited the local autonomy issue each time he wished to adopt an environmental posture contrary to the facts. As his position was often so outrageous, in exasperation, I once drafted a memorandum to the Director of Local Health Services recommending that he be fired, an action which the Director fully endorsed but could not execute because of the prized local autonomy.

Cat Keels Over

Of a lighter nature the following episode illustrates what can and does happen. One morning a memo from one of the health units arrived in my 'In' basket. It stated that a cat, while eating shellfish, had 'keeled over'. An investigation was requested. After a few pertinent phone calls a reply was drafted advising that samples of shellfish taken from the area be dispatched to the laboratory for analysis.

A few days later, a further memorandum reached my desk asking in what were the samples to be dispatched? A little taken aback, as I knew the health unit and the laboratory were in constant touch with one another, I contacted the laboratory and asked that the necessary sampling containers be sent to the health unit. A memorandum was dispatched to the unit advising of the action taken.

Again, a few days later, yet another memorandum reached my desk asking who was supposed to get the samples? An oath of exasperation escaped me. I telephoned the Medical Health Officer of the area involved to clarify what the health inspector's duties were. I was advised that there was some difficulty involved with obtaining the samples but that the matter would be reviewed.

A few days later I received a reply which explained that the only time sample oysters could be collected was at low tide and that the only suitable low tides were at 2 o'clock in the morning. The memorandum concluded:

> ". . . the sickness of one cat is not sufficient to warrant collection of samples at night."

Such then are the nature of the uncontrollable conflicts within our bureaucracies which frustrate rational administration.

There is no doubt that administrative failures of the type described, contributed to the climate which generated widespread environmental nonsense. How can the person in the street, in the face of such irrational behaviour, be expected to discern the truth? As a consequence, it came as little surprise when the management of environmental issues was transferred to the Water Resources Service, later to be renamed the Ministry of Environment. The name change was taken to counter both the meddling of federal environmentalists in areas of provincial jurisdiction, and the wailings of the eco-freaks.

Relinquished Position

When re-organization of the administration took place, I had the privilege of being both Director of Public Health Engineering and Executive Engineer of the Pollution Control Board. At transfer, I relinquished my position as head of Health Engineering. Little did I know what was in store for the new administration from those I had left. The Health Branch now saw the possible realization of the dream of all bureaucrats, authority without responsibility. Little-minded bureaucrats were to weave their webs of intrigue. Instead of wholeheartedly supporting the new regime by accepting the fact that authority had been transferred, they adopted an attitude to obtain an authoritative voice in the decision-making affairs of the pollution control legislation, while enjoying the enviable position that the responsibility for the outcome would be borne by others.

As in-fighting between Health and Pollution Control plays only a secondary role in this story, only those points essential to substantiate the disintegration of government administration in the face of environmental anarchy will be presented to show the irrational attitudes, which had, by the close of the '60's, taken hold of various Cabinet Ministers and had virtually destroyed the internal administration of the bureaucracies involved.

Instead of throwing their support behind the newly-formed pollution control administration, the Health Branch personnel fought to maintain a position of dominance over pollution control decisions. It seems to be a fact of life that bureaucratic departments must build onto themselves, futile time-consuming referral systems to sustain their right to exist. While the conflict was solely bureaucratic at the outset, the momentum picked up under the influence of the power-hungry Minister of Health, whose preposterous activities were touched on in chapter four.

Sources of Contention

Health officials, of course, could argue that they had a position of sorts, though much at variance with the *intent* of legislation changes. At the time, within the Health Act, there still remained the original and somewhat traditional authority pertaining to approval of public sewer systems. This had been a source of contention between the health and pollution control legislations for some time. When the two Acts were administered by the same staff, conflict could be curtailed.

Being cognizant of the hazards, at the time when transfer of pollution control administration was under discussion, the Deputy Minister of Health was advised in a memorandum that amendments would be needed to the legislation.

The advice of the memorandum was ignored. This, as much as

anything else, led to the administrative chaos created by the Minister of Health. It was this redundant legislative authority which had allowed the Minister to assume the role of the White Knight. He, like some of his bureaucratic underlings, revelled in the idea of authority without responsibility. Again, in 1967, when it was proposed to rewrite the Act because of the Buttle Lake mining episode, the powers that be were reminded in memoranda of February 1967 of various changes needed to the legislation to avoid duplication. But all was to no avail.

The following skeleton facts, abstracted from a hundred or so memoranda on the matter, should suffice to illustrate the total break-down in bureaucratic administration which occurred over the next two years and which was common to all agencies involved in environmental issues. These memoranda were in all cases directed to the top level, to either Ministers, or Deputy Ministers. A memo of September 1967 reads:

"During your absence there has been a sequence of events which must be given serious consideration. From a careful scrutiny of the facts and documents, it should be more than obvious that Health has set out to regain a large measure of authority in the field of pollution control. . .

"It is quite obvious from the final two paragraphs of the Health Minister's letter that he is not aware of the untenable situations which can arise . . . "

One year and twenty memoranda later, events were as per this memorandum to my Minister:

"If the situation was not of grave concern to me, I would not trouble you. I attach copies of press statements attributed to the Minister of Health.

"I find the statements in conflict with the intent of the legislation . . .

"On Wednesday, September 4, 1968, I am to address the Canadian Bar Association on the matter of 'Control and Regulation of Pollution'. In the paper which I have prepared, it is stressed that:

' . . . the foremost single factor affecting the development of a dynamic pollution control authority relates to a government declaration of policy . . . '

"I have maintained the position that the Pollution Control Act is this Government's declaration of its policy. The Minister of Health does not seem to agree and as he is a prominent Cabinet Minister I respectfully suggest that the position of the Act be clarified as it is not possible to apply rational administration under the circumstances."

Matters were, in all honesty, chaotic. Duplication of effort was now simply *a fait accompli*. Two groups of technical people were doing the same work, at taxpayers' expense. There was accumulating a mass of correspondence from confused developers, municipalities, engineers and others, seeking to know what was going on. I gathered together a number of significant letters and despatched them to the Deputy Minister and Chairman of the Board, with a memorandum which read:

> "The attached pieces of correspondence are irrevocable proof of contradictory and gross duplication of effort within the Government. Someone's efforts are redundant . . ."

A review of the pertinent correspondence clearly showed that the administrative hodge-podge resulted from the Cabinet's inability to formulate a policy to deal with environmentalism in a rational manner. That the Minister of Health had created an insurmountable barrier through imposition of his whims, was quite clear.

Resigned from Ministry

As no change appeared to be imminent, I resigned, *entirely of my own choice.* From my letter of resignation I abstract certain pertinent statements, which in a sense summarize all of the nonsense touched upon:

> "It is with regret that I must advise you of my decision to resign from the service; a decision I have arrived at with reluctance. There are several related reasons and I feel it is only fair to set them on paper.
>
> "Firstly, in view of the unrelentless pressure placed upon the Director over the past few years, during which support has been lacking in many areas, it is my considered opinion that I should seek a change in occupation to ensure that I preserve my physical and mental attributes. While many have been sympathetic to my position, few have really understood it.
>
> "Secondly, I have long advocated that the legislation, as formed in the Pollution Control Act, is more than adequate to meet the needs of the people of this Province to control pollution, but I have found, regrettably, that the Act has not been *accepted, respected or supported* by many in places of influence in the Service and in the Government. Perhaps the most obvious offenders within the Service have been those in the Health Department where, if sincerity prevailed, one would have expected to find the greatest support for the authority of the Pollution Control Act.
>
> "Thirdly, there are obviously those who cherish the hope that the control of pollution can be best accomplished with a maximum of public and political participation. While I

unequivocally acknowledge that in a democracy the views of the people must be heard, I also recognize an essential need for firm handling of opinions presented by intimidating minorities when such opinions create an improper perspective. I cannot help reflecting that the subject of pollution is a complex technological matter and should be guided and placed in the hands of competent technical personnel and removed from the emotional public arena, insofar as is possible. The decisions to be made under the Act cannot be made with public sentiments and emotions masking the real issues, nor can they be made to satisfy people with devious and ulterior motives.''

My Minister generously responded by saying in part:

"I have publicly indicated my regret and that of the Government that you have decided to terminate your service as Director of Pollution Control. I can understand your decision and appreciate the detailed letter you wrote to explain your position. Under the circumstances, it can be considered as being constrained.

"I am not positive that all of the problems will be removed in short order. However, I agree that there is a definite need for a change in legislation to remove the overlap of jurisdiction that makes the present situation so difficult.''

BUREAUCRACY

Part II: FEDERAL HYPOCRISY — BUREAUCRATIC AND POLITICAL

The internal squabbling of Provincial agencies, just described, is of little consequence when compared to the administrative chaos between the provincial agencies and that grandiose bureaucratic institution know as Environment Canada. This federal agency has, since its inception, been attempting to take over the authority for environmental control within the provinces. It is doing so by duplication of provincial control agencies. To establish themselves, under the guise of environmental concerns, the federal agencies are doing all in their power to intimidate the provinces. (Such should not surprise us as it is all part and parcel of the grander scheme of Ottawa to usurp provincial powers, whether constitutional or not, a position made very evident in the hassle over the repatriation of the Constitution in the early 80's and the offshore oil jurisdictional arguments.)

As for Federal skulduggery, it is perhaps of value to mention now that the Provincial legislation of British Columbia clearly stipulated that wastes shall not be discharged without a permit from the Provincial agency. Provincial legislation prescribes all the powers necessary for enforcement and for absolute control of pollution within the province. These requirements have been province-wide since early 1967. At that time no similar federal legislative authority existed. In the Fisheries Act there was a highly ambiguous clause dating back to 1860, covering, in very general terms, the discharge of wastes to waters frequented by fish. The conditions of the clause were, in fact, virtually unenforceable.

Formidable Powers

Thus, when it was decided by the Federal Government in 1970 to amend the Fisheries Act the clause in question was also changed as such action was purported to be in the best interests of fisheries. However, let us not be deceived. The reason for the change was not to protect the fish *per se,* it was the familiar Federal power play in operation.

Federal politicians and bureaucrats saw in environmentalism the long-awaited opportunity to reach right into areas of provincial jurisdiction and assume authority not given under the British North America Act, which was the legislative force in Canada until the bringing "home" of the Constitution in 1980. Environment Canada could, with some subtlety, through environmental control activities, intrude into the resource and industrial management issues of the provinces. The subtlety was even carried through the House of Commons where the Minister of Environment Canada in 1970, when asking for the amendments to the legislation, inferred that the Federal Government already had "these formidable powers". In his Speech to the House, the Minister said:

> "We have these formidable powers now. . . However, they are not specific enough. They are difficult to administer. They don't deal with wastes in quantitative terms. Nor do they relate, directly, to other pieces of Federal legislation."

All of which raises a question. If they were not specific, difficult to administer, didn't deal in quantitative terms and didn't relate to other legislation, did the legislation really have the powers, as the Minister claimed?

Empire Building

The inevitable outcome of this piece of political folly soon became apparent. Bureaucrats simply started iniquitous empire-building; the market was flooded with sets of Industrial Control Regulations and Guidelines. Neither the Federal legislation, nor its Regulations, took any account of provincial requirements where they existed.

For example, in April 1970, under the jurisdiction of the Provincial Pollution Control Act, a public inquiry was held in Vancouver "to resolve what technical considerations and measures must be provided by the Forest Products Industry in British Columbia for control of discharges to water, land, or air to satisfactorily ensure that pollution will not be caused. . . " Environment Canada was represented at the Inquiry by the presentation of a brief on behalf of the Department of Fisheries. The Brief contained, among other things, specific representations from the Minister of Environment Canada, which shall be referred to in a moment.

As a result of the Provincial Public Inquiry, pollution control Objectives for the forest industry were prescribed in September 1971. Shortly thereafter Environment Canada issued its objectives for the same industry. There was little or no correlation between the two. In many discussions which I personally had with those involved, it was apparent that the Federal Agencies had no intention of recognizing the jurisdictional rights of the Provincial legislation. They made it quite clear that they wished to impose their own statutes and made it equally clear that the best course of action for the province to follow would be to abdicate their position, by simply adopting the Federal Regulations and administering them on behalf of the Federal Government.

Duplication of Effort

In view of my knowledge of what happens when there is conflicting legislation causing overlap of jurisdiction, I wrote to the Federal Minister of Environment Canada in 1971. I pointed out that as a consultant to pulp and paper companies it was necessary for me to be fully cognizant of the true intent of the new Federal Regulations for Pulp and Paper Effluents. I also pointed out the intrusion of the Federal regulations into areas affecting resource management, a provincial right, and the fact that we already had Provincial regulations covering exactly the same area. After two attempts, I eventually obtained an answer. The reply said:

> "On your first comment, the regulations are not intended, nor will they in any way be used for controlling natural resource development. However, it is our desire to be . . . assured that adequate consideration will be given, in advance, to the installation of suitable pollution control equipment.
> "With respect to the regulations being developed in British Columbia, I agree that there *does appear to be some duplication of effort here,* * but the development of Provincial Regulations is consistent with my philosophy of the usefulness of national standards. *Not all Provinces have the strong pollution control authority which has been built up in British*

*Columbia** and will therefore not be in a position to develop meaningful industrial effluent standards. With the Federal Standards taking effect in those instances, a sense of uniformity will be conveyed across the country. The 'pollution havens' which could otherwise develop to the detriment of industrial progress in provinces such as British Columbia would not exist. . . "

Making a Name

The letter was signed by the Minister of Environment Canada. Just as in the case of the not-to-be-deterred Provincial Minister of Health versus Pollution Control, as recounted earlier, the Federal Minister was obviously hell-bent on making a name for himself through environmentalism. The fact that blatant duplication, admitted to in the above letter, was to occur, was of no consequence.

I was working on behalf of several forest industry clients to obtain provincial pollution control permits. In one particular case, negotiations had dragged on for over four years without resolution, the obstruction being Federal bureaucrats. A detailed pollution control program was presented to the Provincial authorities, showing how compliance with their regulations were to be implemented. In discussions, the Provincial authorities indicated agreement with the program. However, it was pointed out that there were certain differences with Federal Agencies which required resolution. Remember, a Provincial approval is here under consideration; the Provincial agencies were provided with all material necessary which in turn was made available as a courtesy to the duplicators in the department of Environment Canada. But the Environment Canada bureaucracy was in no way going to kow-tow to provincial underlings. And so the flow of letters started.

In 1972, the first action by the Federal bureaucracy was to advise all companies of the existence of their regulations and assumed authority. There then followed more specific letters. In the case I am presenting, in 1973, a letter arrived which said:

"We advised you early in 1972 of the promulgation of regulations under the Fisheries Act. . . We subsequently contacted you requesting your cooperation in forwarding, on a monthly basis, data on effluent quality . . . We wish to request now that you submit a detailed outline of your plans for water pollution abatement pursuant to the requirements of our Regulations. Following receipt and study of your plans, we will undertake an assessment of the proposals with you and with the B.C. Pollution Control Branch, with the objective of developing a mutually acceptable time frame for compliance . . ."

How is that for bureaucratic duplication? Not only that, the letter demands that the applicant prepare a second report showing how the Federal Regulations to control pulp mill effluents are to be met. Note the absolute lack of consideration for the applicant, who has already prepared a report showing how it is proposed to meet the Provincial pulp mill objectives. The request openly acknowledges, without so much as an apology, that there are two sets of bureaucrats and two sets of standards for the same discharge.

Hostility

About this time, I met with the writer of the letter in his office in the presence of another senior member of his staff. When I expressed concern about public waste and the fact that they were duplicating the provincial activities, I was told, with a little hostility:

"Why should it concern you, you're not there any more", an inference to the fact that I had formerly been Director of Pollution Control. So much for bureaucratic arrogance. A reply to the above-quoted letter was dispatched. It said, in part:

" . . . we have put forward a program aimed at meeting the objectives for the forest products industry as set forth by the Province. It is clearly apparent that we cannot have two different environmental control programs in the same mill and we have been proceeding on the assumption that any objections you may have to our program would be taken up with the Provincial agency."

A reply made it clear who wished to crack the whip:

" . . . we wish to reaffirm our request of August 30, 1973, for a detailed outline of your plans for a water pollution abatement program to comply with the requirements of the Federal Regulations."

As a result, a meeting was requested with the Provincial authorities to seek clarification of jurisdictional rights. The various pieces of correspondence were placed on the Provincial files, as copies of the Environment Canada correspondence had not been sent to the Pollution Control Branch, showing a basic lack of courtesy. Or was there in fact, a deliberate attempt to disguise the bureaucratic nonsense and duplication which prevailed?

The correspondence was left with the Provincial authorities with a covering letter which concluded:

"We do not want to play games and waste our time and the taxpayer's money. It would be much appreciated if we could have the benefit of your good advice as to how we should proceed in order to put an end to this nonsense."

Several Meetings

At the same meeting with the Provincial agency, it was pointed out by the Director of Pollution Control that the matter raised had been under review by the respective parties involved and that a meeting was scheduled within the next few days, at which it was hoped a reconciliation could be worked out. There had already been several such meetings. I found it hard to suppress cynical comments. Needless to say, nothing came of the meeting, as shortly thereafter a further letter arrived from the Feds which concluded:

> "We would be pleased to meet with you to undertake a full discussion of your Company's present effluent pollution abatement plans."

Another meeting with the Pollution Control Branch was arranged. After all, the application was for a Provincial Permit. The Federal agency was advised. It was explained that a meeting had been held with the Director of Pollution Control in Victoria and that we had been assured that the efforts to coordinate the Provincial-Federal regulations were progressing towards a satisfactory and early conclusion.

This brought forth a response from the Feds containing two very significant statements, leaving no doubts as to where the attempts at Provincial-Federal cooperation stood. The letter in part said:

> "As you noted, discussions are presently underway to coordinate the requirements of the Federal and Provincial agencies. . . This will in no way alter the fact that pulp mills must meet the Federal requirements as well as the Provincial Objectives. . . We would appreciate a reply to this letter outlining your intentions and the timing for the mill to comply with the Federal Pulp and Paper Effluent Regulations in order to avoid the necessity of Environment Canada having to unilaterally stipulate a schedule of compliance."

Well, that was plain enough! First of all, the statement "must meet the Federal requirements as well as the Provincial Objectives" makes it quite clear that the bureaucrat writing the letter fully condones duplication, waste of taxpayers' money and all the other things we usually say at such moments of exasperation. Secondly, the reference to "unilateral" action illustrates the pompous arrogance by Ottawa's bureaucrats in the environmental field, which rightly comes under Provincial jurisdiction. That this arrogance and assumed authority were condoned at the political level is readily illustrated. In the appendix of the 1970 Fisheries Brief, presented to the Public Inquiry in Vancouver, the Minister of Environment Canada said:

> "We have a number of world firsts to our credit. We (the Fisheries Department and industry together) can boast about

building four of the cleanest pulp mills anywhere in the world."

Mind you, Webster's definition of "boast" is "to speak with vanity, to brag, to crow, to praise extravagantly oneself" so if you wish to put this interpretation on the statement, then what follows is redundant. However, I don't believe that the dictionary definition is the way the statement was intended. Taking the statement at face value, it is fatuous. The four mills were built under Provincial Control permits prepared and issued, I might add, by myself. With regard to the first of these four mills, I recommended to the Provincial government that we retain an eminent consultant from the United States to prepare a comprehensive report on the matter of effluent discharge. This recommendation was accepted, a report was prepared and a permit was issued, in accordance with the recommendations of the report. The report, in its findings, took into account the wishes of the Department of Fisheries.

Good Relationship

At the time there was a close and extremely good working relationship with the Fisheries Department, as evidenced by kind remarks from the Director of the Pacific Region on the occasion of my resignation:

"You joined the Board just at the time when pollution matters were really beginning to receive public attention. I know that the task must have been difficult at many times, since there is generally an element of emotionalism attached to pollution. . . During this time we in the Department have enjoyed an excellent spirit of cooperation with the Board and this has been primarily due to yourself."

Lest any reader be confused about the Minister's claim that the Fisheries Department built four mills "cleanest anywhere", it should be noted for the record, that the mills were built by private companies, having no connection whatsoever with the Department of Fisheries, or any other agency of government for that matter.

Another point of outrage in the "brief" material occurs in the discussion relating to mercury contamination, found in Howe Sound from a chlor-alkali chemical plant. The Minister said:

"Interestingly enough it was our own Fisheries people who insisted on a settling pond being built in the first place. . . not our Provincial authorities."

File Revealing

Note the arrogant disregard for Provincial jurisdiction. A review of the file on this matter is most revealing. At that time, the working relationship between the Provincial Pollution Control organization and the Department of Fisheries could not have been better, as demonstrated by the earlier quote from the Pacific Regional Director of the Department of Fisheries. There was a free exchange of information and data; this was, of course, before present-day irrational environmentalism took over. When the permit was issued for the chlor-alkali plant it had been agreed what precautionary measures should be taken. Fisheries had indicated the desirability of a settling pond. The Provincial authorities had concurred, indeed we felt that a larger two-cell pond should be used and had advised both the applicant and Fisheries of our thinking. The applicant felt that we were being overly-cautious and requested deferment of the second cell. Fisheries, based on their experience, felt that a one-cell pond would do. As a compromise, a permit was issued by the Provincial body for a one-cell lagoon with a special condition which read:

> "The area immediately south of the lagoon shall be retained unencumbered for a second cell to be provided if the single cell fails to retain solids to the degree stipulated."

It is interesting that the cure prescribed for the later malfunction at the plant was the construction of the second cell, as originally suggested by the Provincial agency, not Fisheries. But the vanity doesn't end there; in discussing remedial actions, the Minister goes on to claim credit for the second cell in the settling pond:

> "We asked the Company to take on a crash program to stop mercury spills. . . They have done so. Not only that but they have built a second settling pond as well."

No reference at all to the fact that extensive discussions had been carried on between the Company and the Provincial authorities, or that the additional cell was a prescribed condition of the Provincial Pollution Control permit. Yet the Minister of Environment Canada had the gall to say, in writing, that it was "Fisheries" who "insisted"; not the provincial authorities.

Hypocritical Meddling

When discussing enforcement, in the same Federal Brief, the Minister states with respect to dischargers who may be uncooperative, ". . . then I will have to take the company's case to Ottawa." We are here discussing a resource industry mill, built and operated in British Columbia, subject to Provincial Pollution Control legislation. In a 1972 Brief presented by Environment Canada to a Public Inquiry held under the Provincial Pollution Control Act, the Minister of Environment Canada said:

> "Within its Boundaries, the Province of British Columbia exercises its mandate for environmental protection in a most responsible manner."

Why then all the talk that he must go to Ottawa? Surely he meant Victoria, the Capital and seat of the Provincial Government? Let us not then be naive; the battle for jurisdictional rights between the provinces and the Feds over environmental issues is there for all to see. But where are the provincial politicians with cries of outrage against this wasteful and hypocritical meddling?

The reason for all this utter waste of manpower and money is clearly indicated in the next few lines of the brief, when the Minister pursues his self-serving discourse:

> " . . . under today's conditions, with the tide running heavily against the polluters, industries' pleas for special treatment aren't likely to be too persuasive insofar as the Canadian Government is concerned."

It is ironical to conclude that this same Minister, after losing his Federal seat, turned to provincial politics and became a Cabinet Minister in the very Provincial Government whose authority he had so vehemently undermined. He even changed to a different political party to get elected provincially and then managed to lose all credibilty, as well as a Provincial Cabinet post, over an unbelievably naive juggling of travelling expenses. And we are expected to believe that elected leaders function with wisdom.

BUREAUCRACY

Part III: A "BELIEVE IT OR NOT" CASE HISTORY

That the administrative failures of government hierachy cause chaos at the working level should not surprise any of us. Here is a revealing case history with which I was involved, as a consultant, after resigning from government service. It is on the files of the Waste Management Branch, formerly called the Pollution Control Branch. The files, of course, are available, due to a court decision ordering that all files be open to the public. Again, this was a decision which the Government of the day, for political reasons, did not wish to challenge, even though such procedures hamper objective functioning of government administration.

Hide-bound by Regulations

In April 1970, an application for a pollution control permit was made. In August of the same year the applicant was advised that his application had been "refused due to late submission of proof of publication." Purely a technicality. The regulations required that proof of publication must be submitted within 40 days. The application had, in truth, been published but inadvertently the bureaucracy had not been advised within the time limit prescribed to record the fact. The applicant, when advised by telephone of the omission, gathered together the pertinent cuttings from the press and submitted same, but to no avail. The bureaucracy, hide-bound by regulations, simply advised the applicant to start all over again.

In fairness, the bureaucracy was not entirely at fault. The attitude displayed resulted from intimidation of the Pollution Control Branch through abuse of the court system. During the early '70's when environmentalists wanted to thwart an application for a new discharge permit, they resorted to legal technicalities, namely, challenging that the letter of the law had not been met, thus invalidating administrative proceedings. This technique, or skulduggery to which the legal profession resort to achieve their ends, is today being pursued by those opposed to progress.

To make the bureaucracy function efficiently and effectively, regulations must, at all times, retain sufficient discretionary powers to allow quasi-judicial administration to offset this type of destructive public mischief. However, over the years, the administrative effectiveness of the legislative powers pertaining to environmentalism have been substantially weakened in order to pander to the vocal radicals. For example, the 1967 Pollution Control Act stated:

> "The Director shall decide, *in his sole discretion,* whether or not the objection will be the subject of a hearing. . . "

After the author, in the role of the Director, refused to acceed to the protests of frivolous objectors the wordings was changed to read:

> "A person, not qualified. . . to make an objection to the Director. . . may file an objection with the Board, and the Board shall determine whether the public interest requires that the Director shall also take such an objection into consideration in making his decision."

The subject is, of course, much more complex than these brief references illustrate. There are many ramifications, which, if presented, would further illustrate how authority was destroyed, through use of the Board, to appease the environmental anarchists. One should not be surprised at the action taken, as the Board, like most such bodies, was set up initially to act as a buffer in contentious environmental issues between the Government and the people. The Board came into being to deal with the volatile issue of where to locate the treatment plant for the city of Vancouver, as the politicians were cowed by the anger of the local people.

It will no doubt be of interest to the reader to understand what is involved when making an application for a waste discharge permit.

Start All Over Again

The application form is filled out; six to eight copies are necessary, depending upon the circumstances. The forms, after signature by the applicant, are then taken to the Regional District Office for signature of that office; one of the copies is deposited there. The applicant must now proceed to the point of discharge. Hundreds of miles could and often are involved. A copy of the Application is "posted" at the point of discharge. Two of the copies are now sent post haste to the bureaucracy. They must arrive within 10 days, or the applicant must start all over again.

Upon receipt of the Application the bureaucracy reviews it and advises on where it must be advertised, generally in two newspapers and in the Provincial Gazette. Having completed this, one must now gather together the proof of advertising and submit same within 60 days (Originally, it was 40 days, but was later extended, as a result of the events being recounted.)

Imagine then how an applicant feels being told, after all this input, to start all over again, because of a mere technicality. The time and expense is not insignificant. And so it was in the case I am recounting. Not only that, the original application had been circulated to four other government agencies as per the regulations. This too must be repeated.

This type of incident was so frequent that the bureaucracy, instead of making a simple change in the regulations, seized the opportunity to add yet another pillar to its C Y A administrative empire. (C Y A are the letters for Cover Your Ass ploys used by bureaucrats to make sure their posteriors are never left exposed and they are found responsible for what they may, or may not have done.)

It created a new post with the title of Expeditor. The Expeditor has a form letter which goes:

". . . it is noted that to date no proof has been received of publication. . . Your attention is respectfully directed to Section 2.06 of the Regulations which states that proof of publication must be filed. . . within sixty days. . . otherwise the Director will have no alternative but to refuse to issue a permit."

This piece of bureaucratic nonsense is despatched shortly after the application is received, but the onus is still on the applicant; nothing has changed, except that the taxpayer supports a few more parasites.

And so it was that in August 1970 the application was re-submitted. This time a further snag was encountered. The newspaper publishing the advertisement created an error in printing. This, I might add, is also quite common and necessitates placing another advertisement, with the ensuing delay. Most papers bear the cost of re-publication, which is poor recompense as the matter of time lost is generally of greater importance. Eventually, in our case, after six and one-half frustrating months, a permit was issued. All this delay was a result of bureaucratic administration and regulations, since there was no public objection to the application. When public objections occur, the processing rate is slowed down considerably; sometimes it takes years *to be told no.*

C Y A Principle Fulfilled

However, let us press on for the above is but the introduction to bigger and better botches to be recounted. In mid-1974, it became necessary to request an amendment to the permit under discussion, which relates to treated domestic wastes. At the same time and by coincidence, an amendment was also being processed respecting an industrial waste permit held by the same company.

The two discharges were in the same general area and totally confined within the company's property. During discussions between the writer and various officials within the Branch, it was agreed that ultimate combination of the two effluents, one industrial and the other domestic, would be a reasonable and satisfactory way in which to resolve the matter. There was no physical, or technical problem involved with combining the effluents, as all regulations could be readily met. The only issue at stake was how to go about it administratively within the Branch to ensure that the principle of C Y A was fulfilled.

Elementary

It might be of value if I mention now, in order to better appreciate what follows, that the matter to be resolved was elementary, from a practical point of view. Without red tape, it would require no more than a day or two of input at the working level to complete. All that was being requested was permission to make a connection between two effluent systems, both under permit, so that a small quantity of excess treated effluent from one system which might become overloaded could be transferred to the other system which had a large excess of capacity.

And so it was agreed in discussions that some means of administratively effecting the desired change would be found and for the permittee to put the request in writing, which was done by letter of July 1974.

And so the wheels of the administration were set in motion. Admittedly, no one had been positive as to how it would all come out. Those at lower levels, charged with the processing of the facts, had not been given any positive directives, nor could they get any when they asked for them. The bureaucratic procedures were to be followed to the letter. The facts were to be reviewed, recommendations written up and submitted to superiors. All were to proceed in good faith. All C Y A techniques to apply.

Became Alarmed

One month later I was advised that there was an unforeseen administrative problem. There were two permits covering two separate points of discharge. If they were combined, only one permit would be needed. However, those wrestling with the problem suddenly became alarmed when they found out they could not, under the legislation, cancel the superfluous permit. It was pointed out with concern that the holder of the permits could, at a whim, resort to using the original method of discharge. In discussion, it was suggested that all would be resolved if the permittee wrote a letter promising not to use the superflous permit, which was done in the following words:

> "In accordance with discussions held between officials of the Pollution Control Branch and our consultant, Mr. Keenan, . . . we . . . agree that (when amendments are completed) . . . further exercise of the permittee's rights under Permit No. (so-and-so) shall cease."

Two months later I phoned the Branch to determine how things were going and to ask when the amendments would be authorized. I was advised that there was a minor problem. Other agencies, the Health Department, Fish & Wildlife, etc., had not been kept fully advised of the matters discussed. A further needless delay was to occur. So much for duplication of effort.

In passing, it is interesting to consider the inept roles played by these agencies to whom applications are referred. Here are two typical replies to routine applications. The first one is from Environment Canada:

> "With reference to the above application for a permit amendment, we have no particular comments to make at this time."

The second extract is from the Health Department:

> "The Application has been reviewed. Based on the information contained in the application we can find no conflict with the Health Branch requirements."

Invariably, the processing of applications are held up for months while awaiting such nebulous C Y A decisions.

In evaluating what is happening, the reader should bear in mind that the Pollution Control Branch carry all the expertise needed to evaluate all aspects of an application. What then are the roles played by the duplicators? Why can the matter not be left in the hands of those hired to do the work of processing the applications? Only once in a while a need may arise when it would be necessary to refer such matters to other Departments. It is not too difficult to appreciate the monstrous waste going on. I might add in all of this assertion of authority, *not one agency assumes any responsibility whatsoever* if environmental problems later arise from the applications they have reviewed and approved. Such responsibilities are carried solely by the permittee. Is it any wonder then, that we refer, in moments of exasperation, to our bureaucracies as useless white elephants? Yet society today is being conditioned to accept the thesis that we must have more government controls if we are to survive the future; 'tis but shades of *Orwell's 1984.*

Permit Rejected

In mid-December, I again inquired as to the progress of the amendment. I was now told that there was still considerable doubt as to how the proposed amendments would be written. The engineer to whom I was talking advised that his resume, with recommendations, had been written up and would be presented to those above him. While he was optimistic that all should come out well, he hinted, rather strongly, that he was more than a little uncertain as to what the administrative policy was at the higher level, as he had failed to get a positive directive in response to many questions. The resume, dated January 1975, recommended in favour of the connection of the two systems. As I said earlier, it was such an elementary request, with no physical obstacles, that it could have been resolved in a couple of hours.

In early February 1975, I received a somewhat apologetic phone call from the processing engineer advising that his recommendations to issue the permit had been rejected. I immediately visited the Branch offices and inspected the file. I read the resume written by the processing engineer. In the margin, one of the senior staff members had written: "No, this is to be covered by permit No. (so-and-so)." The permit referred to was that which it had been agreed to abandon, at the Branch's request mind you, as per the letter quoted earlier. After six months of internal administrative bewilderment those responsible for processing, at the working level, were finally given a firm directive.

After a thorough review of the file, I then met with the official who would be assuming the responsibility for the further processing of the matter. We discussed the recommendation of the resume and the margin note of rejection. He expressed surprise, stating he did not personally agree with the decision and promised to discuss the matter internally. A few days later I received a letter setting out the context of the discussion and prescribing the ground rules for the next phase of the exercise, with the usual ambiguities created by ill-defined administrative procedures.

At the time of writing, a new dimension was added to the episode, involving use of a portion of the effluent for spray irrigation at a reclamation project. This threw the whole matter back to square one. Once again the bureaucracy could not decide if one or two permits were needed. Their letter stated:

> "If the application is acceptable, we will determine after appropriate processing whether the discharge will be authorized by two separate permits . . . or if one permit with several appendices will suffice."

All of which goes to prove that our bureaucracies are lost in their own self-created labyrinth of red tape.

Self-Sustained Bureaucracy

Is it any wonder then in the midst of all this incompetence that one day in the press we find the following:

"POLLUTION BRANCH 'BUREAUCRACY' HIT

"A pollution control branch engineer has resigned from government service with a blistering attack on what he calls bureaucratic fumbling in the branch. In his letter of resignation made available to the press, he said, 'My original conception that government employment is unrewarding, boring and unbelievably awkward in its operation has been more than confirmed.'

"He called for 'overwhelming improvements' to end the 'degenerating, self-sustaining bureaucracy known as the pollution control branch.'

'As a taxpayer and voter in this province I am appalled at the waste of public funds and human resources as exists in the pollution control branch,' he said. 'Expenditures of large sums of money are approved for unnecessary and inane projects, monitoring apparatus and additional over-qualified staff with total disregard for the source of these funds.'

He complained that branch staff, especially university graduates, are given unrewarding and unnecessary tasks.

" 'I refuse to continue to check spelling, correct grammatical errors, fill in details for standard letters, etc., for three-washer laundromats in Oyama, B.C.' He said the staff should be reduced by at least 50 percent and university graduates should act in supervisory positions while technicians make up the majority of employees. He also complained that because the staff members refused to accept responsibility for their decisions, 'feeble decisions' are being made.

" 'A great deal is being done to establish this great bureaucratic government agency known as the pollution control branch but very little is being done about pollution,' he said."

While the charges are, in the mind of any reasonable person, correct, there is another side to the story, as always. When the report appeared in the media, I penned for the record the following pertinent thoughts:

"Due to public pressure, fostered by the news media and blindly followed by politicians, we (the public) created the Pollution Control Branch and its policies. Let us make sure that criticism of the Branch be placed in the proper quarters: the public arena. The public got what it asked for, a provincial bureaucracy to administer pollution control in accord with public whim.

When Director of Pollution Control, I repeatedly pointed out that pollution in British Columbia, on the basis of fact, was more emotional than real. I have not changed my mind one iota. No amount of reasoning prevailed against the psuedo-experts of the day (they are still around); encouraged by the press and condoned by politicians, they made their woeful mark."

BUREAUCRACY

Part IV: EXECUTIVE FLOUNDERING

In the late seventies, the Government of British Columbia undertook restructuring of several of its Ministries. Particular attention was directed towards the prolific nebulous environmental groups which had sprung up within the organizations. The Environmental Engineering section of the Ministry of Health, and the Fish and Wildlife Branch of the Ministry of Recreation and Conservation (which Ministry, at the same time, was totally demolished) were both unceremoniously dumped into the Ministry of Environment, all of which prompted a reorganizational stampede within that Ministry.

The Ministry of Environment was founded originally around the Water Resources Service, an engineering-oriented agency developed to manage water resources. The frantic attempts at reorganization have resulted in the destruction of this once effective Service in favour of a great nonentity, housing frivolous groups dabbling with little or no purpose in environmental issues. In attempting to come to grips with this task of reorganization, the ministry exposed its ineptness by distributing "AN OPEN LETTER TO ALL MINISTRY OF ENVIRONMENT PERSONNEL". The purported purpose of the letter was to seek ideas. It struck me as a "cover-up", an attempt to ensnare all-and-sundry into being party to the administrative mess which had arisen. I responded:

> "The invitation in the open letter is an affront to the administrative competence of those in charge. It begs the question: 'Is the Ministry so lost in its own labyrinth of administration that those in charge, the Deputy Minister, the Assistant Deputy Ministers (four of them) the Directors, Managers and Chiefs, (totalling over 50) no longer comprehend nor recognize where the problems are?' It is them who must be asked and held responsible, not the rank and file. Does the General ask the Private if the battle plan is sound?
>
> "It is those in charge who must define the inadequacies, the inefficiencies, the duplications, the redundancies and the priorities. If they cannot provide the answers, then they have indeed reached their level of incompetence and should be replaced with those that comprehend the needs. . . ''

Wondrous Achievements

The January, 1981, issue of *Environmental News,* published by the Ministry of Environment, provides ample proof that all is chaos. The Deputy Minister, in a *Message,* on behalf of the Ministry, woefully attempted to enumerate accomplishments. Of the 1980 highlights he said: "To me, each and every member of our staff, from the clerk in Fernie to the biologist in Smithers, can feel proud of their contribution", a statement followed with a list explaining the wondrous achievements. One staff member is mentioned as the recipient of a Chemical Institute award; another is recorded as having been declared "wildlife officer of the year", while a third member is recognized for being "co-winner of the British Columbia male athlete of the year award". Accomplishments of the Ministry?

In paragraph three we are given a list of "valuable employees" who retired during 1980 — another accomplishment of the Ministry? In paragraph four we are told, "Many staff members will remember 1980 as the year they added to their families" — indeed, a fine accomplishment of the Ministry — well done!

In paragraph five it starts to get heavy. The Waste Management Branch established a "Paper Save Program in Victoria and introduced oil recycling to some communities". Words of praise (or should it be condolence) are dispensed to a few who "became heavily involved in environmental conflicts", while a pat on the back is extended to someone for illustrating "the importance of the shellfish industry and the increase in the use of sea kelp as a food product". This paragraph ends by pointing out that one member of the staff was elected Mayor of a municipality. Fine accomplishments all, which the Ministry gratefully claims to bolster its own conspicuous failure.

Paragraph five also lists a number of routine promotions of little people condoning the hypocrisy to further their own ends in the system. Paragraph six proudly announces "the successful culture of sea-run cutthroat trout for the first time." The article ends, "I remember 1980 as the year we made significant progress *in achieving our objectives.*" Is it really true that these are the highlights of the accomplishments of 1,500 people supported with a budget that had reached the level of $85 millions in 1982?

Christmas Letter Propaganda

One can only wonder who is the Ministry's script writer, for, not to be outdone, the Minister stooped to using the goodwill of the 1980 Christmas season to bolster the sagging morale of the Ministry's staff, when he broke with the traditional handshake to each of his staff and substituted a letter. No one disagrees with the abolishment of the handshake, for it savoured of hypocrisy. For Christmas 1980 we all received a goodwish letter from the Minister; if it had been left at that it would have been graciously accepted. But in keeping with Christmas commercialism, the greeting was used for propaganda. Along with wishing us all well, the letter said:

"Your efforts made 1980 an outstanding year. The Ministry adapted superbly to a major re-organization; . . . Together, we accomplished a lot to be proud of. Our Ministry is better known; *the abilities of our people respected and listened to in wider circles.* Perhaps best of all, we've established a united foundation upon which further achievements will stand. Everyone contributed to this accomplishment, and I especially want to thank you for your contribution. I hope you are as proud of the job you've done as I am."

Too bad the missive did not tell us who respected our "abilities" who didn't before, or who it was that was listening to us "in wider circles". It is pertinent to add that two years later, at the close of 1982, much of the reorganization was still in limbo.

After some three and a half years, in May 1983, the Minister responsible for all these great accomplishments left. In his parting letter to the staff he claims to have had tears in his eyes as he wrote, "I am leaving a Ministry I believe to be the finest in government . . . It is admired by other Ministries; by business, industry, and the general public." One must wonder when the Minister last discussed the subject matter with developers, consultants, contractors, builders, mining corporations et al. Is it really possible that other Ministries envy such accomplishments?

In the *Times-Colonist,* June 23, 1983, across the top of the front page of the Financial section was the headline, **"Junior bureaucrats, studies hold up B.C. mines"**. The headline referred to a speech by the president of the Mining Association of B.C. to a convention of the Canadian Institute of Planners. The substance of the article was that junior bureaucrats involved in decision-making and the resulting government-ordered studies, the number one activity of the environmental bureaucrats, are hurting industry. If the Minister would remove his fawning political blinkers just for a moment, he might grasp at whom the above remarks were addressed. Does he really believe his beloved Ministry of Environment is admired by business and industry?

Media Support Radicals

Of course, the media, in its never-ending support of the radical cause and socialized government, produced an editorial under the title, **" 'Junior' Planners Protest the Public"**. The main theme was that "The motives of civil servants are likely less selfish than those of miners who are entirely devoted to getting ore out of the ground for profit."

This begs the simple question, "If industries don't work for profit, who pays taxes to support the civil servants?"

Shortly, thereafter, the media appropriately published a brief letter from the President of the Mining Association, which, in part, put the matter back into honest perspective, something the media seem to be loathe to do of their own accord. The President, in opening his letter, protested that his speech had been given "a bum rap" by the paper. The letter went on to state:

"... One problem that has been identified has been that... many critical decisions trickle down to some very inexperienced people... If someone is proposing to invest $100,000,000 or more, it deserves the attention of the most senior people, not the most junior... As to the plethora of studies required, again that should be something dealt with by people with extensive experience, not someone two years out of school... You suggest I am questioning the motives of civil servants. I am not. I do question a process that sometimes takes two and three years. That kind of delay is unconscionable."

The author trusts that the example given in the preceding sub-chapter fully vindicates the position taken by the President of the Mining Association.

Are governments not aware that the seemingly endless call for studies is simply a part of the public-financed self-education strategy of junior social science bureaucrats, who find themselves dealing with projects where their experience is zero? By having masses of studies to hand, prepared by others, they attempt to cover up their woeful inadequacies while frustrating the rational progress of the system that has elevated us to a standard of living that would have been incomprehensible to our forefathers. To show how questionable are the activities of these groups within government, I quote from a Branch Reorganisational Memorandum to staff members from a Branch Director:

"... some of our activities will wane, while new challenges will also arise to take their place. Flexibility and innovation will be the key to survival..."

If ever there was an admission that their activities are redundant, that is surely it.

Another Failure

Towards the close of 1978, the Government took what appeared to be a daring and much needed action. With the usual political fanfare, it proclaimed the establishment of a Ministry of Deregulation. Unfortunately, but inevitably, this daring and unprecedented clairvoyance to rid us of needless regulations, imposed to satisfy the whims of pressure groups, quickly fell on its face. What started out with a flourish to be a Ministry, degenerated to a "Program" within the Ministry of Finance, never to be heard from again. This is not hard to perceive, since both politicians and bureaucrats have much to gain from over-regulation. Getting there has taken "Big Brother" generations.

Empire Builders at Work

As I write, there comes to mind a delightful anecdote on how self-interest bureaucratic empires perpetuate their existence. The incident occurred back in 1963, shortly after I became Director of the Division of Public Health Engineering. I had noted over a period of time that my secretary was always busy entering great masses of coliform drinking water sampling data in a ledger. When this started to interfere with the handling of my routine correspondence, I decided to look into the matter.

I found that the Health Units, of which there were 18, were submitting hundreds of water samples each week to the laboratory for bacteriological analysis. The results were reported back to the Health Units with a copy to us in central office. My first query was, "Do we need the results in central office?", since they were reported to the field Units where such information was of some practical value. Before discontinuing the central office ledger, I decided to contact the Health Units and ascertain that the results were being kept. On the side, I asked the Health Units to check to see if all of the samples were needed, as my review of the data suggested that a large proportion could well be valueless. I even went so far as to suggest that every effort should be made to keep the data gathering to a practical minimum.

The outcome was surprisingly good. Most Health Units advised that sampling could be reduced by anything from 20 per cent to 50 per cent. I was delighted and advised the Health Units to advise the laboratory of the reduced workload.

In a matter of days I got a call from a rather upset Director of the Laboratories, asking me what-the-hell I thought I was doing. It was explained to me, in irate tones, that only recently the laboratory had expanded its facilities and staff to cope with the larger workload. I was asked what was proposed for the staff in the laboratory, who would have nothing to do if the workload was reduced!

Since such decisions were not mine, as I had no say in the administrative hierarchy of the Health Branch, the matter was turned over to others to resolve. As far as I was concerned, I was able to discontinue the recording of redundant data at central office. I recall that the outcome of the laboratory issue was that all reverted to their old schedules.

Important Lesson

There is an important lesson to be learned from this critical review of bureaucracy. Because bureaucracy, to all intents and purposes, *is unmanageable,* the only really effective measure which society has available to control the tax burden created by the public service is to keep it as small as possible, certainly much smaller than needs would dictate. This is even more true in recent years since the formation of public service unions, which have effectively destroyed what little power of management previously existed. To a greater extent than I care to admit, this book has been written out of the sheer frustration of trying to cope and reason with government, both from inside and outside the Public Service.

Chapter Eight

THE PUBLIC INQUIRIES FARCE

In the early 1970's a series of Public Inquiries to determine measures needed to control pollution were held in British Columbia. The environmentalists with — as usual — the aid of the press, condemned the Inquiries as being biased, farcical and highhanded. The irony of the situation is that the charges were all too true. But the charges should have been made by Industry, rather than by the eco-freaks.

The Public Inquiries spanned the period 1970 to 1973. They were held to "resolve what technical considerations and measures must be provided . . . to satisfactorily ensure pollution will not be caused in accordance with the Pollution Control Act, 1967." The five inquiries, in chronological order, dealt with Forestry, Mining, Chemical Products, Food Processing, and Municipal Wastes. I participated in all but the one relating to food processing.

The Inquiries were, to put it bluntly, an affront to impartial Government administration. One could go so far as to say that they bordered on public deception. As a result, the Province of British Columbia is saddled with harsh unrealistic regulations, which have been drawn up as a sop to environmental pressure groups. Their irrational contributions at the Inquiries went virtually unchallenged by the panels who had the opportunity to publicly confront these groups and expose them for what they are. One of the most vociferous objectors later became notorious as a leader in the Greenpeace movement.

While the material offered by the industrialists was challenged in every detail by the panels, the material presented by the environmental groups was given, in public and the press, an air of credibility to which it was not entitled, simply because the inquiry panels did not have the fortitude to denounce the material presented for the drivel it was. A theme or hypothesis was allowed to develop at the Inquiries to the effect that cost was of no importance, environmentalism the only worthwhile goal.

The Inquiries purported to be technical in nature. The word purported is used with precise deliberation, because the final "Objectives" which were prescribed, were not based on the technical data presented but were, in fact, arbitrary. This point was driven home, time and time again to those involved. All preferred to ignore the facts. It was obviously more expedient to pursue the course openly adopted by the Minister of Environment Canada when he confessed that "industries' pleas for special treatment aren't likely to be too persuasive."

Abdicated Responsibilities

It is quite obvious, from a scientific point of view, that those charged with making decisions abdicated their responsibilities. To prescribe "objectives' to appease the environmentalists, is to prescribe unrealistic goals. One panel member conceded to me, in private, that such was the case. This should not be too surprising as the Chairman of the Inquiries, on occasion, referred to himself as a missionary in pollution control. There is little doubt that the philosophy behind the Inquiries was evangelical, but unfortunately, the good tidings were only for the ecological gods. Industry, the mainstay of our society, was made the sacrificial lamb, so that the bureaucrats could consolidate and increase their empire and power. Under the Chairman's guiding hand, as Director of Pollution Control, his staff increased over the period of the Public Inquiries from between 30 and 40 to over 200. In honour of his contribution to the bureaucracy's empire, he was eventually elevated to the level of Assistant Deputy Minister.

The Inquiries were used solely to arm the bureaucracy with a set of arbitrary rules giving it absolute power, without any sincere or responsible thought for the intricate economic relationship between Industry, Society and environmental issues. They were used, to a great extent, to kill the idea that there was an alliance between Industry and Government, a fatuous proposition used by environmentalists and socialists to intimidate; and — by God — they succeeded because of a spineless administration.

No One from Industry

That industry was to be crucified is not hard to grasp, if one simply considers the composition of the Inquiry panels. Not one representative of industry sat on any panel, yet four of the Inquiries were solely related to industrial matters. It is worth repeating: *not one representative of industry sat on any panel;* it's like playing poker with a stacked deck.

Before presenting details of the Inquiries, a few words of

explanation are in order. As all of the Inquiries followed the same general pattern, there is no point in going into great detail for each one. For the purposes of this book, the second of the Inquiries, that dealing with Mining, is chosen as the base to enlighten the reader as to the autocratic procedure under which the Inquiries were conducted. Brief references to the other Inquiries will be made only to support the general thesis being presented.

FOREST PRODUCTS INDUSTRY INQUIRY

The Forest Products Industry Inquiry was held in August 1970. Being the first of the hearings, it was approached by all with considerable caution and misgivings. Overtures to the bureaucracy before the event were somewhat futile as no one seemed to know what was required. It was even hinted that it might well be a whitewash job to get the environmentalists off the Government's back. As events turned out, the industry got tarred and feathered.

As the Inquiry proceeded, it became painfully obvious that Industry was expected to get down on its knees and ask forgiveness. At one point in the proceedings, the Chairman castigated the representatives of the forestry companies, who presented a joint brief at the inquiry, for lack of specific data, in spite of the fact, as stated by the spokesman for the Industry at the time, that they had not been given precise terms of reference to meet and that the Chairman had in fact, misled them as to what was required. However, the Chairman, from behind the environmental veil and in concert with the intimidating news media, made it quite clear that Industry's pleas were not going to be too persuasive.

Unrealistic Philosophy

The main brief presented was that of the Council of Forest Industries in that it spoke collectively for a large segment of the industry. There were, of course, the expected array of meaningless and unsubstantiated briefs from the environmental groups. As to my brief, it is worth noting that it was written only months after I had resigned as Director of Pollution Control, thus the thoughts presented were obviously developed while in Government Service and in close association with the environmental hysteria which had been unleashed over the previous years. My statements were based on facts and needs. Under the usual magnified headline "Expert Discounts Pulp Mill Threat" the press had summarized my contribution this way and I quote only a small portion to give the general tone of my address:

"A dollars-and commonsense lecture was delivered by Charles Keenan, former chief of the Pollution Control Branch, to the government's Inquiry panel, 'emotional' volunteer groups and the public on the role of pulp mills in our economic and environmental structure. . .

"Keenan made unfavourable references to 'ad hoc pressure groups' for meddling in affairs of which they had no expert knowledge. He inferred that such groups did more harm than good. (It was the first time in the lengthy hearings that any person had directly criticized the Society for Pollution and Environmental Control (SPEC) and other such groups or individuals.)

"Keenan, who said he was an adviser in drawing up the present Act, said: 'Authority to dictate conditions to the pulp and paper industry without responsibility for the consequences, is a position which all government opponents and ad hoc pressure groups wish to enjoy and exploit. It is vital that legislation ensures that our future well-being is not left to the whims of the uninformed.''

Disconcerting Aspect

As a consequence of all the briefs and data presented, the panel duly distributed, some nine months later, to the various participants, for comment, copies of tentative "Objectives" which it was proposing to recommend for adoption. As a result, I submitted a supplementary brief touching on the technical incompatibility of much of the data that it was proposed to adopt in the "Objectives". In addition, I was retained by one of the pulp and paper companies to assist in preparation of their supplementary brief which dealt heavily with the purely technical aspects of the proposed "Objectives" as they affected the company's mill. For present purposes, reference shall be restricted to the more general comments submitted. Technical discussion is to be kept to a minimum and only in general terms, in so far as is possible.

While it was not difficult to find fault with the proposed "Objectives", the most disconcerting aspect was with respect to the philosophy being pursued. An honest plea for a rational position was made, and I quote from the submissions with which I was involved:

". . . none of us can, in all truth, fully escape the consequences of over-legislating Pollution Control, no more than can we justify the results of no legislation at all. . . those setting 'objectives' must assume responsibility to ensure that they are readily attainable within the economic structure of a particular company . . . we must allow use of the resource, but prevent abuse. It is hoped that 'objectives' will reflect this basic fundamental of practical waste control management. The writer is very much in agreement with the general approach of using 'objectives' in the first instance. In due course, with evidence collected over the years, the 'objectives' can, in many cases, be adopted as standards once realistic achievement is proven.''

That such philosophy was not being used was brought out in the discussion on toxicity. While somewhat technical, a few lines are abstracted to illustrate the conflict:

". . . the bio-assay test (a product of concentration and time used on fish in tanks to test their resistance to specific wastes) is no more than an index of the effluent toxicity and in no way directly relates to the receiving water conditions . . . Research has not yet established any relationship between the bio-assay test, higher levels of dilution and tolerance for fish life. Such a parameter must be specified as an 'index' and used to show the relative toxicity of a waste. Its use as a regulatory standard should be avoided.''

No Automobiles can be Allowed

The point at question here is, that even if an effluent is toxic to fish within the outfall, it is totally irrelevant. The only question of importance is whether or not it is harmful when diluted in the receiving environment. To say that an effluent must be non-toxic at the point of discharge is like stating that automobile emissions must be harmless as they leave the exhaust pipe, something we know is not so. Yet we all know that exhaust fumes discharged to an open atmosphere with good dilution and dispersion become harmless.

If we are to follow the rationalization associated with the bio-assay test and apply it to our automobiles, then no automobile can be allowed. Such is the hypocrisy and stupidity which was developed in the Objectives as a sop to the environmentalists. Throughout all the Inquiries there are dozens of similar irrational, arbitrary conditions which are not practicial. Some insight into these are given in the next few pages, when dealing with the other Inquiries.

However, before moving on, let me disclose the skulduggery carried on by the bureaucracy to trap Industry into accepting the impractical and wasteful "Objectives" developed at this first Inquiry. In the first draft of the proposed "Objectives", which was distributed for comment to the participants, was the following:

"The technical considerations and measures arising from the Public Inquiry, along with information available to the Panel Members, have been interpreted in numerical terms, and are presented in the form of suggested guidelines and *recommended objectives.* . . ''

Diabolical Subtlety

I had personally served on other committees which had drawn up pollution control "objectives" and felt the approach a practical and proper interim procedure to follow, the word "objective" being given its dictionary meaning of "something to be aimed at or striven for." Overtures by Industry and individuals to the bureaucracy during the drafting of the Objectives got the comforting verbal assurance that the Objectives were something to be aimed at, but not likely to be rigidly requested in many cases. But a diabolical subtlety took place.

While the draft report used the wording "recommended objectives"the final report came out with the wording *"recommended minimum objectives"*, the additional word having been slipped in furtively after the first draft by a devious panel. Now, because of the subtle insertion of the word "minimum", the objectives were to all intents and purposes "standards". This and other important points are enlarged upon in discussing the next Inquiry. As a result of the author's subsequent dealings with the bureaucracy there is no doubt that the rank and file apply the "Objectives" as standards.

MINING INQUIRY

I was privileged to be retained in a professional capacity by the Mining Association of British Columbia to assist its Environmental Committee with the preparation of Briefs for the second of the Inquiries to be held in March 1972.

That the Inquiry was to be used by the bureaucracy to railroad through environmental dogma became evident from the outset. Important philosophical sections, dealing with areas of some concern to the Industry, were to be cut from the presentation. The Briefs had been submitted ahead of time to allow preview by the Panel. As a result, certain sections and statements were ordered to be deleted "as not substantially meeting the terms of reference for the Inquiry. . . " In truth, the deletions in this case were to cover up the power struggle going on between the Federal and Provincial governments on the subject of jurisdiction in environmental matters. The pertinent sections were under the heading, "LEGISLATION AND MINING". One statement said:

> "The Mining Association, in coming forward at this Inquiry, does so in the belief that the jurisdictional powers for controlling pollution rest with the Province."

Feds Challenged

The position of Federal agencies was challenged. In support, the mining brief pointed out that at the previous Forest Industry Inquiry, the Federal Department of Fisheries, in their brief, acknowledged that conflict between the Provincial and Federal agencies created problems for Industry. It said, "objectives. . . will only be met if the various government agencies responsible for pollution abatement work together in harmony." It also emphasized the need for realism, in the words: ". . . new standards. . . must be capable of attainment. . . without creating undue financial hardship."

The need to have the authority of the Inquiry clarified was requested in the mining brief in the words:

> "It is imperative that ambiguity of authority for the control of pollution be removed. The Mining Association is here to help in the development of realistic 'objectives'. . . for the protection of the environment in those instances where it can be shown that a viable environmental asset is likely to be jeopardized."

Not an unreasonable position in view of the nonsense and chaos prevailing in jurisdictional matters, as discussed in earlier chapters. This wasteful state of affairs exists to this very day, indeed, it appears to be getting worse, as the respective bureaucracies grow in size with each vying for ultimate power.

Herewith, in condensed form, are pertinent philosophical statements from the introduction of the Mining Association Brief, to show the practical approach advocated by the Industry.

> "Environmental quality control programs must be based on a well-researched and equitable balancing of government interests and objectives. Since improved standards of living and continued economic growth are two of these objectives, it must be recognized by everyone that attainment of these goals is not possible without making some changes in the environment. Actions to limit environmental alteration must be guided by sound scientific evidence. Only in this way can industry and government avoid critical waste of time, resources, money and effort. . .

> "To establish realistic controls it is necessary to measure the economic and social returns from the industry against the environmental losses incurred. An objective examination of the balance sheet at this point in time clearly demonstrates the advantages of continuing to encourage mining development . . .

> "In economic terms, the return to the province per square mile from mining lands is considerably greater than any other resource industry."

Disregarded Counsel

The philosophy just quoted was used throughout the Mining Brief in the development of technical controls. It was presented as a logical basis for discussion. It is pertinent to observe, indeed very pertinent, that the philosophy was not challenged at the public hearings. On the other hand, the panel, the Branch, the Board and the Government disregarded the counsel therein, preferring to bed down with the environmentalists.

The abstracts are offered to show the reader the effort made to have realism prevail. While the great mass of detailed technical data presented to the Inquiries is not quoted here, an astute reader can readily see from the philosophy presented that a very conscientious and practical approach was taken. This was particularly true with respect to detailed technical issues, some of which were enormously complex, particularly the matter of controlling ambient air quality at one of British Columbia's great smelter complexes. Dozens of pages of complex data were submitted to back up the case made. But all was to be in vain.

By letter dated October 19, 1972, the Inquiry participants were presented with the first draft of the proposed Objectives for comment and further input. *The proposed Objectives came as a shock*. As far as the Industry was concerned, the Objectives in no way related to the factual evidence presented at the Inquiry. A supplementary rebuttal brief was immediately prepared, presenting forceful arguments on the basis of facts. It was wasted effort. The bureaucracy had obviously made up its mind and, like the environmental parasites whose side it now took, did not want to be confused with reality; in short, "Industry's pleas were not to be persuasive".

Deplorable Situation

In March 1973, the bureaucracy duly issued to the participants, the Objectives in final draft form, without, needless to say, the fundamental changes requested by the Mining Association and deemed vital to make the Objectives tenable. The Objectives had, simultaneously, been forwarded to the Board for adoption. The whole situation was deplorable. The Objectives were and still are, untenable and useless. They cannot be complied with, other than through the waste of enormous sums of money to achieve no end; not even a better or more useful environment. The callous indifference of those charged with the development of the Objectives constitutes a monstrous crime against the taxpayers of this province.

After considered deliberation of all the facts, the Mining Association advised the Board that it wished to appeal against the adoption of the Objectives. The Board Chairman duly responded that the Board would entertain the submission of further arguments by the

Mining Association. While this appeared hopeful, it transpired it was nothing more than the Board going through the motions, to put it bluntly, of covering its ass.

Indifference of Bureaucracy

And so it was that an Appeal Brief dated May 8, 1973, was submitted to the Board. Much of the material related to technical matters and makes rather heavy reading for those not attuned to the subject. Thus, only condensed, or paraphrased references will be made to a few of the statements in keeping with this discussion, to illustrate the total indifference of the bureaucracy towards the facts and, of course, to allow the reader to make some value judgments on his own account.

In the Appeal Brief, the Mining Association stressed that a basic fundamental of the presentation was one of *"economic realism"*. The Association *"unequivocally opposed the imposition of objectives which incurred the expenditure of monies to a limit where there would be no environmental benefits."* In this regard the Pollution Control Board's attention was directed to the preamble of the proposed Objectives prepared by the Inquiry Panel, where it was unashamedly stated: *". . . economic considerations have not been examined to a depth as initially visualized."* In truth, they were not examined at all. That this was so, was quite evident. One member of the Inquiry Panel, Dr. P.H. Pearse, had the courage to publicly disagree with the Objectives in a written "Dissention" of some length which commenced:

> "I dissent from those parts of the (Panel's) Report which deal with recommended objectives . . . The approach taken . . . does not . . . provide a satisfactory means of controlling pollution . . . "

It is ironical to note that Dr. P.H. Pearse was held in sufficient esteem by a later government to be appointed as a one-man Royal Commission to review forest ownership and management throughout British Columbia. He also had the distinction of heading a Fishery Inquiry. . . Yet the Panel *et al*, totally disregarded the cautions of this sole economic representative on the panel — a sorry reflection on this whole scene. This incident of fact, portrays the essence of these farcical hearings; firstly, there were no representatives of industry on the Panels and secondly, the voice representing economics was smothered.

The Appeal Brief pointed out that Dr. P.H. Pearse had stated:

> "Pollution control requires attention, in the first instance, to the environment — its assimilative capacity, and the quality of air and water desired. The recommendations in the Report (of the Inquiry Panel), for the most part, are not based on these considerations.

"These standards take no account of the condition and assimilative capacity of the air and water into which the wastes are discharged.

". . . and where they exceed the requirements of air and water quality protection, they impose wasteful use of capital and labour in control measures. . .

". . . but when applied. . . in a remote situation where the discharges have an insignificant effect on the receiving environment, they will require excessive expenditures on abatement."

In short, the "Dissention" report of Dr. Pearse, the sole socio-economic discipline on the Panel, supported the general position of the Mining Association. The Appeal Brief contended that the Panel had ". . . failed to satisfactorily resolve the issues for which the Inquiry was called." The Board was reminded that the Inquiry had been called:

". . . to determine the measures which must be adopted. . . to satisfactorily ensure pollution will not be caused in accordance with the Pollution Control Act."

and that the Act stated:

" 'pollution' means the introduction into a body of water, or storing upon, in or under land or discharging or emitting into the air such substances or contaminants of such character as to substantially alter or impair the usefulness of the land, water or air."

There is little doubt that the rules had been changed, if indeed, there ever had been any. The Board was cautioned that it was not being objective. It was emphasized, with supporting evidence, that the "A" Objectives were ". . . unrealistic for many existing operations and unattainable in many cases, *nor are they needed.* There is no evidence to suggest that such idealistic goals should be imposed. . . the objectives. . . far exceed the definition of 'pollution' as set out in the Act."

No Interference Tolerated

And what of the outcome? To their everlasting shame, the Board scuttled behind the environmental wall. The Objectives were adopted on November 30, 1973, with barely a change in the text. As a final show of contempt and to ensure that further appeals would be prejudiced, the Board ordered that the Objectives be printed and published forthwith, even though the Appeal Brief had concluded with the remarks:

"The Association is fully prepared to diligently pursue whatever course of action it deems necessary to ensure the industry in this province is not placed in jeopardy as a result of the proposed "Objectives" in their present form."

The inference in the statement being that the matter would be taken to higher authority. The Board had obviously made up its mind that no further considerations or interference would be tolerated.

That this was the case became evident over the ensuing weeks as several further appeals and meetings ended in the Mining Association's overtures being swept aside by a smug administration, serving the wishes of the socialists in power in the Provincial legislature.

Monstrosity Created

As an impotent Board, to all intents and purposes, had abdicated its responsibilites, an appeal to either the Lieutenant Governor in Council, that is the Cabinet, or to the Courts, had to be considered. The reader should note that the legislation only allowed an appeal to either party, not both. Since the matter was obviously a monstrosity created by incompetent bureaucratic administrators, it appeared appropriate that the next step should logically be to the Cabinet, rather than to the Courts, to attempt to have sanity prevail. Thus it was that a further appeal was launched; what an absurdity that turned out to be.

The appeal hearing was held in the Executive Council Chambers of the Parliament Buildings, with a Cabinet Committee of four members. The matter was dismissed on a technicality. Not one word of the actual material of concern was heard. Think about that — *not one single word of the subject of the appeal was allowed to be presented.* The Cabinet, like Pontius Pilate, was only too pleased to find an excuse to wash its hands of the affair. Unfortunately, for British Columbia, those were the days when the Socialists were in power. *Never was the alliance between socialism and environmentalism more explicitly portrayed.*

Three years of conscientious effort by an industry and its committees, voluminous briefs, technical data, learned expert testimony, etc., not to mention the cost, all gone for nothing. And remember, it was the Government that initiated the Inquiries — not the Industry.

As stated at the outset, the Inquiries proved to be nothing short of outright public deception, shams of collosal proportions, contributed to, in the final analysis, by the Cabinet elected to govern. How true was the bias expressed by the Minister of Environment Canada when he said that Industry's "pleas for special treatment aren't likely to be too persuasive. . . "

OTHER INQUIRIES

With regard to the other Inquiries, here are a few of the highlights. The Chemical and Petroleum Inquiry followed the same futile pattern as the others. When the draft of the proposed Objectives, implying to be based on the findings of the Inquiry, were released, one group of industrial participants contacted me for an exchange of opinions, as they were extremely upset with the arbitrary, highhanded and impractical nature of the document.

Here are a few extracts from the Industries' rebuttal:

"Experience has shown that unnecessarily restrictive regulations are economically harmful to the region they purport to protect. The costs of pollution control, like all other costs of manufacture, must be passed along to the consumer. The result can be that the products of industry in the region become too highly priced to be competitive and their manufacture is discontinued.*

"The permissable maximum emission of oxides of nitrogen from new nitric acid plants is set at three pounds per ton of nitric acid. Oxides of nitrogen are not harmful in themselves and at low levels of concentration they are not only environmentally beneficial but essential for the support of life on this planet."

"Formed in vast quantities by natural processes, as well as in comparatively small quantities by human activities, oxides of nitrogen are toxic only if the concentration rises above a certain threshold level. What we need to control is not the total amount of oxides of nitrogen in the environment, but their concentration. The limits recommended in our brief have been found sufficient to completely protect the environment. One must ask why the Province wants to impose additional unnecessary costs upon its economy to keep a benign constituent out of the environment?"

Similar positions were presented with respect to other elements, including iron, an essential constituent of life. The deficiencies of the bio-assay test, as a regulatory device, were underscored. The presentation concluded with the words, "The proposed system of controls tends to be meaningless."

In view of the outcome of the Mining Inquiry, need I add that all was ignored, to the everlasting shame of yet another apathetic Inquiry Panel?

Philosophy Wrong

I decided to omit the fourth Inquiry, the one pertaining to Food Processing. I was getting tired of the obvious *"a fait accompli"* attitudes of those conducting matters. The fifth Inquiry, held in April 1973, related to Municipal Wastes. I submitted a brief. The Inquiry proved to be no different from the others. The same autocratic attitudes prevailed.

---

*This was no idle doom threat. A chemical plant in Vancouver, with which the author was associated as a consultant, closed because, among other economic burdens, it could not meet costly pollution control requirements which did nothing for the environment.

In due course, a draft report of the proposed Objectives, purporting to be based on findings of the Inquiry, was received with the usual hypocritical request for observations and further input (CYA tactics). The facade and pretense presented to the public that justice was being done was nauseating. I knew by now, of course, that any input was to no avail. The philosophy of those conducting the Inquiries was wrong, thus the results are wrong. Indeed, it was all too obvious that the bureaucracy had built a philosophy to suit its own ends, and it made damned sure that no one was given an opportunity to argue the point, as per the facts of the Mining Inquiry. In the letter accompanying the draft report was the following, take it or leave it, attitude.

"Final objectives will not deal with matters of policy and such like."

Could it be, that those responsible fully realized that the philosophy of the Inquiries was wrong, that they were, in effect, in an untenable position?

Rules to Frustrate Intelligence

In response to the appeal for further input, I replied as pointedly as I could, while still showing some reluctant courtesy:

"It is deemed a privilege to have this opportunity *to again argue against the current basic philosophy in pollution control, which has succeeded in subjugating rationality to emotionalism and the whims of those with ulterior motives.*

"Arbitrary regulations, for whatever reasons they may be promulgated, can only create untenable positions for honest professionals who must use their technological knowledge to advise of the proper course of action. Let us make sure that our Bureaucracy is, in truth, geared to help us rather than have a set of rules to frustrate our intelligence. . .

"It is alarming to note that the word *'economic'*, or any of its connotations, *does not appear anywhere in the text of the proposed document.* That 'Objectives', of the nature proposed, should be adopted, by a Government body purporting to act in the best interest of the public, without a pertinent statement on economics, shows either an unbelievable bias on the part of the Panel against economic considerations (bordering on stupidity), or an honest omission, which is hard to perceive. . . "

Without Responsibility

A technical discourse followed, but is omitted to maintain the reader's interest. The response continued:

"The case presented is chosen to illustrate the basic fallacy with the proposed 'objectives'. . . (they) have not been linked in any way to practical engineering economic achievement and resource use. . . (they) make no allowance for the immense variability in site conditions; in short, they are not economically-oriented to the renewable resource capacity of the receiving waters. . .

"The proposed "Objectives" reach far beyond the practical and realistic intent of the Act. They, in fact, create the very situation that I admonished against in my Brief, in the words: *'It would be a travesty of justice if our efforts at these Inquiries simply resulted in the arming of our bureaucracy with regulations which would allow it to function without thought or responsibility to the true needs of the taxpayers.'* "

Need I add that all was ignored?

CONCLUDING REMARKS ON INQUIRIES

Before closing this chapter, let us consider the repercussions of such highhanded arbitrary standard setting. Those who set arbitrary standards must recognize that others, less knowledgeable, will accept them at face value as being absolute. *They will be vigorously applied by the less informed, on the grounds they were prescribed, presumably, on the basis of knowledge.*

Here is what happens. In the mid-1960's when several new pulp mills were being built in British Columbia, considerable thought had to be given to the matter of developing standards for effluent discharge. All available sources of information, both national and international, were reviewed, experts were consulted along with Industry — (the formation of an unholy alliance according to environmentalists). Good protective standards were developed but practical information for one parameter, that dealing with conductivity, could not be found. It was to be tried as a monitoring technique with respect to spill control. All relevant data was examined and in consultation with others a number was chosen which was put in the permit with the understanding of the permittee that it was on a trial basis and would be subject to alteration depending upon data collected.

A Revelation

About a year or two later a new set of pulp mill effluent standards was obtained from one of the American States. I immediately noticed that they were using a similar value for conductivity. A feeling of smug pride ran through me just to think that our guess had been correct. Not liking the arbitrary manner in which we had chosen our standard I wrote to the State in question, asking them for the technical background for their choice. The answer was a revelation. They had got the number from British Columbia and would appreciate our documentation of its origin.

If arbitrary decisions have to be made in choosing standards, they must be done with a great deal of commonsense judgment based on experience and discerning observations. Unless there is evidence to confound past practice, the same course must be followed. To set arbitary numbers, with the purely idealistic idea of maintaining a pristine environment, is folly. The assimilative capacity of nature *is a resource,* which man must utilize to the full, if we are to sustain our way of life.

To impose uniform across-the-board regulations requiring the same degree of controls irrespective of site location, as has been done, is nothing short of stupidity. This point was argued over and over at the Public Inquiries, but to no avail. Surely if an industry locates in isolation it is entitled to be given realistic regulations and not burdened with meeting the same stringent requirements as prescribed for more densely-populated areas. The philosophy of the Objectives raises grave doubts as to the competence of those responsible for their development.

Upstage the Other

But something more damning is happening. Federal/Provincial environmental empires thrive on the public demand for regulations. Each agency is trying to upstage the other with tougher and tougher standards, on the premise that those with the more stringent requirements will have public support, or put another way, those with the weaker requirements will be accused of supporting an unholy alliance with Industry. I have been told this on numerous occasions when I have been so audacious as to challenge the bureaucrats involved, as to who really has jurisdiction. Each side has claimed that their standards are the more restrictive and therefore must apply.

That I had no doubts in my mind that the regulations and policies adopted by the agencies were purely arbitrary, is illustrated by the following abstract from one of my reports for a pulp mill client:

> "While this report has attempted to show the main pollution control factors confronting the mill and has estimated the costs of remedial measures, the Company must appreciate that sound technological conclusions may not prevail in arriving at an accepted solution, as many of the decisions being made, in an attempt to regulate waste discharge to the satisfaction of the public, are quite arbitrary in nature."

It is, perhaps, poetic justice that the mill now belongs to the people, through a government takeover which occurred under the rule of the socialists, from 1972 to 1975. It would be most educational to find out how well the mill discharges and emissions measure up to the Objectives?

Source of Energy Buried

As a consultant, I was personally associated with two projects where unwarranted use of the "objectives" forced the shut-down of two hog fuel burning power plants, just at the time when the energy crisis was on our doorstep. All appeals against such a course of action were dismissed. The hog fuel, a long standing source of energy in this Province, was, instead, hauled away to a land dump and buried, while the power load needed was imposed upon B.C. Hydro and Power Authority. For economic reasons, the company in question has since closed down. In the light of such actions, it is not hard to perceive the crash of our economy.

Technology is being used by the activists to accentuate problems — not solve them. This attitude must be stopped. Technology is not part of the problem, though it can, where indifference exists, cause problems, but this is as a result of human frailty, not the fault of technology. The blunt truth is that technology has liberated masses of people from drudgery and the sheer struggle to survive. Technology is a force, a powerful force, which can be used to society's advantage. But this will not be possible if we place it in a straitjacket, as has been done through arbitrary and useless regulations, developed in a futile attempt to appease the confrontationalists.

Legislation Ignores Realities

In 1981, the Provincial Government made yet another attempt to bolster its environmental image by introducing the Environmental Management Act. Some never learn. The mandate of the new Act ignores the realities of the issues just presented, while addressing itself to the nebulous theme of the environmental scenario. It proclaims:

> "For the purposes of this Act a detrimental environmental impact occurs when a change in the quality of air, land or water substantially reduces the usefulness of the environment or its capacity to support life."

That the legislation lacks logic, is not hard to perceive. Any development, whatsoever, including your home and the roads you drive on, deprives some species of its natural habitat and lessens the environment's "capacity to support life".

The legislation, in all honesty, was introduced to simply legitimize the activities of the massive staff of pseudo-experts now within the Public Service. It is an open invitation to build academic and bureaucratic empires, as has happened within the Ministry of Environment. Policies, stratagems, standards and objectives are to be developed to further frustrate the progress of the industrial potential of this province, while in no way dealing with the realities of the unavoidable conflict between nature and industry.

In 1983, an Assistant Deputy Minister of the Ministry of Environment, who, by marvellous coincidence, was Chairman of the Public Inquiries just discussed, outlined at an Environmental Government Affairs Seminar in Ottawa some of the Ministry's high priority stratagems as, "production of 500,000 harvestable rainbow trout by the year 1987" and an "average moose population of 30,000". Surely the taxpayer is not to believe that we are sustaining a Ministry of 1,500 people on a budget of $85 million in 1982 for such reasons. Surely the Ministry's primary goal must be directed to developing factual material to counter the persecution of our resource industries?

Anarchist's Cause Growing

That the persecution of Industry is real and that the position is not understood is very evident. Across the top of the front page of the newspaper in bold letters was a headline, "MINING COMPANY Aided Draft of Permit"*, an unquestionable inference that some diabolical impropriety took place. The article states, or rather, accuses representatives of the mining company of helping ". . . draft permits allowing it to dump tailings. . . " and ". . . huddled frequently with top government officials. . . ". The paper, while inciting the public, is saying in effect that our high-priced bureaucracy is not supposed to extend a helping hand of any sort to Industry; that it should not sit down with them and ensure that each understands what the other expects and what can realistically be achieved.

All too many of the little-minded bureaucrats dealing with industries have little or no practical working experience in the areas they claim to understand. And what is the purpose of all the studies and stratagems at public expense, if they are not to be used and discussed to determine practical solutions? Until the media and public recognize and accept the need for some "huddling" between industry and government, the cause of the anarchists will continue to grow.

*Original headline had company's name.

Chapter Nine

ENGINEERING DIFFIDENCE

Where does the civil engineer stand in all of this environmental nonsense? The media, the academics, the environmentalists and the politicians have all been taken to task. Has the engineer done what must be done to ensure that environmental issues have been put in proper perspective? Has he striven with all diligence to ensure that common sense, that blessed ingredient to successful engineering, as well as to progress, will prevail? Or has he taken the easy way out? Has he abdicated his responsibilities to others, and if so, why? Has he forgotten the charter under which he was first spawned?

In 1828 the Institute of Civil Engineers in Great Britain was founded, the forerunner of the North American engineering societies. The society described the profession as *"the art of directing the great sources of power in nature for the use and convenience of man".* Thus, from the outset, civil engineers were charged with the responsibility of working with nature. Where then have they been during the hysteria which took root in the 1960's and which has had a direct and brutal impact on many facets of Society and the profession?

Conspicuous by Absence

It can be said without reservation that the profession has been conspicuous by its absence. It has been delinquent to the shame of all its members. When Public Inquiries were called to debate environmental issues with direct and lasting impact on the future of our social structure, the voice of engineers, as a society, was not raised.

To get a feel for what was going on in engineers' minds let me review some extracts from editorials, correspondence and articles in various engineering journals over the period 1960 to 1980. Perhaps the first symptom to note is apathy. Many articles appeared on this subject.

One started:

> "A deplorable state of apathy now besets the engineering profession in Canada", followed by a list of facts to support the charge. It then goes on to say:
>
> "Can the Engineering profession in Canada fulfill its obligation to society. . . on the basis of such limited effort and attention to technical and professional matters? The purpose to which Canadian engineers profess to be devoted is the efficient development and use of our natural resources . . . Canada cannot effectively take her place in this highly competitive world unless her engineers excel."

Absorbed into Other Groups

About ten years later the following was printed on the same subject:

> "Throughout history, the pattern of groups who neglect their own affairs is that they become absorbed into other groups, or become restrained from acting as they would like. Such groups get and deserve little sympathy from the public at large and are frequently the subject of arbitrary legislation imposed by government. The track record would indicate a high probability of this happening to engineers in B.C."

Another editorial comment excuses its non-committal policy with the following:

> "Some members object to speaking out on the grounds that we should only analyze purely engineering problems. Even then they feel we should be careful not to take sides in supporting a particular solution. This attitude, which we have stuck to over the past years, has been adopted in case we might offend some members. By sticking to this line we have left the field open to other individuals and groups who do not seem to be shackled by the same restrictions."

Further on, the article continues with:

> ". . . critics claim a position should not be taken by the 'Association' unless approved through full exposure to the views of the members. . . If you agree with the critics, the Association will never make significant comment on any matter more contentious than motherhood. . . "

Almost nine years earlier in an editorial in the same journal on the subject of specialized training for engineers, I had written:

> "There is no dispute that the technological control of the physical environment is engineering, but if engineers do not train or equip themselves to competently cope with biological problems in the environment, they need not complain if they find that large sections of their field of endeavour come more

and more under the control of government agencies."

From time to time, articles appear extolling engineers for their practical capabilities and imploring them, because of their practicality, to go into politics, and set the record straight. First of all, there is probably no one around today, politicians included, who does not agree that politics is a hypocritical and conniving business.

Rationalized Answers

A great deal of rationalization has gone into explaining why engineers don't go into politics. The usual reason given is that his basic training teaches him to rely heavily on rationalized answers and to leave hunches and intuitions to those of lesser capability. Politicians love futuristic intangibles, so widely used by the environmentalists, such as talking about a doomsday with no date in mind. Such is not to the liking of a man who chose to be an engineer, because his inherent nature directed him into a calling where he could get peace of mind from finite numbers. If his calculations say the project is safe, then he sleeps well. On the other hand, if his equations do not balance, he will toss and turn all night, and recalculate the whole problem next day until all intangibles are deduced to fall within acceptable confidence limits.

Another argument often put forward relates to possible conflict between the engineering code of ethics and those tactics known as political expediency. Some will recall that a certain structure in British Columiba, which was built in spite of studies confirming a better alternative, was described by a certain Cabinet Minister "as a triumph of politics over engineering". Ethically, an engineer must consider the "well-being" of the public. On the other hand, a politician only needs to outwardly reflect the popular views of the public, while inwardly pursuing the party policy directed solely to ensure re-election: Watergate, et al. Policy, as derived from certain segments or groups may not truly represent the "well-being" of the public. Indeed, what purports to be public opinion, is all too often based on the ideology of minority self-interest groups. Politicians, of course, outwardly respond to such public demands, even when unsubstantiated.

Engineers are trained to respond to demonstrated needs. They must make positive decisions; there is no room for waffling, for political whims. Those gifted and fortunate engineers who must break new ground are conditioned to take calculated risks, provided the data shows a confident chance of success. If the fathers of science and engineering had not had the fortitude to make value judgments, modern society would not today stand on the pinnacle which it occupies. If today's Society does not soon show some of the fortitude which put it on the pinnacle, it will go but one way — down — and fast.

Mostly Superficial

However, such arguments against the engineer entering politics are for the most part superficial. The real reason that engineers avoid politics is because of possible conflict of interest. It is often pointed out that doctors and lawyers go into politics with great frequency, why not engineers? The day-to-day work of doctors and lawyers does not deal with public works, public funds, etc., which provides the bread and butter work of engineers. After all, the word "civil" means "pertaining to a city or state". If the principal of an engineering firm sat in government, would there not be criticism if his firm got government, municipal or other contracts involving public funds? In the light of today's adversary politics, it takes little imagination to answer that question. And so it is, practising engineers do not stay out of politics by choice, they are forced by circumstances to stay away.

That this analysis is all too true, is well summarized by reference to comments attributed to one of the few engineers who have gone into politics. *The Daily Colonist* of January 25, 1979 advised that the Chairman of the Capital Regional Board in Victoria announced he would not vote on, or chair any more meetings that had to do with questions of other engineers' standards, his reasoning being:

> "Neither the Board, nor the public we serve should expect me to preside where these kinds of questions are at issue. The code of ethics and standards of the Association of Professional Engineers are very specific that you have to avoid comment where other engineers are involved."

It is worth observing that the same engineer, before entering the political arena, resigned his professional position as manager of an engineering firm. Indeed, part of the need to take the position stated above, arose from the fact that the firm from which he resigned before entering politics, was then involved in matters affecting the Regional Board, creating a conflict of interest dilemma. It would appear then that for the engineer to function effectively in politics he must divest himself of all association with his calling.

Present Powerful Lobby

But if engineers find politics incompatible with their professional activities, and interests, it does not follow that they cannot present at every opportunity a powerful lobby to government to rebuff the type of irrational and emotional hysteria generated by the environmentalists. Much environmental nonsense now pervades many aspects of the civil engineer's professional activities and challenges his very right to study, develop and control natural forces for the benefit of man, in accord with his professional calling.

Why then are engineers not out in the forefront at public inquiries into environmental matters? To answer this I must draw from experience and set out thoughts based on personal knowledge, which regrettably reflect on the sad state to which the profession of civil engineering in British Columbia has degenerated. In common with most of the human species, today's consulting engineers are money-conscious, which translates into self-interest, rather than professional ideology. It is this self-interest drive, above all else, that has weakened the will of engineers to *speak-out collectively*. They are forsaking the society which they built, to worship instead the idols of gold. That consulting firms should do so, is not too difficult to comprehend in a world of commercialism. Indeed, in the March 1978 edition of the *Journal of the Association of Professional Engineers of B.C.,* an editorial is headed, "It Pays to Advertise" and concludes with the advice to engineers, ". . . get out and sell." Such advice and thinking could well hasten the end of professionalism. For example, I am well aware of an executive consulting engineer who has held some of the highest honourary positions in the engineering associations of this land using expressions like, "More lolly for the boys" and "Pennies from Heaven" when contemplating proposed needless expenditures of large sums of money in the name of environmentalism.

Justly Called Professionals

In the early days when engineers were first entrusted with the task of "directing the great sources of power in nature for the use and convenience of man", they were justly called professionals. Monetary return was secondary to professional competence, status and dignity. Consultants did not ally themselves with commercialism and form limited liability companies, the practice used in the business world as insurance against poor judgment or even downright incompetence. When I first came to this country in 1956, I was more than a little surprised to find that consulting firms were, indeed, limited liability companies.

Today, in Great Britain, where the engineering profession obtained its first charter, the formation of limited liability consulting firms is still taboo. In 1974 the profession in Britain took a close look at the situation. The entire matter of allowing companies to carry limited liability was laid before the membership and council. The proposal to change was soundly defeated by a margin of 3 to 1. Pertinent comments which were published at the time, made it clear that the answer to the quandary:

> ". . . hinges on the contrast between professionalism and commercialism. A commercial concern is there to make money, period. But the professional man is there to put a skill at the service of his client and money comes second. . . That

is why the consultant can adjudicate between a contractor and a client in big claims. If he first thought of his percentage, he would lean to the contractor and if he were anxious for another job, he would favour the client. The consultant's professionalism is measured by the extent to which he does neither . . . This 'alone standing man' could never keep shareholders happy and his professionalism would soon perish.''

Walking Tight Rope

Never were truer words spoken, as I know from personal experience. During one period in my career, I was a shareholder and director in a limited liability company. Over a period of about three years I recall, with documented proof before me as I write, the insatiable devotion of the Board of Directors to matters of profit, shareholdings and equity.

At one period, to upgrade the efficiency of the Company, management consultants were hired to prepare a report. It is interesting to note the delicate manner in which the money-making goal of professional companies was put: "to achieve maximum profitability consistent with excellent professional performance". Now there is a tight rope wire on which to balance.

In the comments published in the British discussion on limited liability are the following highly significant words:

"It is admittedly difficult for firms to build up reserves to allow a partner to take his capital out of the firm at the end of his active engineering life. Corporate structure would ease this problem and critics have suggested that this is the strongest argument now in vogue and hint that most pressure for the change comes from senior men facing that difficulty."

Again I say, from personal experience, how true, but how tragic that professional idealism must take second place to monetary goals. When a top shareholding executive retires, a Company loses on two counts. Not only does the Company lose expertise, but in exchange makes a heavy financial commitment to pay off shareholdings. Those left behind, must now pay off the debt incurred and this can only be done by committing the company to monetary goals, at the expense of professional ideals.

Avoid Taking Position

It is little wonder then that incorporated engineering consultants must pursue policies which lead to monetary gains and by the same token they must, at all costs, avoid taking any position, no matter how strongly they personally feel, that places them, or their company, at variance with popular public opinion, which might tighten the purse strings. This then is why engineers have not come forward to do battle with environmentalism. If the town council wants a tertiary treatment plant, even though it is not needed, the engineer agrees.

The situation is rationalized, of course, somewhat as follows, and I quote from an article in an engineering journal;

". . . engineering work rarely gets started unless a policy decision has been made by a social, political or economical body functioning at a higher level of authority. . . The important thing to recognize is that policy decision responsibilities are not usually given to the engineer to make. . . "

Let me illustrate what happens when an engineer attempts to use his full professional capability to advise a client, who has preconceived notions based on whims. In 1957, as an employee of a leading consulting firm, I was assigned to the task of studying how a certain city could best supplement its water supply. The Mayor of the city decreed that the best way to supplement the water supply was by constructing storage dams in "them thar hills" behind the community. My investigations showed that there was not enough water in "them thar hills" and the economics were poor. Having spent much of the previous seven years of my life studying water resource projects, I was able to quickly deduce that the extensive lake system, on which the city was situated, was the obvious source of water for the city's future needs. I presented my calculations and deductions to my boss, a director of the company, who agreed, without hesitation, that a report should be prepared accordingly.

Withhold Payment

The following week the report was presented to Council. No sooner had the presentation been completed, than the Mayor rather curtly announced that the engineers had been retained to study building dams in "them thar hills". The report, he claimed, was not in accord with the terms of reference, it was unacceptable and he recommended to council that payment for same be withheld.

The upshot of the matter was that we were discharged; the company never got paid. Ironically, dams were never built. A few years later, the recommendations of my report were implemented, to the letter, by the City, under a new council. The very routes suggested for the pipelines were followed, as was the location and method to abstract the water from the lake system. Such incidents are all too numerous and should illustrate the need for engineers to become involved and take an active and aggressive role in the basic decision-making process. Such a vital area cannot be left to the whims of politicians.

Pleaded Their Case

Let us look for a few more moments at the inevitable repercussions of the low key attitude of engineers in the public arena. There is no doubt in my mind, and it was made abundantly clear to me in my official capacity as head of pollution control, that engineers were deeply concerned about the way things were going. Many called at my office to plead their case.

I often openly acknowledged agreement with the points made and invariably recommended that the matters be presented to the Cabinet. Those with whom I talked were in some cases members of the Council of Professional Engineers, or held office in Association affairs. I exhorted them to take their cases through the Engineering Association Council to the Government. There was a common response to such exhortations: The majority of the engineering council were not directly involved with environmental matters and the concensus of council, when such matters were raised, was that individual firms would have to fend for themselves. Taking a cursory glance at the composition of the Councils over a number of years, I note only a few faces who are readily recognized as knowledgeable in the field of environmental engineering, thus giving credence to the case made by those who spoke with me. Is it any wonder then, that engineers have lost their voice in the environmental fray?

Increasingly Concerned

As a result of the discussions and proddings, bits and pieces of correspondence directed to members of the Cabinet reached my desk. Such presentations are most enlightening and of particular interest to this review, as they set out explicitly those matters which were causing grave concern. In addition, the material confirms the points which I have earlier recounted. One leading firm, perhaps the forerunner in the field in the province, put the matter this way:

"We are becoming increasingly concerned with the manner in which pollution control is being handled in our province, not only from a professional standpoint but also as taxpayers. Pollution control has become a very emotional subject and in too many instances reason has not prevailed. In addition to this, duplication of effort and obvious disagreements between the departments now involved in pollution control, have done little to gain the confidence of either the public or those involved in attempting to determine what is required. . . We feel that the situation has reached the intolerable position where development is apparently going to be stifled. . . As 'free enterprisers' in an ever-increasing bureaucratic society, we are more than somewhat concerned with the trends toward the development of larger and larger administrative bureaus which sometimes become autocratic as well as inflexible and expensive."

Reviewed against what I have disclosed in earlier pages, the above abstract shows that the private sector were all too conscious of the nonsense which was going on, and of the wasteful conflict between the bureaucratic departments.

However, while a few letter briefs and the like from engineering professionals appealing for a more rational approach by the body politic did, from time to time, appear, they were in essence, of a cautious character, lamenting that all was not well and pleading for a change. To my knowledge, no forthright factual hard-hitting document appeared, certainly none from the engineering association, with the thrust needed to counter the irrational propaganda of the environmental activists.

Reluctance to do Battle

The reluctance of engineering firms to do battle with the bureaucracies is not too difficult to understand, when reviewed against their monetary goals and the fact that government departments are prepared to squander vast sums of money on useless research, which would naturally go only to those firms which paid lip service to the cause. For example, one news item puts the matter this way:

"Seek out the enemy and perhaps you can get rid of him. This is the latest approach to pollution by Environment Canada. The federal department is going ahead with a Canada-wide inventory of sources of most popular* pollutants. Inventories of this kind are an essential part of the process of clearing up, says the Environment Minister. Toronto-based engineering consultants have a contract to do the evaluation. . . "

Or take this quote:

"Federal Government officials will contract out almost all of its research and development programs to private industry under a major policy shift, says the Minister for Science and Technology. . . It will mean that private industry will receive most of the $635 million now being spent."

The above statement omits to say what happens to those currently doing the work. A rough estimate of the number of employees in governments, masquerading under the cloak of environmental activities in Canada, could well exceed 15 to 20 thousand. Based on the bureaucratic expose presented earlier, it is not unreasonable to suggest that this army is so enmeshed with its own paper-work that its staff can no longer do the job for which they were hired, thus the need for consultants.

---

*I wonder which is the more popular pollutant, cigarettes or beer?

I am sure the reader will have little trouble relating to the fact that money-oriented consultants, are all too willing to take their cut of the monstrous waste without challenging the morality of the issue. How about this for the prize in lunacy?

> "Consultants have been retained at an estimated cost of $90,000 to do an 18-month study to determine whether municipal sewage can be transported under high pressure . . . The Environment Minister said that current methods of moving sewage are based on gravity flow and go back to the days of the Roman aqueducts. I hope we can improve on that. . . "

Rivers have been flowing under gravity a lot longer time than that which has elapsed since the Roman Empire reached its zenith. Maybe the Minister should set up a study to see if we can improve on that. The wheel, too, predates Roman times, yet we still use it. How backward can we be? Indeed, if energy costs keep soaring, we might well in the not too distant future, be converting many of our present day pressure systems over to gravity.

Guilt Complex

Due to the incessant attacks by environmentalists on the engineering profession as a whole, engineers have, in some cases, developed guilt complexes, as if they are responsible for many of the world's development woes. One engineer put it this way in an engineering journal:

> "Since the earliest beginning of our profession, engineers have been intimately involved in all forms of pollution. We have been responsible for designing and building it. . . "

Really! Engineers who glibly admit to such complicity have a very limited knowledge of what went on in the evolution of Society. In the beginning of our modern social structure, the engineer, invariably, appeared on the scene after the problem had arisen. He was called in to find a solution and I might add, always at a cost in keeping with funds available and other priorities. Cities were not created by engineers. Man from the earliest of times decided, through instinct, that the security of his future evolution and well-being necessitated that he form communities, for reasons which we need not cover here. And because man chose to live in communities, many of which eventually became cities, problems of pollution arose from his inherent biological nature and other habits.

One of the top priorities for survival was a supply of potable water. In one answer to this solution those forerunners of the modern engineer provided the magnificient aqueducts which, as I understand it, Environment Canada would be loathe to approve today, because of their gravity-using design.

With the arrival of the much-needed life-sustaining water, of course, came the problem of disposal of waste water after use. If man had contented himself with only using that needed to sustain his thirst and a sponge bath, no problems would have arisen. But water was put to many uses, with the result that vast quantities of offensive waste liquids occurred. The early engineers met Society's immediate need, by building drains to take the water away. For instance, the great sewer known as the *cloaca maxima* was constructed in the first century to drain the Roman Forum. Believe it or not, it is still in service. A gravity system too!

Pestilence and Death

To better understand the evolution of the control of the wastes created by society, let us look for a moment at what was happening in the middle of the Nineteenth Century. With the rapid growth of population, Society in England in the Nineteenth Century was being enveloped with a hideous problem. Let me quote from the 1842 Report from the Poor Law Commissioners of Great Britain:

> "Dwellings of the poor were arranged round narrow courts having no other opening to the main street than a narrow covered passage. In these courts there were several occupants, each of whom accumulated a heap. In some cases, each of these heaps was piled up separately in the court, with a general receptacle in the middle of the court for the general use of all the occupants. In some the whole courts up to the very doors of the houses were covered with filth."

It is not hard to understand that such conditions could only lead to pestilence and death. The apocalyptic horsemen rode rampant through the cities. Then, about the 1850's, the engineer was commissioned to provide sanitary sewers. His immediate task was to get the sewage out of the house, the courtyard and off the street. In some cases, a form of treatment was provided, in others, the waste was removed to large rivers or the sea where nature took over and stabilized the situation, though man at the time did not understand how. As a result, improved public health swept the nation. Phase one had been successful. Phase two is still going on, namely the development and provision of adequate treatment to protect the health of people and the aesthetics of the environment.

The purpose of the brief review given above is to show that charges that engineers, through use of their technology have created problems, is not in keeping with the facts. The truth is, that while there are problems, they are greatly reduced by the use of engineering science.

The problems are made by societies and their needs. Engineering is the foremost and only worthwhile tool we have to lessen these problems, short of going back to caves, of course, which appears to be about the only answer acceptable to the environmental cult.

A Technological Moron

The Engineer is often charged with the creation of utilitarian structures, with all of their inherent unaesthetic characteristics. He is cast as a man without a soul for beauty, a technological moron, who has but one goal, at least in the eyes of the environmentalists, to subdue and crush nature. If the engineer does today build utilitarian structures, or appears to take "short cuts", which may leave him open to ridicule, then perhaps his critics should ask themselves, why?

There are many striking examples of engineering achievements down through the ages, all of which incorporate in their design a grand magnificence which holds us awe-spelled even today, with all of our modern technological wonders. The magnificent aqueducts of the ancient Romans, is but one example. When there were no restraints on the engineer, he could pour his soul into his work as well as his technology, both of which, when combined, often produce works of sheer beauty and genius. If one cares to look at the engineering works carried on around the turn of this century, you cannot fail to observe in every phase of work, the pride of those responsible, though by today's standards, as dictated by monetary restraints, they would be deemed extravagant. Pick up any engineering book and look at the illustrations of the older works and note the total absence of any semblance of utilitarianism. All were not, of course, beautiful; some tended to cater in style to a bygone era; some were gaudy, much to their loss, but all at least attempted to enhance the surroundings. The foregoing also applied to bridges, those great structures for spanning gaps left in nature to the inconvenience of man. Tut! tut! Mother Nature, how could you?

But over recent years, compelling changes have been taking place, due to the influence of many factors affecting costs. As a result, social priorities have had to be re-evaluated, as money is needed in other areas. Houses, hospitals, schools, roads, and other public services, to name but a few of the more obvious. And so the granite or masonary buildings with their parapets, cornices and gargoyles are replaced with utilitarian concrete boxes, and in no time at all, these austere works become the order of the day for the engineer, who has only so much money allocated by Society to produce a solution.

Rapid growth

But a more insidious change has overtaken the engineer in rapidly developing communities in British Columbia. I recall being involved with the development of a treatment plant for a village in northern

British Columbia. The community, as is the case with most small communities in this province, was growing rapidly. There was a need for some treatment of the wastes. In such cases the choice of the best size of plant requires judgment that would make Solomon think twice. Questions to be tackled are: how rapidly is the community growing, when will its population double, treble, etc.? In what direction is development going, what degree of treatment is needed, where is the best location for a plant, and so on?

Obviously, there is little point in building a plant just large enough for the present population, because next year the plant will be too small. Conversely, if a plant is sized to meet the needs of the too distant future, capital is used up and maintenance costs accrue for works which are not being put to use. As a compromise to this, engineers have stretched ingenuity to the breaking point to get maximum return for expenditures. In the case under discussion, it was decided that the plant should be designed in such a way as to allow duplication in the future. One-half would be built first, sized to take the present flow, plus the increase expected over five to seven years, at which time the second half would be built. The scheme was approved, and half the plant built.

And what of the outcome? There occurred, over a three year period, an unforseen growth in population because a new forest products industry moved into the area. It was found that duplication of the plant, as had been planned, would barely meet the newly-created needs. New engineering economic studies showed that the plant should be abandoned in favour of a larger one designed to meet the new population criteria. It is not hard to understand in such cases the reluctance of communities to provide monies for ornate works. On the other hand, if the works are going to be around and admired for the best part of a century, or longer, then the cost of aesthetics becomes a worthwhile consideration. Because of the increased rate of progress and development in recent years such acts of compromise are an inescapable part of our modern day system.

Count Down to Doom

Perhaps this is where I should recount a futile attempt to join the environmental battle on behalf of engineers. Back in 1970, while I was perusing my copy of the *B.C. Professional Engineers Journal,* a headline caught my eye:

"Pollution — Do You Believe It?"

My curiosity was aroused. I read the article which started:

"Some authorities are maintaining today that, if the present rate of population and industrial expansion and the present rate of environmental pollution continue, the earth will be unable to support life in its present form within a generation or so. In fact some of the authorities give us as little as ten years before we must succumb to the filth that we are generating."

The article continued by summarizing many of the general environmental fads of today and concluded with an appeal to the Engineering Profession to take a closer look at this matter with the hope of finding the answer. I responded by offering my services and a few forthright comments to boot.

I received no reply, nor have I heard of any earth-shaking policy developments by the Association's Committee, though in 1977 a so-called "Environmental Policy Statement" was made which is so non-committal as to be useless. It states for example, "The Association and the Society encourage public input during consideration of all major projects." This pandering attitude is what has engendered the wide-spread environmental nonsense which now pervades every aspect of our social structure.

Hamstring and Control

Before concluding this chapter, I quote a letter written by an Ontario engineer. Part of the content of the letter contains a number of thoughts which I have presented in this book, the main one being the alliance between environmentalism and socialism:

"Whether Engineering knows it or not, it is being used to foster and promote world totalitarian government. . . The emphasis on doomsday ecological and environmental propaganda aids those in society who would subvert our politically libertarian and economically competitive free society to one of suppression and state monopoly.

"It is a fact that the ecology movement has been created in the United States by certain wealthy, tax-exempt organizations which fund radicals. . . with the hope that enough concern will be generated among the populace that strict environmental legislation will be enacted.

"The real purpose of this legislation is to hamstring and control business in order to destroy competition, create shortages in key industries, and give government ever-increasing power. These aims were partially attained in the National Environmental Policy Act passed in 1969, in the United States. . . It is not surprising that the U.N. is tooting the 'ecological disaster unless world government' horn. The U.N. represents the most important and dangerous tool of the one world dictatorship lobby.

". . . engineers (must) not be conned into accepting and even promoting world or federal pollution law. Municipal law where necessary will do the job and will not be prone to political misuse at a national or international level. This principle is important if we wish to pass freedom and liberty on to our children.''

Stewards of the Land

I can find no better conclusion to this chapter than the following challenging words of Robert F. Legget, a prominent Canadian engineer, given in a 1979 speech at the University of New Brunswick. In his address he asks: "Why are engineers silent?"

"Where is the voice of the engineer in the Canada of today? Engineering has as its greatest responsibility the development and husbanding of the physical resources of this land, in the broadest sense of that term — in effect being 'Stewards of the Land'. . . In earlier years the voice of the profession was heard on many national resource issues. It issued public statements and made submissions to the Government when it seemed appropriate to do so. . . But today? When was the voice of the profession last heard on any national issue?. . . Why has the voice of the engineer become so muted?"

The author hopes the reader will find the answer to Mr. Legget's searching inquiry within these pages, but more so, that this brief review of where engineering stands will prompt the profession to shake off the lethargy which has enveloped it, so that it may again assume its rightful position in the decision-making process. It is not being proposed that engineers rush into politics, God forbid!; but rather that a powerful engineering lobby be presented at all times in the decision-making process.

Chapter Ten

BRITISH COLUMBIA

Part I: WHAT IS THY DESTINY?

And now the time has come to look at British Columbia in all its present grandeur and to contemplate its future. And what an exciting and rewarding future it can have. But first, the "no-growth" and "tourist paradise" proponents must be laid to rest. To speak of "no-growth" and British Columbia in the same breath, is so nonsensical that one wonders at the sanity and marvels at the ignorance of those who propound such themes.

There are some very self-evident facts which must be recognized and accepted about British Columbia. The case for industrialization of this great Province is overwhelming. British Columbia and industry are so inevitably inter-related that to ignore such evidence is tantamount to ignoring destiny. From the very first day I saw British Columbia (after working and travelling all over the world), it has meant two things to me: spectacular beauty and industrial power, particularly the latter, for there is, in truth, much wondrous natural beauty to be seen in most places in the world.

Those who live in British Columbia are fortunate. They are surrounded by rugged beauty in such abundance that it may indeed be taken for granted. But, while British Columbia has unsurpassed natural beauty, it is not quite the "Utopia" that the money-hungry tourist industry would lead us to believe.

British Columbia offers a rich variety of scenery to captivate the travelling, sightseeing tourist, which makes up the greater majority of those that visit the province for a short time each summer. Some come, of course, to fish and hike and climb, or in the winter to ski, but the greater majority prefer to stay close to their automobiles, campers and trailers, and gaze on the wondrous landscape. Most are, in truth, windshield tourists.

Compensation to Non-Tourists

For short seasons, in many areas, British Columbia can claim to have true recreational potential to suit specific tastes, but to portray British Columbia as the recreational paradise of North America, is rubbish. Those renowned resort areas which are universally acclaimed as such, and to which, in truth, British Columbians, when possible, escape each winter, have balmy, holiday inducing atmospheres, with glorious golden beaches washed by tepid sea waters. Yet the tourist industry, academics and environmentalists, would like us to believe that the destiny of British Columbia is as a recreational paradise, that the land should be protected for posterity. Nothing could be further from the truth.

Indeed, when one considers the congestion created all summer long on our highways and ferries, one cannot, in all honesty, but question the wisdom of subsidizing this type of activity, since the loss to others, going about their normal day-to-day business, is substantial. Perhaps the tourist industry would like to consider paying compensation to non-tourists for lost time at ferry terminals, or for the added expense of having to use aircraft. Maybe the time has come to give priority on the ferries to those on *bona fide* business.

The winter climate in most of British Columbia is harsh, making it unsuitable for any but a few specialized winter sports. The great mountain ranges of British Columbia are awesome and perilous. A frantic struggle goes on all winter long to keep the lines of communication open. To leave the highway, is to get lost. Even great perils overtake those that stay on the beaten track from destructive floods, snow, ice and rock avalanches. Such is the nature of this great land.

Held Spellbound

I have travelled British Columbia from end to end, in winter and summer. In the exercise of my profession over 25 years, I have virtually travelled every strip of major highway in the Province, on more than a few occasions, when weather conditions would permit. I have viewed it from aloft as I have criss-crossed the Province in the air. I have, for both business and pleasure, sailed on its coastal waters; I have enjoyed its scenic wonders; hiked in its mountains; anchored in its inlets; I have been spellbound.

British Columbia, in truth, is a great panorama of rugged beauty. This is from where it gets its reputation. The great mountain masses, the powerful rivers, the glistening lakes, the snow capped peaks, the pine forests, the long narrow inlets, the coastal islands, all combine to cast their spell. British Columbia is, indeed, "Steeped in eternal beauty", to use the words of Robert Service. But, take heed that the spell it casts does not deceive you. What Service said of the Yukon equally applies:

> "Wild and wide are my boundaries, stern as death is my sway
> From my ruthless throne I have ruled alone,
> For a million years and a day.
> Hugging my mighty treasure, waiting for man to come . . . "

British Columbia is, above all else, a storehouse of industrial wealth. If common sense is to prevail, industrialization is our destiny. To contemplate maintaining great areas of wilderness, to the exclusion of resource development, is nonsense. The economy of British Columbia is almost solely dependent on the exploitation of the natural resources of lumbering, wood processing, mining and fishing. This is why we are here, to wrest our living from the mighty environment which surrounds us.

Rotting Forests

While many people seem to think that vast wilderness areas and public recreation are synonymous, nothing could be further from the truth. Without the aid of well-developed access and trails, wilderness forests are most uninviting places; they are even unacceptable to many forms of wildlife indigenous to British Columbia. Few will deny that the retention of small carefully selected wilderness areas should certainly fall within the scope of any scenario of the future, purely as natural monuments for man to gaze upon. As for recreation, it is fair to comment that our citizens at large, gain their enjoyment in other ways. In any event, the day is not too far off when society will be confronted with a wood crisis, as with oil. We simply cannot allow our forest lands to lie dormant and rot away. It does not serve the best interests of man *nor the animal kingdom.*

British Columbia has all the natural resource ingredients to make it one of the world's great industrial empires. Abundant energy is available through hydro-electric, coal, oil and natural gas. Natural mineral resources abound in the mountains and their valleys. The surface is cloaked with massive forests of timber. Raw water supplies are available equal to, or in excess of any needs which may arise. The coasts, inlets, and rivers abound in fish of some commercial value. The coastline provides unsurpassed natural harbours for trade on the high seas to offshore lands, where goods must go. The climate is conducive to productivity, the Province lies in the same latitude as the great industrial nations of Northern Europe. Why then all the reluctance to get on with the inevitable? If we don't do it, another generation will.

Industrial Needs Ignored

During the years that I served in Government, it became distressingly apparent as the pressures of the subversives mounted, that our so-called free enterprise politicians, lured on by the vain hope of capturing environmental votes, one by one turned their backs on the needs of industry, the very blood stream of our society. Openly, they paid lip service to the environmental nonsense as described in earlier chapters. Governments come and governments go. A Cabinet Minister in charge of resources in the only socialist government to hold office in British Columbia simply ignored the pleas of industry while referring to them as "bloody capitalists". Any elected government which fails to give high priority to the needs of industry is delinquent. As a result of the socialists, a decline in industrial activity in this resource-rich province was aggravated during their years of office in the 70's.

The world needs our industrial potential to be harnessed. To do so does not mean a destruction of the natural beauty around us. The land must be reshaped to better serve man's needs. Reshaping the land will not destroy it. Those emotional phrases such as permanent environmental damage, fragile environment, unique ecosystem and the like, are nothing more than the perfidious wails of the ecological gods. Just as the lands across the Atlantic have been reshaped and yet retain all their beauty, so too can British Columbia. Indeed, reshaping the land will in many ways enhance it for the future. There is always an immediate adverse effect with any development, but in time, generations perhaps, the final outcome will be better for man and equally as good as the old, as far as nature is concerned. There is no evidence to confound this, and experience supports it.

Recuperative Powers of Nature

Nature in her own way is a harsh, ruthless, brutal shaper and reshaper of the face of the earth. And the face of British Columbia has felt this ferocity. A mere twenty thousand years ago, British Columbia was a great block of ice with only the peaks of the mountains emerging to look at the sky. The ice age lasted thousands of years. When the ice, estimated to be at least a mile thick, receded, it takes little imagination to visualize the gouged and denuded landscape. No lush vegetation or forests, no animals, fish or life as we understand it. This was just over 10,000 years ago and yet today we are surrounded by the wonders of a vigorous biological and very alive environment.

I even have a more recent example right from our own day to day doings to illustrate the recuperative powers of nature. There is a small confined inlet on which is located an older pulp mill, where the effluent is discharged untreated. Some years ago, I was retained by the Company to study the matter. During my review of the situation, a most interesting event occurred. Due to the older and poorly-conceived method of discharging the effluent, the waters in the immediate vicinity of the mill discharge suffered from oxygen depletion with the result that fish and other forms of indigenous sea life were generally absent.

The waters were highly coloured and the inlet bottom close to the discharge was coated with wood fibre. There was much foam and other scum evident. In short, the area was not too appealing, if one was looking for a water hole in which to relax.

During this period, the mill, due to labour unrest, was forced to shut down. Effluent discharge ceased. In a matter of days the waters quickly took on the appearance of the natural waters in the surrounding area. Fish, bottom life and other biological forms all reappeared in a matter of days. Indeed, their rapid reappearance was to create a problem for on restart-up of the mill there was in the vicinity of the discharge an inevitable fish kill, quite small of course, and of no consequence, though it did lead to a prosecution due to little-minded Federal bureaucrats seeking their day of glory to justify their existence.

However, the point of the incident is that within days, once the polluting discharge stopped, the natural environment started to rapidly return; thus the cry of permanent damage which is often levelled at such operations, is without substance. No matter how desecrated an area may become, if the time ever arrives when such is needed for natural production, it can readily be effected.

Frightening Consequences

Perhaps the ultimate evidence needed to convince the reader of this truth is by reference to Hiroshima. While no one can deny, and all must surely deplore, the awful holocaust created by nuclear bombs and the frightening consequences to those immediately affected, it is a simple truth that in spite of the desolation created, the city of Hiroshima in a few short years arose from the ashes of what we were assured was "permanent destruction". Today, Hiroshima is a beautiful, vibrant city demonstrating that almighty nature is anything but fragile.

One of British Columbia's renowned conservation writers, the late Roderick Haig-Brown, an avid proponent of the environmental cause, in an article dealing with salmon, said with respect to the Fraser River:

"This is the environment that produced the great salmon runs, and by digging into this environment we have created many problems."

It is interesting to speculate that because of the ice age, there were no salmon runs in many, or all of British Columbia's rivers, just 10,000 years ago, yet the species, *per se,* goes back for millions of years. Obviously the fish by their own instincts sought out and adopted suitable alternative spawning grounds during the ice age, assuming of course that they frequented British Columbia waters before that era. It is recorded in more recent times, and to the "amazement" of biologists, that salmon which were displaced by the Mount St. Helens eruption have sought out spawning grounds in other waters.

Fish "Ranching"

A reality of fish enhancement, which is played down by government fishery agencies, is the fact that prolific salmon runs can be created just about anywhere along the British Columbia coast by the introduction of hatcheries, or by fish "ranching". The Capilano River hatchery is a typical example, where millions of fish returned in the late summer of 1979, of which only a few thousand spawners were needed to replenish the run, the remainder going to the canneries. Such methods would eliminate many of the traditional, but antiquated methods of catching fish at sea. Many, no doubt, would be opposed to such a change, as the fisherman's love of the sea dies hard.

In mid-1983, a Provincial Government proposal to implement such a scheme got this response from a well-known newspaper columnist:

"... a frightening plan that could threaten the very future of sport fishing. It could also see the start of the end of the commerical fishing fleets..."

This outburst, believe it or not, was generated by a fear that his personal fishing interests would be threatened. To bolster his cause, he even stooped to dragging in the threat to the fishing fleet, something he had attacked in earlier articles when he perceived the commerical fleet might one day take all his fish. Such are the vagaries with which the decision-maker in society must contend.

On the homefront, consider for a moment, all of the home gardener's efforts of soil-turning, grass-cutting, pruning, spraying, and the interminable war against the dandelions, which goes on year in, year out in his battle to keep the natural species from taking over; weigh it against such phrases as the "delicate balance of the eco-system", or "fragile environment". Then look at the glorious biological environment which surrounds us and contemplate that just over 10,000 years ago nature crushed it. By comparison, is not man's interference puny? And what of those abandoned ancient cities now buried in jungle growth to such an extent that natives looked upon such mounds as phenomena of nature, little realizing that the remains of an ancient civilization lay buried in the lush vegetation. The irony in all of this is that those who understand will agree in private that such is the case.

Author Considered Right

At the time I resigned from Government, the head of one of the most forceful environmental pressure groups in the province made such a confession to me in the confines of my office. This man had spearheaded the attack against the discharge of mine tailings into Buttle Lake, without doubt the most effective method to handle the tailings. After I had announced my resignation, during a discussion in my office, in wishing me well in my future, he said, "off the record" he considered that my position had been right, but as he was heading up an anti-everything organization, he was obliged to take the militant position he had. Here is a letter he wrote to me at the time:

> "On behalf of the officers, directors, and members of our Association I would like to convey to you our appreciation for the manner in which you have carried out your duties as Director of the Pollution Control Branch.
>
> "We recognize that we have been at odds on occasions. However, we have always recognized the difficult position in which you have been placed, and have appreciated the overwhelming task that you have been forced to undertake. While we may have disagreed with you from time to time on details, we have always had the highest regard for your personal ability and integrity, and I can assure you we have been aware of the complex social and political factors that were bound to affect your Department."

He is now an environmental consultant, one of those who advocate that we must do an environmental study before we take a pee behind a tree. He is in truth the epitome of the intellectual environmental parasite. When we last met he was working primarily on Government studies, financed lavishly by taxpayers' money, to come up with reports which end by telling us what we already know, and recommending that further studies be undertaken — just in case. It is somewhat ironical to note that he has subsequently been before the courts for flagrant violation of wildlife regulations, needed to protect the animal kingdom from rapacious hunters, which he proved to be, in spite of his professed concern for the outdoors environment. I have always questioned in my own mind the environmental sincerity of the many Fish and Game clubs, whose only goals seem to be to preserve wildlife to satisfy a lust to hunt and kill. Perhaps they see environmentalism as a form of penance.

"Unholy Alliance"

Let us look more closely, for a moment, at the destiny of British Columbia and the posture of the doom-and-gloom proponents. Leading environmentalists in British Columbia have for years talked in disparaging terms of the "unholy alliance between Government and Industry". In blunt language can I ask just what-the-hell is the relationship between Government and Industry supposed to be? Are these people not aware that Industry is the source of wealth in our modern society? Without Industry our society collapses, and this is not a mythical collapse like the ones the environmentalists predict. Do these people think that industries produce goods just for their own amusement and use?

If you don't happen to earn your bread and butter directly in association with Industry, be assured that indirectly that's where your meal ticket comes from. Industry produces to meet the needs and demands of the people; does government not purport to represent people? A government, which alleges to serve people but not Industry is not only hypocritical but downright irrational and dishonest. Such hypocrisy cannot survive. An alliance of understanding between government and Industry is so fundamental to the progress of our system that we must be leery of the motives of those that advocate otherwise.

Indeed, if there is an unholy alliance it exists between the environmentalists and the socialists. Some years ago, as a result of contemplating those with which I had to contend in the exercise of my duties, and as a result of studying numerous briefs and petitions, I formed a very definite feeling that socialism and environmentalism were common bedfellows. As recent proof of this allegation I have a cutting from the press published a few days after the socialists lost power to the Social Credit Party in the December 1975 provincial election in British Columbia.

Under the headline, "ENVIRONMENTALISTS WARY OF SOCREDS", is a summary of spokesmen for most of the leading environmental groups in the province, which, of course, includes the Sierra Club, as a front runner, followed closely by SPEC. No time was lost in casting brickbats at the incoming free enterprise party, while distributing bouquets to the defeated socialists.

Regretted Defeat of Socialists

One environmental group leader signified that he regretted the defeat of the socialists by suggesting they had done "a hell of a good job". If you place "hand-outs" to environmental parasites high on your list of priorities, he is correct. A spokesman for a second group endorsed the hand-out sentiment by commenting that he hoped "the new government will continue with the environmental programs already in progress." A third group expressed fear that the new government would go back to "the old ways of ripping out resources without much concern for damage done." A fourth group, with international overtones, expressed concern "that the new government with its promised stress on resource and industrial development will create new problems."

While condemning the media throughout these pages for its role in the cancerous growth of environmentalism, it is ironical that the same media provides us with the needed antidote, provided we are immune to the intrigue going on around us. *The Daily Colonist,* September 23, 1978, carried a headline which read, "Labour next hope — Sierra Club".

The article accompanying the headline states that workers may start refusing to carry out environmentally-damaging assignments, according to the American president of the Sierra Club. Since this book documents the humbug surrounding environmentalism, it is with grave concern that all must view the possible alliance of labour with such intangible and emotional forces. Such a union would create utter chaos within our decision-making process, as rationality obviously could not be a part of any reconciliatory negotiations since environmentalism is devoid of such. Such an alliance conjures up thoughts of our society being blackmailed to an even greater extent than at present by bullying labour unions.

Tourism Rates First?

In the article the Sierra Club president states, "Instead of cutting trees, people would be catering to tourists, there would be a need for services, for outfitters and guides, camping facilities, stores, transportation and motels. If the tourist industry (in British Columbia) builds up, there will be a continuous demand for wilderness areas".

The Sierra Club is surely naive in suggesting that we abandon our primary source of income, forestry, and replace it with the tourist business; that we set the mighty and wealthy resources of British Columbia aside as a wilderness for tourists (Americans presumably), who make their untold wealth from exploitation of their own natural resources, while we take up some more menial task and be their humble servants.

To contemplate curtailing, in any way, development of our vast resource industries in favour of tourism that is forever whining for government concessions to fill their own selfish pockets is ludicrous. Society must be wary not to allow such attitudes to destroy our technical and economic capability, as is now happening. We must surround ourselves with the will to fight this socially cancerous doctrine. Labour too should be wary of aligning itself with the eco-freaks. Surely the working man must feel that being part of the prosperous forest industry is a much nobler occupation than selling trinkets to tourists. In any event, the development of our natural resources will not lessen tourism. The wondrous beauty of the landscape is too massive and eternal.

Opposed to Any Mining

To illustrate the typical attitude of those opposed to industrialization of the Province, let me quote a revealing example involving a protest by a school assistant superintendent against a small mining operation secluded in a treed mountain valley. The letter of protest, with copies to various cabinet ministers and others, has been condensed:

> ". . . I am opposed to any mining in the area. It should be retained as purely recreational land. No mining or logging . . . In late fall I hiked adjacent to the area in question. Numerous claim stakes, ribbons, survey marks were found.

If the area in which these materials were found is to be mined, I feel sorry for the burgeoning population of the lower mainland who need all available recreational space — ponds included.

"In my position as Assistant Superintendent, I am charged with the responsibility of making instruction in the district relevant to both the present and the future needs of students. To this end I have circulated my concerns to all district schools for discussion in social studies and senior geography classes. . . Already, our students who frequently utilize the area heavily for geography science, community recreation and outdoor education classes are fed up with the treatment the area is receiving. On one occasion one of the groups was not permitted in to hike by a couple of men on a bulldozer.

"You can begin to appreciate how I feel. Any person who makes a statement (as reported)' . . . the lake is a natural tailing disposal site. It's a dead pond, there's no life in it, so what else is it good for?' raises the hackles of teachers, particularly well-trained biology teachers and biology students, throughout this district."

An analysis of the above shows the all too prevalent blatant disregard for facts. The mine is isolated. It is surrounded by hundreds of thousands of acres of similar type of heavily-treed land where hiking can be carried on, if one so wishes, though, in truth, hiking off the beaten track in such country, is neither pleasurable nor recommended. Indeed, once the mine road is completed, it actually makes the surrounding area more accessible for public use, if not immediately, certainly when the mining activity ceases, which in this case will be within a decade or two.

Ideology is Idiocy

The objection is typical of hundreds which I received, over many years, from every corner of the Province. Note the blanket "no mining or logging". Such ideology is idiocy. Just where does the money come from to sustain the misguided "intellectual" if we close all our mines and stop all our logging? Here is a member of society, who has his salary paid by taxes (from industry) and because our society, whether we like it or not, provides him with a couple of months holidays each summer, he wants the wealth of the countryside retained in a pristine state for his hiking activities. Just what-the-hell do such people think life is all about?

On top of that, here is an educator exhorting his students to protest the very means of their future livelihood. Is it any wonder then that in the press we get plaintive cries from our mis-informed students? Here are a few lines from a lengthy letter in the media to the Government. It protests an extensive in-depth review of the respective values of forestry, wildlife, fishing and recreation made prior to granting permission to log in the Tsitika valley on Vancouver Island.

"As young citizens we are deeply concerned about the. . . decision to allow logging in the Tsitika River watershed . . . The. . . management plan. . . appears to have ignored the scientific and educational values of the area . . . Conventional logging will disturb this ecosystem. . . a living laboratory will be destroyed. . . "

Few would deny that the letter arises from academic indoctorination and none can deny the emotional appeal. But, in truth, the position taken is totally out of perspective with reality.

Focus on Cities

Each time I fly over the land and look down, I never cease to wonder at the enormous amount of undeveloped countryside lying below. British Columbia, viewed from the air, is one great mass of forests and mountains with fine ribbon-like roads, barely visible, linking communities, which from the air appear to sit in the middle of a vast wilderness. The settled areas comprise less than one percent of the land area and contain over 80 percent of the population. Indeed, four out of every five people in our society live and work within the totally unnatural confines of urban areas. To improve the quality of life for society, attention must be focused on cities and the working environment.

Perhaps the truth of the environmental issue lies in the following incident. At the time of the public Inquiry to determine the pollution control measures to be adopted by the mining industry, the head of one of the largest environmental pressure groups in British Columbia contacted certain mining companies to obtain data to help prepare a brief. In a meeting with company officials he was told that the next time he was driving up to the interior of the province he was welcome to call at any of the Company's mines. His response was incredible. He advised that he never visited the interior of the province, or any of the areas where the mines were. Yet here he was, spearheading a pressure organization, hell-bent on condemning our resource industries.

Cultivated Landscape

Much of the scenery in countries across the Atlantic is in complete contrast to that of British Columbia. Instead of tree-clad mountains rising to dizzy heights, one can enjoy the beauty of the patchwork quilt-like rolling hills, cleared of trees, where the eye can feast on the maze of cultivated fields with their hedgerows, ditches, stone walls and cottages. If it's not raining (one reason, why I left) one can see the higher peaks, denuded of trees of course, but still all beautiful, covered in purple heather, with the massive outcrops of ever-enduring granite. According to environmentalists, the environment of these highly-cultivated lands should be in a state of collaspse. No birds, no animals, no insects, just desolation. But it simply isn't so.

One evening I was watching an enlightening television documentary about the Lake District, in Britain. It was fascinating to observe that one of the primary concerns of those trying to preserve the Lake District beauty, is how to retain the changes made by man. The commentary said that every effort was to be made to maintain the beauty of the fields created by the farmers as they had reshaped the landscape over hundreds of years. To me, this was full recognition of the beauty created by man in harnessing and reshaping nature to his needs. The commentary went on to say that a bleak and unkempt wilderness will occur if the area is not cared for along the lines of the farmers. It is pertinent to note that one of the hysterical claims of the Scenic Hudson environmental group goes:

"We believe that ugliness begets ugliness and that nature's beauty, once destroyed, may never be restored by the artifice of man. . . "

One of the most beautiful gardens in the Victoria area, the world renowned Butchart Gardens, was created out of an abandoned quarry. Haven't the ecologists heard?

Nothing is Forever

One statement was made in the Lake District documentary with which I must disagree. No doubt it was used with poetic licence, though technically inaccurate. It is one of those phrases used by environmental fanatics, when attempting to alarm their subjects. The comment was: ". . . if they are to survive forever".

Nothing survives forever; the sun will one day cease and so will all life on earth. Those who profess to understand ice ages predict that the ice will once again return within a matter of thousands of years to cover British Columbia and not one tree, one pond, one river, one lake will be spared the ravages of the glacial monster on the move. We can only hope that Mother Nature will first submit her environmental impact statement for the blessing of her gods, wherever they be.

The true interests of proponents of environmentalism is put in some perspective in an article by William Tucker, published in *Harper's Magazine* under the title "Environmentalism and the Leisure Class", which deals in no uncertain terms with the Storm King Mountain controversy, on the Hudson River, near New York. He said that environmentalism suited people who found the present circumstances to their liking; it offered the extraordinary opportunity to combine the qualities of virtue and selfishness.

Each time an industrial development is proposed, politicians evade the issue of where they stand with statements such as, and I quote a cabinet minister of a former socialist government:

". . . biologists, environmentalists, local residents and politicians will have ample opportunity to register opinions and advise before a decision is made."

This statement was voiced with respect to a possible new steel mill to be located on Vancouver Island. Certainly it is the politician's duty to consider the impact on the local people but discussion must be on the basis of commonsense not emotional doomsday nonsense. If people are affected, then the impact on their lives must be given realistic consideration. That the environment will be disturbed, goes without saying. Is it really too much to expect our elected managers to display leadership by presenting a balance sheet to society showing the pros and cons of a situation so that choices can be based on realities?

"Demise of Democracy"

Look for a brief moment at what is happening with the development of electric power in British Columbia where hydro sources and coal deposits still abound in vast untapped reserves. That we are being cheated of our destiny by subversive forces is evidenced by statements from the Chairman of the B.C. Hydro and Power Authority.

Speaking publicly, the Chairman stated that it looked as though nuclear energy, because of public attitudes, would in all probability have to become part of the power scene in the not too distant future of British Columbia. This, as the reader should now expect, drew immediate response from the environmentalists. The Sierra Club instantly jumped in with the frenzied charge that the Chairman was "advocating the demise of democracy".

The Hydro Chairman was, in truth, simply presenting the available alternatives for power generation, as made necessary by irrational attitudes of environmentalists. The Chairman put the matter in astute perspective in an interview quoted in *The Daily Colonist* as follows:

"Many public utilities feel foreclosed from taking advantage of the natural attributes of the country, namely, coal and water. Groups that oppose coal burning or hydro-electric dams are driving people to the consideration of nuclear generation. Assume that hydro is foreclosed from rivers and coal. . . In the face of that we believe that the only power left to us is nuclear."

In direct reference to the position of the Sierra Club, the Chairman is quoted as saying, ". . . groups like the Sierra Club and SPEC are part of the energy problem, not the solution."

Nuclear Neglect

That politicians have succumbed to the whims of the environmentalists, is not hard to document. The Minister of Energy, Mines and Petroleum Resources of the Province of British Columbia released in February 1980, a pamphlet called, "An Energy Secure British Columbia", in which the hydro, coal, oil and natural gas potentials of the Province are advanced. On the final page is a heading, "Alternative Energy Sources", followed by brief statements which go on to list additional energy forms such as geothermal, solar, wind and biomass. By adopting the stance that British Columbia is only interested in looking at areas akin to its own present natural energy sources the pamphlet surreptitiously avoids the word "nuclear".

It is none-the-less astonishing to read and reread the pamphlet and not find one single reference to nuclear energy, possibly the greatest single opportunity the whole world has for unlimited and cheap power. Indeed, the future survival of society may well depend on overcoming the present disadvantages associated with nuclear energy. While British Columbia may wish to advance the case for fossil fuels, it is still a possibility, according to some scientists, that our atmosphere may not be able to sustain the combustion of such materials, which require enormous amounts of oxygen, maybe more than our plant life can replace. There too, are the consequences of a build up of carbon dioxide, though there is a considerable divergence of opinions as to what this could all mean. But the position taken by the Minister in charge of energy matters should not surprise us, as nuclear energy has become the centrepiece of attack by the environmentalists; it is now a "dirty" word, so much so that few politicians have the fortitude to freely acknowledge the great potential of this source of energy.

The subject of energy faddists was put in succinct perspective by the Chairman of B.C. Hydro in a talk to the 20th Canadian Regional Conference of the Parliamentary Association in September 1980, when he was quoted as saying (I paraphrase slightly in the interest of brevity):

"Rock-concert mentality and popular articles make much of wind, tide and varieties of sunlight or heat entrapment as energy sources. The facts are that at today's levels of technology these exotic alternatives will make exceedingly limited contributions to gross energy requirements for years to come. . . the dream of self-sufficiency via solar, tide and wind energy production is a mirage popular on the hustings."

Society must surely start asking how much longer it is going to allow this insidious destruction of the logic that has successfully brought us out of the Dark Ages to an incomprehensible level of material wealth in little over a century of time.

BRITISH COLUMBIA

Part II: ISSUES OF CONFRONTATION.

Since sparsely populated British Columbia is relatively undeveloped, with abundant untapped natural resources, it is not hard to understand that there are many, many issues of confrontation, because of the devious political attitudes of the environmentalists. Let us consider for a few pages some of these issues and the diverse opinions being expounded.

Some years ago a proposal was put forward to divert waters from the Shuswap — Thompson watershed into the Okanagan watershed. This proposal was made on the basis of Government engineering studies which looked at general needs, economics and feasibility. It was a recognized fact that there was only a marginal amount of water available within the Okanagan watershed for future development. On the other hand, there was an excess in the Shuswap — Thompson watershed. The pros and cons of the engineering report is not the subject of this discourse. The matter is raised to illustrate the humbug generated. Radicals, with the expected support of the media, had the scheme blocked on the basis that people of one watershed have no moral right to demand growth at the expense of another watershed.

In addition, briefs prepared and submitted to the Government put forward the thesis that the problems of each watershed should be resolved within the watershed and that the development of each watershed should be planned and limited by its own water resources. Although many briefs claimed to represent the sentiments of citizen groups, anyone familiar with the philosophies of the eco-freaks will readily recognize the origin of the attitudes.

Perhaps the foregoing, more than anything else, illustrates the environmentalists' total lack of comprehension of how our society functions. First of all, when people live within the common boundaries of a province, or country, they are citizens of that regime and are entitled to benefit from the planned use of the resources available within the total area under the jurisdiction of their government. From where do the people who live in cities get their power, food and all of the necessities needed to sustain their way of life? Certainly not within the confines of their own parochial boundaries.

The second point, namely, that the development of each watershed should be planned and limited by its own water resources is equally fallacious. Are the anti-growth freaks not cognizant of the fact that in our modern society no nation lives within the limits of its own resources? This fact is so fundamental and self-evident that it needs no explanation, other than to reflect for a few minutes on the chaos that can be created if the natural and plentiful sources of energy and food are not placed at all mankind's disposal. These protagonists obviously do not understand what Trade Commissions are all about.

Waste Sustained by Politicians

Another issue worthy of passing consideration in this presentation is the grandiose water management, social and economic study completed in 1974 of the Okanagan Lake system. This extensive four-year study does much to illustrate the wanton waste sustained by politicians in the name of environmentalism. The study cost the taxpayer over $2 million in direct outlay and certainly more than half as much again, when the hidden costs of the input from the unwieldly Public Service system is added.

Back in 1968-69 when the study idea was first imposed on the Province as a joint Federal-Provincial effort, its purpose was questioned by certain senior Provincial officials, including myself, who wanted to know what the study would prove that we didn't already know. There was available a considerable amount of information on the Okanagan basin which, with a little intelligent thought, would have provided the answers to most questions. But the environmental humbuggers in Ottawa were not to be denied. The Provincial political attitude adopted was that such a study would get the people off the Government's back. That alone was deemed sufficient reason to go ahead.

There was also the Federal bureaucratic skulduggery with which to contend. Ottawa certainly saw such a study as a golden opportunity to secure jurisdictional influence in the Province. The pretext offered was that they were, ". . . anxious to test techniques in water resource planning. . . ", which begs the question, "Are those who made the proposition, unaware of the elementary fact that water resource planning techniques have been understood by engineers for centuries?" Such matters were routine for the Water Resources Service, a once active engineering body of the Provincial Government before it was renamed the Ministry of Environment. This once strong Service has been swamped with pseudo-expert groups with philosophies tempered to satisfy a whimsical mandate to appease radical pressure groups.

Implications Too Obvious

During the early negotiations of the Agreement to undertake the study, in 1968-69, the implications were all too obvious. The initial overtures of Ottawa left little doubt as to the intentions. To initiate the matter, the Federal Government prepared a draft agreement, which contained devious and presumptuous features. It inferred that they had jurisdictional rights. The Provincial response through the Deputy Minister was: "the Okanagan basin does not seem to be a major interjurisdictional or international basin."

But the Federal Government were hell-bent on taking over. They had proposed to walk right in and revamp the whole institutional, legal and administrative structure, to which was said:

> "Regarding the 'institutional, legal and administrative' studies which were included in your draft, I would suggest that these aspects of water resource administration and management are of a magnitude and complexity which is beyond the level of the studies we visualize under the Okanagan basin study.

> "For example, I do not believe that such matters as the British North America Act, the Boundary Waters Treaty of 1909, the Federal Fisheries Act, the structure of the Department of Energy, Mines and Resources, the B.C. Water Act, etc., could be usefully studied or discussed under the Okanagan Basin Agreement."

The tentative negotiations went on to suggest that joint Federal-Provincial public hearings be conducted. Again the idea had to be rebuffed, as politely as possible, with the words:

> "Your draft Agreement includes provisions for holding public hearings . . . Public hearings are being held under the Water Act and the Pollution Control Act . . . It would create undesirable confusion if a federal-provincial study group would also hold public hearings on water matters."

Those who were close to negotiations had little doubt as to the purpose of the study. While the public might like to think that it had been executed in their interest, the facts make it quite obvious that it was simply one more politicial ploy. And so the best part of 3 to 4 million dollars has been used to tell us what we already knew, namely, to quote from the 1974 Summary Report, that phosphorous is "the major nutrient promoting undesirable algal blooms" and "the future of the Valley rests primarily in the hands of local residents". To illustrate the intent to get the public off the Government's back, as suggested earlier, the report states:

> "As the plan was specifically designed to provide for the social betterment of the valley residents, a sincere attempt was made to educate the public about water management problems and *to receive and consider ideas from citizens regarding their preferred future life-style.*"*

Such statements are meaningless. It is the type of nonsense engendered by environmentalists. While it is all very jolly to allow people to express their "preferred future life style", just how does one propose to go about implementing same if the chosen future life-style necessitates curtailing growth so that the inhabitants may enjoy a degree of solitude?

*Emphasis by author.

How does one sustain such a paradise? Only individuals can choose a preferred life-style and then only if financial capabilities so allow.

The best that can be said for the 4,000 page Okanagan Study is that it will appear to lend credibility to the value judgments which still must be made on the basis of people's needs, resource availability, engineering practicality and a great deal of commonsense. At worst, it simply ensures jobs for numerous bureaucrats as they continue to spend our taxes implementing various facets of the report.

That the study is virtually worthless, has been shown by subsequent events. To the consternation of many, a weed known as milfoil, a rather harmless plant whose present sin is to interfere with swimming in certain areas, has appeared in abundant quantities in Okanagan Lake. The grandiose Okanagan study, which was "to test techniques in water resource management", has nothing to offer in this issue, nor any other issue for that matter, as it was simply an exercise to con the taxpayer into thinking he was getting a return on his tax dollars to Ottawa. The Government, in an ill-conceived attempt to meet the milfoil challenge, poured millions of tax dollars into researching the situation, but all to no avail, as the whole matter became enmeshed in the all too familiar environmental hysteria.

The sooner the people in the semi-desert Okanagan Valley recognize that the only long term rational solution to all their water problems is the diversion of water from the Shuswap, the better. The decision to divert or not must be based on man's needs, not environmental humbug.

Opportunity for Speculation

The milfoil incident offers a delightful opportunity for speculation. Had the diversion of water from the Shuswap occurred, there is no doubt, no doubt whatsoever, that the ecologists would have hailed such action as inexorable proof that we must not, on the peril of our existence, tamper with nature. It was on the basis of this very attitude that the McGregor River dam diversion, a valuable economic asset in the development of this Province's hydro-power and flood control program, was stopped. It was claimed by the environmental bureaucrats of the Federal Government that an obscure fish parasite might find its way into the Mackenzie River Basin and destroy the whole something-or-other. No evidence, just hypothetical nonsense, and the Provincial authorities bought it. If the environmentalists had been active when the Panama and Suez Canels were built, we would have been subjected to horrifying tales of the devilish consequences of linking the Atlantic Ocean with the Pacific Ocean, or the Red Sea with the Mediterranean Sea through the Suez Canal.

Here is something to ponder. How is it that if there is a natural marsh, it is a magical thing, a purifier of water, a habitat for wild life, in short, an eco-system par excellence, which must be preserved and treasured as if all life depended on it? Yet, how come, when weeds appear on a body of water, truly a marsh in its infancy, all hell breaks loose and we are told that the area, through nutrients, is being polluted, that the balance of nature is being upset and that society, irrespective of the cost, must build tertiary treatment plants to reduce nutrient discharge, a somewhat futile effort recognized by those who understand the subject. Such is occurring today in many areas, including the Okanagan, where reason has not prevailed. Are such people unaware of the ceaseless natural evolutionary process called eutrophication, which changes sterile water bodies into biologically productive ones? Such is the nature of the forces controlling the earth's destiny that from time immemorial nothing stands still. As in the past, so it is today, man must learn to make the best of the ever-changing environment surrounding him. In the final analysis, nature will win, just as she will with each of us, who one day must return to the soil whence we came.

Another Absurd Study

There is yet another absurd federal-provincial study, this one for the Thompson River system. It is formulated much along the illogical lines of the Okanagan study, where, as explained, the primary purpose was only to satisfy the Federal policy of encroachment into Provincial affairs, environmentalism being nothing more than a pawn in the ploy. This study, in common with most environmental studies, displays contempt for rationale in order to placate the political conniving of the federal system.

A perceptive reading of the Pre-Planning Study findings is most illuminating. The study addresses itself to alleged complaints about such environmental intangibles as colour, algae blooms, foam, taste and odour in fish, to name the more specific items. The report says, "In response to these concerns a federal-provincial study was initiated in 1973 to identify the various problems and if possible find the sources." It is hard to believe for one moment that those condoning the study were not aware that extensive detailed work has been carried on for years in the subjects questioned and much of it in British Columbia by the B.C. Research Council. The amount of work done is so voluminous that it is not considered necessary to offer references for the purpose of this story.

In truth then, the reasons for which the study was initiated were political and emotional. The investigators were determined to have a study at any cost, so neglected to acknowledge the fact that the problems which it hoped to identify were already fully documented in government files, research institutes and technical literature. The report presumes to be *revealing* when it identifies the City of Kamloops and the adjacent pulp mill as the main offenders. Frankly, anyone with a basic understanding of the subject already knows this. However, in this sophisticated age it seems that the more blatant and naive the protest, the more likely that tax dollars will be forthcoming from the public coffers.

Tax Dollars Forthcoming

To put the proposed Thompson River Study into some perspective, it should be noted that the drainage basin contains 56,000 square miles of land and a mere population of 120,000, of which half live in or around Kamloops. To suggest that such a population density and its associated industries in any way endangers the river regime is ludicrous. The Thames valley in England is about one/tenth the area under consideration. yet contains a population in excess of 14 million people. Using the logic of the eco-feaks, life should be extinct in such an area. Why, then, is it not?

At the time the Kamloops pulp mill was proposed in the mid-1960's, extensive investigations and studies were carried out by Provincial agencies and the Federal Fisheries and again in the early 1970's when it was proposed to expand the mill. At that time I was invited to be a guest speaker on a public panel in Kamloops. The panel contained a number of experienced professionals who could speak authoritatively on fishery and environmental matters. The consensus of the panel was that the proposed expansion of the mill, with the treatment and control measures proposed, would not endanger the fishery resource of the Fraser-Thompson River system which contains one of the world's great salmon spawning areas, the Adams River.

Possibly because of more front line experience in environmental issues, I was more outspoken than panel colleagues. This resulted in a very pointed and heated question being directed to me from the audience, which in effect said that it was all very well for people like me to get up and say that the river would be unaffected. but what was I prepared to do in ten years time when all the fish were dead?

There was but one answer to such doomsday nonsense. I replied that I would be delighted to meet with the gentleman ten years hence and give him my answer. The ten years are now up and the river continues to carry unabated one of the world's great salmon runs. As for doomsday prophecies, all will recollect that every now and then some of the far-out religious sects take it upon themselves to predict the end, but to their mortification the day comes and goes without catastrophe.

Cheekye-Dunsmuir Transmission Line

And now to consider a few excerpts from one of those massive, costly, needless, environmental impact studies imposed upon B.C. Hydro by government regulations. Let us look at the one for the Cheekye-Dunsmuir transmission line, which became a bombing target of environmentalists as presented in the opening chapter. The study was carried out in accordance with "Guidelines" prepared by the Secretariat of the Environment and Land Use Committee. This is the same Secretariat whose questionable function was raised in chapter 1. In enunciating the methodology, the report states:

"The process used has two basic functions,

1. To consider *as many** geographical routes as possible.

2. To consider *as many** environmental and engineering factors as necessary to permit a rational selection of the preferred route."

In short, no stone is to be left unturned to find the answer, since the public is paying, of course. And what of the findings? It would not seem too much to expect from a study costing several hundred thousand dollars, an astute or even helpful answer. The recommendations are indeed extraordinary, an admittance without parallel that such studies only pretend to solve the problem and I quote:

"The result of the study is the selection of three preferred routes. It is recommended that the final route be selected from these three routes after discussions between B.C. Hydro, Provincial and Federal Government Agencies, Regional Districts and municipalities, and with the general public."

What has been accomplished? The participants, of course, got their fees, and the objectors got their kick at the cat, but note that the final decision still has to be made by others and the issue is now a little more bedevilled by suggesting there are three possible routes. Look again at the terms of reference ". . . to permit a rational selection of the preferred route." How blatantly obvious must the failure of such studies be, before they are forever banished along with the parasites who live off them?

But that is not all. The study report for the project is distributed to fourteen major groups within the bureaucracy. Within each group it is passed to anything from two to four sub-groups or persons. In short, it is reviewed by something in the order of forty to fifty bureaucrats, not including the various supervisory and administrative desks over which it must pass. Weigh this against the abysmally ineffective bureaucratic system described earlier and you must surely be shocked with your conclusion.

*Emphasis by author.

Encroachment on Freedoms

And what of the feed-back to B.C. Hydro? Here are a few typical comments: One major section within Government made the assinine comment, "the report unnecessarily favoured shorter routes over longer ones." Surely anyone can grasp the simple truth that, in general, the shorter the route the better, provided it is feasible. Others opted for a route which "would develop less new access roads to uninhabited areas". Here again, the perverse mind of the eco-freak is evident. How would we thrive in this great land if we did not take every opportunity offered to open up the countryside? Indeed, some went so far as to recommend that all roads built to facilitate construction, be "reclaimed". One statement recommended "closure of the road to vehicles, even on private land".

It is evident, and indeed there is much material to support it, that the environmental cult feels it has the right to harass and dictate to private land owners; such encroachment on the freedoms of the silent majority must not go unchallenged.

Final Ignominy

But the final ignominy is yet to come. That the environmentalists have infiltrated and intimidated the political scene is evidenced by reference to a February, 1980 news release from the office of he Minister of Environment on the Cheekye-Dunsmuir transmission line route:

"Recognizing the *sensitive environmental qualities of the Sunshine Coast**, the chairman said that B.C. Hydro has been directed to use the utmost care in designing and clearing the right-of-way for this twin, 500-kilovolt transmission line."

This humbug, coming from the Minister of Environment's Office, is hard to believe. The Sunshine Coast (just a name; it has no more sunshine than anywhere else) is no different, environmentally speaking, than any of the rest of the B.C. coastline; it is, at best, typical — nothing more, nothing less. The news release continues:

"B.C. Hydro will now proceed with completion of detailed route alignment studies for this area in order to mitigate — as much as possible — the environment impacts of the project. Such studies are mandatory under the environmental assessment requirements outlined in ELUC's guidelines for linear development."

This, mark you, after all of the studies done to date. I trust the reader sees the bluff going on and now comprehends why I have coined the phrase "environmental parasites" to describe those involved with such activities. At the opening of the Spring Session of the Legislature in 1980, the ever-critical press carried on its front page a photograph

---

*Emphasis by author.

of students of the Malaspina College carrying placards with the somewhat inept words, "We don't want the Cheekye-Dunsmuir Line", a group in no way connected with the issue, but no doubt with sympathic feelings towards socialism as preached by today's academics and encouraged by the press.

The people who are opposed to the transmission line crossing the Sechelt Peninsula conveniently forget that the power which they themselves use, is carried by transmission lines which cross extensive tracts of British Columbia land to get there. The lifestyle so many of us enjoy today, resulted from earlier foresight to develop the resource potential around us. Because of a low population density, we are still at a stage in our growth which allows us few to reap the benefits, while *pretending* to live with nature.

Excused Sabotage

A member of the NDP socialist opposition, to curry favour with anti-government factions, actually excused the dastardly act of sabotage at Qualicum by trying to shift criticism to B.C. Hydro. He is quoted as saying:

> "I can understand the frustration of people deeply concerned about the project, because there were never meaningful public hearings and we don't know even now whether it should have proceeded in the first place."

So, after all of the studies and all of the involvement of those earlier listed, it is sanctimoniously suggested that right has not been done, simply because the public interest to best serve the majority prevailed. It is such devious political mentality that has been fostering mythical environmental concerns over the past two decades.

But the final admission that environmental studies are a sham comes from a senior official of the now defunct Secretariat and I quote from a file note:

> "I feel that Hydro has developed over the past few years a much more comprehensive process, but I am concerned that it has tended to take a 'scatter-gun' approach hoping that by considering every possible impact, somehow there will be enough data to satisfy government and public concerns."

That Hydro, with all the eco-freaks and environmental consultants they have been forced to hire, were unable to zero in on a precise solution demonstrates the worthless nature of the environmental impact study. For those that are not yet convinced that we are surrounded by environmental madness, the following should provide ample proof:

In November 1980, B.C. Hydro issued an Information Bulletin about the proposed Murphy Creek dam on the Columbia River. In the section headed Environmental Studies we are advised that:

"Hydro has engaged *six* environmental consultant firms to conduct studies which, *along with additional environmental and engineering feasibility studies being undertaken by Hydro staff, will assist** . . ." in arriving at a decision.

The consulting firms were to look at the impact on recreation, tourism, water quality, fish and aquatic habitats, wildlife, agriculture and forestry. In addition, the bulletin advised that ". . . the Fish and Wildlife Branch are conducting a survey of anglers", and the Okanagan College are to look into possible effects on "heritage resources".

Realities Numb the Mind

Let us now consider the area which necessitates this demanding scrutiny. With the army of pseudo-experts which were to be turned loose at public expense, one could not be blamed for harbouring ideas that the area is somewhat special, maybe pristine or even *environmentally unique.* Disillusionment is the reward of such high hopes. The realities numb the mind of any rational person, for we find that the area has been the recipient of intensive activity over the past century. The 20 mile long narrow valley area, the bottom part of which is to be flooded, is traversed by a major highway, numerous secondary roads and a railway. It contains a city and six communities, with a mighty pulp mill at the upper end of the proposed dam pool. At the other end of the valley, close to the site of the proposed dam, is located one of the world's largest lead-zinc smelters. A population of some 15,000 inhabits the area, with another 30,000 nearby.

Immediately upstream of the area which it is presently proposed to flood, there already exists the Keenleyside Dam, which is larger by far than the one now proposed. The Keenleyside Dam was completed just a dozen years ago, at which time all the tangible and practical information was assessed. There is surely little doubt that the impact of the presently proposed project must be well understood by B.C. Hydro who built the earlier dam, plus, of course, many more — so why all the pseudo-experts who, in truth, between them have no comparable experience on which to draw. Because of the smelter complex, the valley has for years been subjected to the media's *acid rain plague,* which is predicted to destroy us before our natural life span is run. Ironically, the most significant result which could come from the needless studies is proof that the acid rain "end of the world" theme is without credibility.

Incredible as it may be to the pseudo-experts hired to evaluate the impact of the proposed Murphy Creek dam, there already exists within the Columbia River system over a score of major dams, half of them upstream of the study area. In short, the Columbia River is, in every sense of the word, a "tamed river". We should be most thankful that

*Emphasis by author

it is not one of those sacred, virgin, wild rivers that is under consideration, otherwise the taxpayer could go broke hiring all the consultants deemed necessary to seek out and document all the intangibles surrounding the environmental myth.

The folly of the related exercises are well summarized in the words of renowned journalist and author Walter Lippman:

> "The notion that public opinion can and will decide all issues is in appearance very democratic. In practice it undermines and destroys democratic government. . . . It is not in fact possible for all the people to know all about all things, and the pretense that they can and that they do is a bad illusion."

The Skagit Valley

Nestled in the mountainous wilds of British Columbia on the borders of the State of Washington is a valley called the Skagit, visited by few because, in truth, it has nothing special to offer; just one of a thousand such places. Yet, over the past decade it became a focal point of environmental confrontation. Why? Because a mere eight square miles of it which lies within the Province of British Columbia was to be flooded by the State of Washington; Americans — dammit!

The area has been logged since 1860 and dammed for years on the American side of the border to provide power for the City of Seattle. The present reservoir extends into Canada for about a mile. International agreements were initially drawn up in the 1940's to allow this and to facilitate raising of the reservoir to provide more storage for power generation when the need arose.

But because of so-called public outcry created solely by the environmentalists with the never-ending aid of the media our hypocritical politicians have reneged on the earlier commitment to allow flooding. Many pathetic excuses have been put forward in lieu of dealing honestly with the realities. The former Federal Minister of Environment Canada (and later a Provincial Cabinet Minister), whose political two stepping was dealt with in the chapter on The Public Inquiries Farce has said, "My attitude is that it must be stopped . . ." A former socialist Cabinet Minister of the Province said ". . . irreparable damage to the Province will occur if the natural water level of the Skagit River . . . is allowed to rise. . . ."

Throughout negotiations on this issue the press displayed its usual lack of responsibility. A leading daily in referring to hearings on this matter carried the headline "STUDENT PLEADS TO SAVE SKAGIT". The article contained such drivel as ". . . the young want to see the Skagit Valley saved because there is nowhere else to go . . ." In British Columbia?

British Columbia occupies an area of 366,000 square miles. Eighty percent of the population occupies a mere half of one percent. We have a population of under 2.5 million. If such statistics are reviewed against any of the older established countries it is not hard to see the drivel presented. In the Skagit Valley a mere eight square miles were to be flooded. The whole valley watershed covering close to 400 square miles would still remain for those who want to hike in the area, or do they think the mountain peaks rising to 8,000 feet are to be enveloped in water?

Fishing would remain a viable sport. Whether the fish were more plentiful or not would be a function of enhancement programs, if the area warranted it. One bleeding heart government officer tried to make much of the matter with statements to the effect that flooding would replace a "unique" stretch of stream fishing with a mediocre boat fishery.

One group evaluating the Skagit talked of such intangibles as "optional values", defined as the value persons not planning to use the area place on the knowledge that the place is there for future use, if they ever wish to use it. If such values are really credible, why don't we all get out of British Columbia so that we may enjoy the knowledge that the land is there to be rediscovered when the spirit moves us. No doubt the Indians would cherish such an attitude.

Ethics Suspect

Environment Canada, in a study report, put the point this way, "Social preservation values are defined as the value to society as a whole, and to the many people who have no intention of visiting the valley, of knowing that it is preserved in an unchanged state". That such a philosophy should be entertained in discussing the Skagit is hard to conceive since the area already has a dam and has been logged and hunted for years. It is not hard to grasp in the light of the intangibles involved that the final recommendations of the report contain such phrases as "they were not able to advise with scientific certainty" and "the total environment requires additional scrutiny", the ever-present excuse for more studies to conceal the truth that today's environmental ethic is suspect.

To show how lamentable is the comprehension of our political leaders, I quote from a letter in the *Daily Colonist* of July 6, 1980, from a member of the B.C. Legislature. In his letter presenting his alleged concerns, he says of the Skagit Valley:

> ". . . . What's there to be preserved? More than 5,000 acres of the finest river valley hiking, camping, nature watching, canoeing and fishing to be found anywhere in the world. This unique (there's that word again)* recreational area lies at the eastern end of our burgeoning Lower Mainland. It offers a

recreational experience unmatched in North America." (Ye Gods, what was he drinking?)*

Do such political dolts really believe that the assets listed would vanish if the dam had been raised another 80 to 90 feet? In March 1981, it was reported by observers on the Skagit River that a mere 60 eagles out of a normal population of 400 were counted in a specific area. The report stated, "The drastic decline in the eagle population is probably due to flooding which washed away salmon carcasses on which the eagles feed . . ." Guess who would have been blamed if the decline in the eagle population had been observed *after* construction of the proposed dam?

In summary, as far as recreation is concerned, the flooding of the valley would have no adverse effects, in fact, the reverse could be the case. There are many ways of ensuring that such developments could enhance the area, if the need is there. For example, a secondary dam could be constructed close to the border which would have the effect of eliminating the "draw-down" on the Canadian side, thus making a permanent lake, one of those pools over which ecologists drool. Frankly, at this time the area does not warrant the expense involved and indeed may never, but if it did, and this applies to all developments, there is no limit to what can be done to enhance an area, but the enhancement must be warranted and in keeping with priorities as well as with all the natural phenomena which can nullify man's best efforts. To keep environmental issues in perspective one must always remain cognizant of the geological truths of the universe. Mother Nature in her own blundering way has wrought changes to the landscape that make the so-called impact on the Skagit Valley inconsequential to her plan for the next billion years or so.

Unique Canadian Heritage?

In a booklet published by the "Outdoor Recreation Council of British Columbia" is the following:

"Can We Afford To Be Careless With Our Underwater Wilderness?

"Olive-green wilderness garden, divers glide soundlessly through kelp jungle, past shimmering greenlings, bristling giant red urchins, lacy white basket stars and a plush carpet of anemones in bonbon colour to find flaming pink hydrocoral paving the sea floor at Race Rocks.

"At the bottom of British Columbia? Unexpectedly, yes. Another dimension unsuspected except by those who have seen it with their own eyes, some of the richest, most varied and colourful undersea life in the world is hidden beneath our slate-grey waters . . . And what are we doing to conserve this

*Inserted by author

fantastic, perhaps irreplaceable, natural resource? This unique
Canadian heritage?"

Saints in heaven preserve us! I have travelled the world by sea and
sailed in pleasure craft on the coasts of the British Isles, West Africa,
Australia, New Zealand and British Columbia. I have yet to find a
coastline which would not fit with but a few details the profuse description of "This unique Canadian heritage", including much of the
16,000 miles of the British Columbian coast. Pray what fools do these
ecological propangandists take us for? The environment of which they
write has been for a million years and will be for another million to
come. Indeed, by contrast, our life span is so brief we can barely even
be looked upon as its temporary guardians.

"The Galapagos of Canada"

To illustrate the hoax being perpetrated, the following is offered.
On the west of British Columbia, some 90 miles offshore, lies Moresby
Island at the southern end of the Queen Charlottes. It is a wild and
rugged area, sitting in the massive and stormy Pacific Ocean. Its climate
is less than hospitable. It supports coastal wildlife in great abundance;
it too contains rich forest lands, the economic mainstay of British
Columbia. Plans are afoot to log the area and as usual the media is
in full array, spurring on the inevitable confrontation. It looks like a
classic in the making. Indeed, guns were introduced to the scene when
the Riley Creek episode arose. The environmentalists are at their wailing
wall with protestations that the area is "unique", a "heritage site" that
has "amazed international naturalists", the "Galapagos of Canada".
All very dramatic, but what are the facts?

The Galapagos Islands are indeed *unique,* there is no place on earth
like them. On the other hand, Moresby Island is but one of hundreds
of such islands and coastal areas, stretching all the way from the
Aleutian Islands to the shores of Vancouver Island, spanning some 2,000
miles. Wildlife of the type on Moresby Island can be found in
abundance throughout the area. *There is no implication here, nor
anywhere in this book for that matter, that we should ignore, decimate,
or wantonly interfere with the basic needs of the wildlife scene.*

Few will deny that the aspirations of environmentalism are
admirable, nor deny the need to provide sanctuaries for wildlife in
appropriate areas to offset the pressures of an expanding population
and the demands being put on natural resources. But all of this can
be done, particularly in the more remote areas, without the "hands
off" attitude being expounded by dictating that we subjugate the
initiative of our resource industries to the type of government controls
and bureaucracy described herein.

In the final analysis, rational people will recognize that the area, with a little intelligent thought, can be logged without undue interference to the overall wildlife scene. Displaced species will quickly re-establish provided they are not hunted to extinction by predator man. If there are species present which will not survive such interference they will certainly not survive the onslaught of nature over the ages ahead, a subject put in some perspective in an astute article on the endangered species conundrum in *Harper's*, entitled "The Sinking Ark" by William Tucker, which concludes,

"Extinction has been the common fate of nearly all species that have evolved on earth. We ourselves are a part of nature, and it is impossible for us to live without changing it in some degree."

It is only because the Galapagos Islands were totally isolated from the other evolutionary forces on earth, that they have remained "unique" in the true sense of the word. To glibly designate Moresby Island as the "Galapagos of Canada" shows well the flaws in the environmental case. That the whole issue is based on surmise to appeal to emotions is readily apparent. Where is the scientific documentation to justify the hysterical claims? It is such attitudes which must surely provide the catalyst to bring about the long overdue demise of this environmental heresy.

To Get Perspective

That the forces of anarchy are active in this environmental scene and in the guise of public servants too, is an ill omen for our society. A most disquieting news item appeared in *The Daily Colonist* on January 25, 1980, under the headline: "Guns of Riley Creek more fearsome than Iran". An exaggeration, of course, but nevertheless disquieting. The incident revolved around the logging of mature forests in the Queen Charlotte Islands, just north of Moresby Island. During legal and authorized logging in the Riley Creek watershed, a landslide occurred which caused mud and debris to end up in the creek, all accidental and in all probability attributable to natural circumstances, as the mountainous terrain of coastal British Columbia is highly unstable, due to the relatively recent retreat of the glacial ice pack. Natural slides and rock falls are as common here as earthquakes are in other parts of the world.

Whether the area should have been logged, or whether improper techniques were being used is not to be settled here, though in passing, one must, to get perspective, look at the extent of the Riley Creek fishery. The Creek is no more than seven miles long; it is but one of a thousand such creeks in British Columbia; its contribution to our extensive fishery resource is negligible. However, the issue to be examined here is the vicious, dangerous attitude of the environmental anarchists within the Federal Public Service. Federal fishery underlings, struggling to assert their meddling rights in the management of British Columbia's resources, *over which they should have no jurisdiction,* moved in, with guns. A forest engineer of the Company involved, who by coincidence had just returned from military duty in Iran, said:

> ". . . in all my time in Iran, I never saw a menacing gun in that country's forests. But three months later and 10,000 miles away there were guns in B.C.'s forests . . . our people were treated like criminals . . . Any forestry firm would seem to be fair game in the climate existing in British Columbia today . . . many discordant voices are challenging the orderly evolution of resource management and development . . . ."

Example of Idiocy Going On

The reader should now better understand the concerns expressed about the devious antics of the federal bureaucrats. What the final outcome of the Riley Creek incident will be, it is too early to say, but that a great deal of humbug surrounds fishery attitudes is prevalent. Here, for example, is the type of idiocy which is going on relative to fishery protection. In *The Daily Colonist* of November 22, 1978, there appeared this headline: "Fish hadn't much of a chance"; the words of a biologist working on a project under the federal Salmon Enhancement Program. The article need not be repeated, as my response, which was published in the Colonist of December 1, 1978, deals directly with the main burden of the issue:

> "Your report, Colonist, Nov. 22, *Fish hadn't much of a chance,* allows me to once again take another slap at the waste and nonsense going on in the name of environmentalism. Here we have the totally naive spectacle of our governments purporting to carry on a salmon enhancement program.
>
> "Look at where they are working: In a stream which enters an industrial harbour; a stream which flows through much development; a stream which carries off waste water from streets, roads and developed areas; a stream which in fact goes dry depending upon the state of the season; a stream surrounded by human predators.
>
> "And our naive biologist expresses surprise that the fish didn't survive, — "dwindling almost to nothing" were the plaintive words used. It's like sending children out on the highway to play; how many do you think would survive?
>
> "Are these people so devoid of the facts of life? Surely the place to carry on enhancement programs is in our multitude of west coast streams, which do not flow through a hinterland taken over by the day to day consequences of urban life.

"Do we also have enhancement programs to return deer, bears and cougars to our back gardens so that our Indians can live as they once did?"

If we were going to have enhancement programs, it takes little intelligence to visualize that they should be directed to areas such as Riley Creek, *after they have been logged,* as such areas will then be free of this environmentally disturbing activity for another fifty or more years and will be in need of and benefit from salmon enhancement programs. If we do not soon start putting our resource management problems into honest perspective, a hideous social calamity is going to occur as the anarchists in our midst become more and more threatening.

Trivial Overflow

That the matter of fish habitat is totally out of perspective is brought out by a letter in the May 1983, issue of *The B.C. Professional Engineer.* It surrounds a court decision dealing with a trivial overflow of sewage to a stream as the result of a power failure:

"The recent round of court proceedings regarding protection of fish habitat are making me wonder whether the Courts are moving to return this beautiful Province to the fish, and move the people out . . . The Court decision . . . fines the municipality for allowing a "deleterious substance" to enter a fish-bearing stream. A sewage lift station failed on a Sunday morning. Repairs were completed the next day. In the meantime the wetwell overflowed through an emergency pipe (part of the proper design of a pump station*) to a nearby creek. In the absence of that pipe, sewage would have backed up into the basements of nearby homes. There was no evidence of faulty design, improper maintenance or negligence . . ."

This loss of perspective by the Courts in the environmental scenario is frightening. Is it really better to endanger the health of people and destroy their houses and contents, when, in truth, no fish were killed, injured, or even made sick? There is little doubt that the Courts are now serving the cause of the anarchists while the lawyers get their fat fees for going through the motions of presenting material with which they are bamboozled. And, as always, the taxpayer foots the bill.

In short, what the bureaucratic environmentalists have done is to open Pandora's box. Our native Indians now see the environmental approach as the ideal weapon to frustrate society. It was reported in April 1983 that the Haida Nation had launched a protest to the B.C. Ombudsman against logging on the Queen Charlotte Islands as an ulterior weapon to bring about a settlement in their aboriginal land claims. The Nishga Indians too, to bring their land claim issues to a

---

* Insert by author.

head, launched an appeal to the Ombudsman over the Amax mining project in Alice Arm.

In opposition to our economic growth, great tracts of valuable forest lands are being set aside as parks and ecological reserves which, as such, serve only the interests of a very small and select segment of the population. While ecological reserves can serve the very worthwhile function of protecting wildlife, one has to question motherhood reasons for reserves such as "protecting the options of our children" as per the Ecological Reserves Unit of British Columbia. Environmentalists speak of ecological reserves as "benchmarks". Evolutionally speaking, these benchmarks in British Columbia only go back, at the best, 10 to 15 thousand years to the Ice Age. Unlike the Galapagos Islands, they are certainly of little value in studying primeval life. As for the protection of wildlife, in many cases the curtailment of hunting and other such predatory activities would probably be more successful. But then, the politicians would have to confront the hunters whose vehement protests in favour of their so-called traditional rights are well known.

Dam the Fraser

There is no better way to demonstrate how irrational attitudes are insidiously affecting the logical development of British Columbia than a searching look at the longstanding idea of damming the mighty Fraser River. The economic equation to be examined contains three basic functions: energy, flood control and salmon.

If British Columbians are to benefit to the full from the natural environment in which we live, the acceptance of dams on the Fraser River is a prerequisite to intelligent development of the Province. Look closely at the equation and reflect on the relevance of the three functions. The economic benefits of the hydro-electric potential of the Fraser is extensively documented in voluminous engineering reports. Its use can no longer be intelligently ignored in this time of energy needs. The financial benefits to the Province would be infinite. Such development would ensure a continued way of life that few other countries can match.

On the matter of flood control, the blunt truth is that in any year the Fraser River has the potential to go on the rampage at the whim of dear old Mother Nature, bringing chaos and hardship to tens of thousands of people, not to mention the many, many millions of dollars of property damage. Unfortunately but true, history reveals that mankind invariably must suffer such catastrophies before action is taken. Yet these consequences can all be prevented by building dams.

In almost sole opposition to the irrefutable power and flood control benefits, we have the Fraser River salmon run which in monetary terms is relatively paltry when viewed against the other side of the equation. But what is even more significant and not, of course, made public by the anti-fanatics is that dams on the Fraser would in effect have little or no impact on the British Columbia salmon fishery as a whole. Dams on the Fraser River *above* the confluence with the Thompson River would not interfere with the much venerated Adams River spawning grounds on the Thompson River system nor with the many downstream spawning areas on the Fraser and its tributaries which, in reality, constitute the greater portion of the salmon environment of the Fraser. It is appropriate too to note in the equation that the salmon resource of the Fraser, above the confluence with the Thompson, constitutes less than two to five per cent of the total British Columbia salmon resource.

Energy Sufficiency

So what have we got in our equation? A multi-billion dollar hydro-electric scheme and a direly needed flood-control device to protect thousands of families and their properties all being set aside for a piece of spawning area of which there is much in the Province. Indeed, the economic benefits to be derived from dams on the Fraser would allow the development of substantial salmon enhancement programs in other areas. This would in effect more than replace that portion of the Fraser fishery which would be lost. More importantly, it would allow British Columbia to maintain a high degree of energy sufficiency in the years ahead.

In addition, and somewhat ironically, environmentalists fail to acknowledge that hydro-power is a renewable resource and indeed as a source of energy, is truly one of the least damaging from the environmental point-of-view, if there is in truth any such point-of-view when all the hypocrisy is shedded. Those who call for use of solar energy should note that the total power stored in a hydro-electric scheme results from the energy of the sun through the hydrological cycle. In summary then, until we have the fortitude to cease idolatry of the salmon — our sacred cow — and dispense with the false doctrines of the environmentalists, idiocy remains part of our decision-making process.

Man is no longer a wilderness dweller and thus must change the wilderness to best serve his needs. This in no way implies that the beauty which surrounds us will diminish. The great mountains, fiords, rivers and lakes, which are British Columbia will all be there when man has passed from the scene.

> "It's the cussedest land that I know,
> From the big, dizzy mountains that screen it,
> To the deep, deathlike valleys below." (Service)

Chapter Eleven

THE PSEUDO-EXPERTS

There is no doubt that much public mischief is being caused today by academics meddling, with bias, in affairs of which they have insufficient knowledge. To illustrate, the following headline appeared in the local press, "ENGINEERING 'WRONG' IN SEWAGE". It related to a special meeting at the University of Victoria purporting to help educate local municipal representatives on the pros and cons of sea outfalls. The article, in part, went:

> "Engineers are the wrong people to consult to clear up a sewage problem — they should be directed instead. An engineer doesn't know how to cope with sewage," said microbiologist Dr. X.
>
> "If you give an engineer a free hand . . . to get rid of sewage he will dream up fantastic ideas, but they will be thoroughly impractical . . . the engineer has no idea what organisms are in sewage, or how long they will live, and he has no idea what happens to the material he sends down the pipe.
>
> "Dr. X advised his audience to look to professional people such as environmental biologists to say what is needed, and to direct engineers . . . ."

Raised Hackles

To see much misrepresentation of facts coming out of our so-called seat of higher learning raised my hackles. Unfortunately the University of Victoria does not encompass the engineering discipline and is thus deprived of the constrained common sense thinking that such a training provides. I wrote to the press and received the courtesy of space. Under the headline "ENGINEER ANSWERS 'MALICIOUS' CRITIC" was printed:

> "Dr. X appears to lack even basic knowledge as to what goes into an engineer's training. The criteria used by engineers is international in concept.

"If 'experts' such as Dr. X wish 'to direct engineers' they must first of all have their own pet 'theories' accepted by their international colleagues, by the U.S. Public Health Service, etc.

"The statement in your article 'The engineer is being given a job for which he hasn't been trained' is not only a malicious attack on engineers but does a grave disservice to all those excellent university post graduate training centres set up specifically for engineers to acquaint them with the precise data which Dr. X says the engineer lacks.

"When Dr. X talks about 'directing' as to what must be done, he must be unaware of those departments of government charged with controlling pollution and health, which retain on their staff engineers (and others) with specific training in sanitary engineering to guide and direct. Why councils in this area, attempting to do their utmost to find the answers, should be misled by the type of article published in your August 15 issue defies logical explanation.

"It is people such as Dr. X, to use his own words, not engineers that 'dream up fantastic ideas' which are 'thoroughly impractical.' "

When Dr. X says that engineers, and I must presume he means environmental or sanitary engineers, "have no idea what happens to the organisms and material he sends down the pipe", he displays a degree of ignorance which can only be explained by his dedication and devotion to the cause of the ecological gods. I have avoided presenting purely technical material in this book but if I may be forgiven just this once, here is an engineer's description taken from an engineering journal of what happens in a simple sewage lagoon:

"When sewage, laden with organic matter and bacteria, first enters the pond, CO_2 and NH_3 are produced and escape to the atmosphere while oxygen is absorbed. As long as oxygen remains deficient the pond will continue to be anaerobic. In an oxidation pond the photosynthetic action of light on the chloroplastic tissue of microscopic algae produces new cell material. The algae break down the carbon dioxide which is produced during the carbon cycle from the carbohydrates in the sewage and use the carbon to produce more carbohydrates and thus release large quantities of oxygen into the water. This oxygen in turn, provides the means for the bacterial respiration needed in the aerobic process. The bacteria supply the algae with their requirements of carbon, nitrogen, and other products of sewage decomposition. In practice the bacterial and algal phases overlap in an aerobic pond and purification is accelerated by an algal-bacterial symbiosis."

And Dr. X says "an engineer doesn't know how to cope with sewage?"

Greenpeace Jumped In

In the midst of a long standing controversy over outfalls versus treatment in the Victoria area, the Greenpeace Foundation jumped in with both feet. They ran a quarter page advertisement in *The Daily Colonist* on August 29, 1980, with the heading, "The Ocean is not a Septic Tank". They enunciated a number of what they thought were valid points, claiming that domestic sewage in the ocean will be detrimental to fish, turn away tourists and depreciate the quality of life on Vancouver Island, all propped up with the statement, "Greenpeace Victoria is calling for a moratorium on the construction of the Clover Point outfall."

That Greenpeace do not comprehend the issue is understandable, but that they do not *want* to understand is more the point to be brought out here. There is of course the inevitable link with socialism to be noted. The two local members of the Legislature for Victoria at the time of these events were socialists. A few days prior to the Greenpeace advertisement, one of these elected representatives was vigorously attacking the matter in the Legislature, using such emotional appeals as, "We are in a crisis situation. We desperately need secondary treatment for Victoria's sewage wastes." He offered the usual drivel about an "environmental disaster", to use his words. He charged, quite rightly, that sewage particles were finding their way to the beaches. This is not a result of what is proposed in the way of outfalls *but rather what exists in the way of non-outfalls.* The truth is, the outfalls (a misnomer if ever there was one) which have served the area for the past fifty years never went beyond the low water mark. This in effect means the sewage has been for all those years simply dumped on the edge of the beach, an appalling state of affairs.

Ocean Treatment Plant

Had the elected representative and his Greenpeace allies wanted to understand the subject they would have responded to two items in the August 1st, 1980 *Daily Colonist* which it is presumed they read in the light of their grave concerns about local issues. The Editorial column in the paper was headed, "The ocean needs our sewage". The facts were clearly presented and I quote, "The ocean is, in fact, an excellent treatment plant for sewage if given an opportunity to perform." As backup to the statement the article quoted the opinions of an oceanographer of the University of California's Institute of Marine Resources:

"Many countries bordering on the sea are planning these extremely expensive and highly advanced municipal waste treatment plants, ostensibly to avoid 'polluting' the sea with organic materials and nutrients. Such plans reflect a serious misunderstanding of science. They neglect these specific facts: that a major part of the adaptation and activity of the creatures of the sea is directed to the conversion of waste particles into new organisms; that most of the sea is starving and particuarly deficient in just those sorts of material that are introduced by domestic waste; that sea water is a toxic material to most land organisms such as disease bacteria . . ."

The Editorial goes on to note that it is the design of the technique used to discharge that is important, that outfalls *per se* are not bad. The item concludes ". . . to devote immense amounts of precious capital for secondary, tertiary, or quaternary treatment to avoid feeding the open sea totally disregards the true nature of the sea."

In the same issue of the Colonist there was a letter by this writer under the heading, "Beach controls tougher here", which called on the Legislative member in question to be more specific. My letter enunciated that sewage is over 99.9 percent water, which has to go somewhere; that defining pollution by "standards" is very misleading, because time of exposure to a hazard is also a vital contributing factor; that the waters in question are not used for swimming because of frigid temperatures and poor beaches. The letter ended, "As for those that fear the impact of domestic sewage on the marine environment, it is a fact that the organic matter in sewage is simply a welcome food source to many species of sea life."

No Response from Greenpeace

Quite a coincidence that the Editorial and my letter should appear on opposite pages of the same issue. Do I hear environmental cries of "collusion"? But what is more astonishing is that there was no response to the challenge thrown down, not even a letter from the Greenpeace Foundation. That their position is a sham is in keeping with their environmental theme. Their claim "The Ocean is not a Septic Tank" shows how shallow is their understanding of the subject they are attacking. While the ocean, indeed, is not a septic tank (a rather crude treatment device), it is instead, a treatment plant, par excellence. Since time immemorial, the ocean has received, treated and stored the organic wastes and salts which are continually washed from the land to the sea through the action of rainfall. The organic matter is absorbed by the food chain, or breaks down into basic elements, while the salts are stored for eternity. If you want to confirm this latter point, try a mouthful of sea water, or better still read this reference from Rachael Carson's, *The Sea Around Us:*

"From the moment the rains began to fall, the lands began to be worn away and carried to the sea. It is an endless, inexorable process that has never stopped — the dissolving of the rocks, the leaching out of their contained minerals, the carrying of the rock fragments and dissolved minerals to the ocean. And over the eons of time, the sea has grown ever more bitter with the salt of the continents.

". . . Nothing is wasted in the sea; every particle of material is used over and over again, first by one creature, then by another . . . Just as land plants depend on minerals in the soil for their growth, every marine plant, even the smallest, is dependent upon the nutrient salts or minerals in the sea water . . . phosphorous is an indispensible mineral."

Without belabouring the Greenpeace issue, it is perhaps sufficient to say that the efforts of these pseudo-experts, in this instance, bear all the same notoriety of their other irresponsible sorties into national and international environmental issues. Perhaps the matter is best summarized in the words of a City of Victoria Alderman, closely associated with the outfall program, when he said, "I take exception to these johnny-come-latelies, who with no in-depth study, launch a campaign to totally change the direction after the fact. I can only assume it's the time of the year, that they're looking for funds or publicity to strengthen their membership."

Nice Little Handout

As to the pros and cons of sea outfalls, the issue had been clouded by the intrigue of the academics, as part of their never-ending quest for public funds to sustain their existence within the sheltered walls of learning, away from the economic realities of life.

When the Macaulay Point outfall was completed, biologists at the University of Victoria saw it as a means of generating research funds. Under the pressure of acute academic criticism, the authorities agreed to an extensive surveillance program to placate the pseudo-experts. In a covering letter to the permitee from the Pollution Control Branch when the program was initiated, the following was stated:

"Although there is a wealth of information throughout the world in support of the proposed method of disposal authorized, we have decided in the public interest to use the proposed outfall as a research project . . ."

Of course, another nice little handout at the public's expense. It is worth noting that this generous gift from the public coffers was concocted by the same bureaucrat who chaired the farcical Public Inquiries discussed earlier, showing again a total disregard for economic concerns.

Following the first two years use of the outfall, the results of the surveillance program were presented. In essence, on the basis of the facts collected, not the conjecture of the survey team, the method of discharge was unequivocally found to be satisfactory, which is no surprise to those who understand the mechanisms involved.

Ecological Footnote

Did the favourable result from the study confound those doing it? They were not content to leave well enough alone but had to inject the "doomsday" theme in order to accomplish their goal. In the report is presented a statement totally out of context with the terms of reference for the study under the heading "An Ecological Footnote Concerning Broader Aspects of Waste Disposal." Frankly, having read the statement which is pure surmise, conjecture and innuendo, I felt it should have borne the title "Environmental Drivel". For example, the two pages of nonsense contained this statement:

"... we don't really know the ultimate fate of the large amounts of waste presently being disposed of in the oceans. To be specific, with respect to the Macaulay Point Outfall, we do not know where the approximately 65 tons/year of phosphate and 120 tons/year of organic nitrogen being discharged there are ending up."

Are the "intellects" who wrote the report really so naive? Or are they deliberately condoning environmental nonsense to further their own interests with the acquisition of more studies and a lucrative return? Are they not aware that every cubic mile of the ocean contains millions of tons, *yes millions of tons,* of dissolved elements which are there as a result of natural phenomena? They express concern as to the destiny of some 65 tons of phosphate and 120 tons of nitrogen discharged per year, yet the oceans of the world, including those of the British Columbia coast, contain approximately 330 tons of phosphorous and 2,400 tons of nitrogen in every single cubic mile, plus of course, in varying quantities, all the other elements of our planet.

Can the authors of the report, as biologists, expect us to take them seriously when they claim they "do not understand the system sufficiently to be able to make an informed guess"? Of course not! The reason for their reluctance to accept the findings of their own work was to be found in the Recommendations:

"... it is recommended that University and Government agencies should coordinate a long-term, broad-scale monitoring program in British Columbia Coastal Waters ...
"... it is recommended that University and Government agencies institute long-term studies on the ecological, social and economic implications of the various methods of handling wastes, including the question of disposal versus recycling."

Already Know Answers

I am sure it does not surprise the authors when I point out the answers to the issues they raise are already in the literature of reputable scientific societies. At the 1970 Public Inquiries referred to in a previous chapter I said:

> "While it is acknowledged that research must play a role in our evaluation of pollution, more research is not the answer to the immediate problem. Man already knows the answers to much of the matters causing concern . . . The answers are not in textbook theory, nor in test tubes, but in the ability to deduce realistic safety factors by using epidemiological evidence and empirical data gleaned over the years . . . ."

On the basis of the findings of the Macaulay Point surveillance study, anyone with experience, even a little commonsense, can readily deduce that further sampling programs were unnecessary. The concerns expressed in the report relative to ecological matters just don't exist; they are purely figments of the imagination by those writing the report. The Ecological Footnote shows the unadulterated surmise being used in such expressions as:

> ". . . we don't really know . . . ."; ". . . they must be contributing . . . ."; ". . . they may be locked up . . . .";
> ". . . The main point is we just do not understand . . . ."

There is an interesting sequel to the above. In 1977, an application was made to construct a somewhat insignificant outfall in the same general area as Macaulay Point. There was the usual rash of objections by the public, supported by unfounded statements from the academics, as they sought to further their academic goals. To appease them they were commissioned to do a study. And what did they find?

Firstly, they reviewed the underwater conditions at Macaulay Point. The findings were:

> "There are still only a few signs of a response to the discharge . . . These are: an increase in the numbers of large hermit crabs and several species of fish . . . ."

Note that the effect is an increase in biological life, not the creation of a biological desert, or dead sea as so often inferred by the fear mongers. The report concludes:

> "These observations strongly suggest that the sea-bed eco-system response to the Macaulay Point deep discharge stabilized soon after operation commenced in 1971, is not presently changing in a visually observable way, and is not a significant distortion of the natural ecosystem."

Of course, to be expected, in the Recommendations we find the usual request for continuation of a surveillance program.

Costs as much as Outfall

And for the benefit of those who may want to shrug it all off, the bottom line of the controversy appeared in *The Daily Colonist* of May 6, 1978, in the revealing headline: "Study Costs Almost As Much As The Outfall". The article started, "It is going to cost the Capital Regional District $560,000 to make an environmental study of the proposed $600,000 new McMicking Point outfall." Without further ado, I penned a scathing letter to the Editor, with a copy to the Premier and other elected dignitaries:

> "As one who played a part in the earlier debate over the McMicking Point outfall, I am now appalled to read in the Colonist, May 6, 1978, that we are to spend half a million dollars on a useless study, which will serve no purpose other than to help educate a few misguided academics."

The Daily Colonist was good enough to publish my criticism, under the caption, 'Sewage Fuss Generated by Academics'. My letter concluded:

> As a taxpayer, I trust our elected Provincial and Regional leaders will see to it that not one single cent is wasted on this totally needless and parasitical exercise."

No action was taken to head off the needless waste of public funds. Two years and untold dollars later, following the extensive studies referred to in *The Daily Colonist* of October 2, 1979, the editor astutely summarised the whole chaotic episode in an article entitled, "Sorry Saga of a Sewer Outfall", from which the following is quoted:

> (the) "committee brought in a report and recommendation . . . amply supported by technicians, biologists and engineers . . . to the effect that an extended outfall from the shoreline to Enterprise Channel (just as Charles Keenan had suggested three years before) would solve the McMicking Point problem . . . . Thus the three year battle came to an end . . . ."

Regrettably, the outfall changes undertaken did not follow the design criteria I publicly suggested, which, while vastly improving the situation, left some room for the unfounded criticisms of some bellicose residents who had bitterly opposed the improvement.

No Warning Bells

To show the irrational and irresponsible exploitation of the environmental scene, I quote from a report prepared by the Department of Biology, University of Victoria, which pretends to deal with the impact on the environment of domestic waste discharges in the Victoria area. The report says in reference to the capacity of the local sea to absorb wastes:

> "What is known is that when the limit has been reached, it

is often too late to do anything about it (i.e. Lake Erie) and changing established environmental use patterns is then extremely costly. The environment rings no warning bells before it collapses.''

Note the subtle reference to Lake Erie. The fact that the two situations in no way relate to one another in either physical or biological terms does not deter the pseudo-expert. Note also the hysteria in the phrase — "The environment rings no warning bells before it collapses.'' It is pitiable to report that this very phrase was quoted as gospel, as proven, indisputable fact, by a member of the public on a television seminar program dealing with waste disposal in Victoria in late 1980. The damage and public mischief caused by such statements is inestimable. If there are no warning bells, just what-the-hell are all the costly and lavish masses of monitoring programs and continuing ecological surveillance studies for?

Lakes Not "Dead"

While I am not intimately conversant with the Great Lakes, I am prepared to risk my professional reputation and state that the Great Lakes are no more dead than you are. I guarantee that there are thousands of miles of beautiful, pleasant shoreline to be enjoyed and that much of the Lakes abound in crisp, clear water, teeming with fish and other biological species. Lake Erie, in particular, has been singled out as the deadest of the dead. Yet, on the basis of technical reports which I have read, Lake Erie produces an abundant fish harvest each year. In the Great Lakes, just as everywhere else, over-fishing has been presented as the primary cause of fish depletion. There is, too, in the Lakes the scourge of the infamous parasitical Lamprey eel with which to contend.

Don't get me wrong, I am not saying that there aren't many areas of local pollution or degradation that should not be stopped and remedied. Nor am I saying that the Lakes are an ideal receptacle for wastes, particularly if untreated. In general, lakes do not possess the same physical powers of the sea to move, mix, dilute and absorb waste materials without showing an adverse impact. Nor are the Lakes an ideal receptacle for exotic toxic chemicals. The disposal of such materials requires the attention of specialists. This is not the subject of this book, which, rather, deals with the attitudes of those advocates of environmentalism who see it as the end-all for society. I am saying though that in spite of the colossal input of untreated wastes from a population as large as all of Canada, the Lakes are anything but dead. To the contrary, I have read reports that the problem is they are too active from the input of life-supporting nutrients. It is too bad that we cannot be given the ungarnished facts obtained with our research funds.

"Stratagems"

In late 1978, the Great Lake Rehabilitation and Restoration group admitted that their efforts over the past decade or two to turn the Lakes back into a "pristine" state had failed. The Great Lakes news item pointed out that the Restoration group were seeking funds to do, in their words, ". . . an eco-system approach" to the problem which, in essence, is nothing more than a good old-fashioned basin-by-basin study of the surrounding rivers. No doubt the designation "eco-system" is surreptitiously tagged on to such requests to ensure funds are forthcoming. Since "studies" are now beginning to be suspect in some quarters, in order to mask the frailties of their proposals, government environmentalists are now attempting to con us with the word "stratagem". This play on words is a subtlety developed to make us believe that they know more than they do, or more than we do, whichever you like.

To develop these strategems of course necessitates the calling of extravagant conferences, at which new and pretentious philosophies are developed to deceive us into accepting that such are necessary. I received in January, 1980, a request to prepare a paper for the Canadian Water Resources Association conference on "Evolving Water Management Strategies in Canada". It is not surprising that the request came from Environment Canada, our national bureau of parasites.

The futility of environmental expenditures is well documented. In mid-1979 the Canadian and United States International Joint Commission (IJC) which, among other things, has been studying Great Lakes pollution for a number of years, observed through its Chairman that new scientific information has made it necessary to question the adequacy of the phosphorous data collected in the Great Lakes and the accuracy of predictive models of Lake responses to reduce phosphorous loads. While offering nothing of value, the statement attempts to justify activities to date, with the less than profound observation that "We know more about phosphorous now than we did two years ago. . . the way it gets into the Lakes and what works at what cost to keep excess phosphorous from reaching the Lakes." The taxpayer would certainly hope so, even though the benefits are of questionable value when balanced against the unnecessary outlay. The sensitive role played by phosphorous in the fertilization of both land and water has been well documented for years. Most people working in the field have been cognizant of the fact that the quantities of phosphorous needed to accelerate algal growths are so minute that little can be done to control increased algae when nature decides the right ingredients are all present.

The Chairman's exposition of justification goes on: "But that is not enough, we need to know enough to choose the mix of programs, which for the least cost will keep the greatest amount of available phosphorous from getting into the Great Lakes system.'' This is nothing more than the unadulterated prelude to a new phase of lavish spending on "statagems", solely to perpetuate a mass of nonproductive jobs, as it would appear on the basis of the available data that all attempts to stop eutrophication, a natural evolutionary process, accelerated, of course, in this case by man's activities, are likely to end in total failure. The futile attempts to control milfoil weed in the Okanagan Lake was referred to earlier. An aircraft that almost flies, is useless. This, in essense, is what environmental studies are providing, over and over again.

Acid Rain

Having now built a parasitical empire on the premise of an "environmental collapse" which has turned out to be false, we are left with the dilemma of what to do with the participants. The ideal solution for the participants, of course, is to pretend that some delicate hypothetical mechanism in the eco-system was overlooked, an area in which the pseudo-expert is never at a loss. And lo! they have found it. We are now told that the latest plague is "acid rain", and that this subject requires urgent attention to protect our lakes and rivers from destruction. The media, as usual, has rushed to aid the hysteria with such headlines as, "Acid rain: Point of no return" or, "Rivers destroyed by acid rain". The note of alarm has that all too familiar wolf! wolf! ring about it.

Before going off half-cocked on this latest environmental fad, it would behoove those that are trusted with dispensing our tax dollars to make a cursory assessment of what the reality is. Acid rain is nothing new; all of the major industrial areas of the world have been producing it for a century or so. Are the lakes really being destroyed by acid rain — *alone* — or are there other factors, like the past development of the land surface for agricultural and/or other uses, or the acid nature of the surrounding rocks? Or could the fish simply be disappearing because of predatory man? What fish are being killed and of what value and where do they fit into the inevitable resource trade-offs essential for society to progress?

One must also ponder if it is true what some say, that environmentalism is being used by a few elitist wealthy groups, such as the Sierra Club, to attain dominance over large parts of our natural living space for their exclusive uses. So powerful is the lobby of the acid rain freaks that during a 1983 Summer visit to Eastern Canada, the powers-that-be stooped to using His Royal Highness, Prince Charles, to further their cause by inserting in one of his speeches a statement to the effect that acid rain posed an economic threat to our forests.

Acid rain has always been with us, indeed, in the early evolution of the planet earth, it was the order. It is documented by research institutes that the largest portion of all the acid-forming ingredients in the atmosphere come from natural processes. It should come as no surprise then, to find that acid rain is not always harmful; on the contrary, it can be beneficial.

It is claimed that parts of southern Saskatchewan can benefit from the vitriolic downpour as the land is high in alkali, requiring the application of acidic fertilizers to get the best crop returns. Acid rain has always been an inescapable part of nature's hydrological cycle since normal rain is acidic because of natural gases present in the atmosphere. Around cities and large industries the concentration of the acid-causing ingredients are more pronounced and in certain instances need to be controlled, which can readily be achieved, at a cost, which raises the question of trade-offs. Will such expenditures ensure the return of the fish and will their return be profitable in keeping with the outlay? The masses of the world's population have long been subjected to this acid environment. If one takes at face value the present hysteria about acid rain, one must wonder why many of the coal-burning industrial areas of the world have not long since dissolved in the vat of acid in which they have been enveloped?

Function of Natural Forces

The nature of the terrain surrounding lakes whether it be acid or alkali also has a major role in the outcome. In short, the environment of which we are but a part has been a function of natural forces since time immemorial. Perhaps it could be explained what it was that man did to cause all the acid bogs on the Pacific Coast of British Columbia, formed since the glacial ice retreated. I recall an incident involving one city located on the Pacific Coast that had severe equipment corrosion problems when the domestic water supply was first fluoridated. (Another area where the anti-pseudo-experts have run amok.) It was found upon investigation that the raw water was highly acidic, a common occurrence in the muskeg country of British Columbia. Acidic values as low as those now being quoted in Eastern Canada as "lethal" are quite routine in such areas. Mother Nature has done it to us again!

Vast Chemical Factory

As in all environmental issues, the search for the truth is not easy. Masses of articles on the acid rain menace have appeared in just about every conceivable form of printed matter. For example, there was published in 1980 an article in a reputable journal which on the surface alleged to document the pros and cons of continuing to use fossil fuels to generate power. The article, as one comes to expect in the environmental arena, touched on the doomsday aspects of acid rain, coining dramatic new environmental expressions to generate fear. It was explained that the atmosphere becomes a "vast chemical factory" and that the emission "rarely stays around to plague those who cause it". Many hypothetical cases were posed, including the totally unsubtantiated theme that it is all "irreversible". The article has been quoted as an authority. However, as always in the environmental scenario, there is a catch. On closer scrutiny it was noted that the article was not free from bias: it was written for the proponents of Atomic Energy who see fossil fuels as a threat to the development of nuclear energy.

As late as June 1983, one more acid-rain report was released by the U.S. National Academy of Science claiming to have found a positive link between acid-rain and the coal-fired boilers of industry. Frankly, there are few who would dispute this. I recall what may well be a disturbing revelation for the pseudo-experts: As far back as 1959, during post-graduate studies at Imperial College in London, I was made aware of the acid rain problem. We were warned to use special "hard" glass vessels for collecting rain samples as the acid-rain would etch (eat away) ordinary glass ware. No one disputes that many industries add to the acid-rain issue but the question is, will the spending of enormous amounts of money to reduce (not eliminate) the problem bear any worthwhile fruits?

And what of all of mother nature's vast chemical factories? In early 1983 it was reported that a National Science Foundation in the United States discovered, "An invisible cloud of sulphuric acid droplets high in the atmosphere. The source of the acid cloud is believed to be the Mexican volcano El Chichon, which spewed large amounts of sulphur dioxide into the air when it erupted in April, 1982." The cloud was described as of "continental proportions. . . predicted to be semi-permanent. . . for years to come."

Scene of Desolation

On Sunday morning May 18, 1980, while sitting at the breakfast table there was an explosion which rattled and shook the doors and windows of my home. I looked out to see which of my neighbours' houses had blown up. More rumbles occurred as the cause was sought. Eventually, I was to find out that Mount St. Helens, 150 miles away in the State of Washington, had blown its top, with an explosion estimated to be equal to the fury of a ten-megaton bomb.

Over the following days we were entertained by superb TV coverage of this spectacular event. Volcanic ash, varying from inches to feet in depth, was spread over thousands of square miles of territory, some reaching to the far side of the continent. Particles travelled all the way around the globe. Rivers in the vicinity of the mountain were filled with flowing mud, ash and debris — the environmental impact was devastating — a whole mountainside was stripped of its mighty forest to be replaced with a scene of desolation. The eruption caused severe hazard to life. Animals, birds and insect populations were obliterated, some sixty human lives were lost. That losses in human life were not greater results from man's ability to take preventive measures to protect himself against nature in the raw.

It is intriguing to note that some scientists were quick to point out that all that happened to Mt. St. Helens is not bad. Much of the fallout would be of benefit to nature, particularly the element phosphorus as a soil fertilizer. Strange, is it not, as mentioned in several places throughout this book, how the pseudo-experts are badgering municipalities and persecuting industries about waste discharges which contain phosphorus. Radioactive materials too, were scattered at random throughout the environment. Those who vehemently oppose mining uranium must be unaware that radioactivity is as natural as life itself. The centre of our planet is a radioactive inferno and we are daily subjected to the radiation phenomena through the warming rays of life-giving sun light. In spite of the awesome display by Mount St. Helens, natural history assures us that the area devastated will certainly recover, the time needed depending upon the dormancy of the mountain. Of course, if it were an act of industrial man, it would be designated "irreversible".

Change is the Rule

This event serves well to remind us that our natural environment initially grew out of such chaos and destructive forces, for in the early evolution such activity was the rule, not the exception. In the beginning, the earth was one great molten ball, which it still is, just a few miles below the surface crust on which we live. Environmentalism, in truth, is in a very untenable position when viewed against the awesome reality of the universe. Since our earth environment and its atmosphere evolved from a fiery furnace, man's interference in such matters is of no consequence to its destiny. Every region of our planet has in the past, due to natural events, experienced extremes of climate and land mass changes that would eliminate most, if not all, of today's higher life forms. Change, which the environmentalists oppose, has always been and always will be the rule. The life forms that survive are those that adapt.

Chapter Twelve

THE OIL SCENARIO

In no area has more nonsense been generated than with respect to the oil spill pollution threat. In spite of all the waste discharges and sea traffic which are claimed to be posing cataclysmic environmental hazards to our coastlines, one cannot help being more than a little sceptical of the doom preachers when the vitality of the marine environment everywhere is observed. While certain marine populations are undoubtedly being endangered in some areas, it is primarily due to the rapaciousness of man, not to environmental collapse.

In common with other aspects of environmental issues, the facts about oil spills have been disregarded in favour of surmise and hysteria. There are those, and among them some quite prominent figures such as Jacques Cousteau, who have brashly predicted the end of our oceans within 20 to 30 years, oil often being singled out as the triggering mechanism. Some of these predictions were made back in the 1960's, so we are rapidly running out of time, if there is just a fraction of credibility to the claims. However, at long last the truth is being revealed. In November, 1982 it was reported from Geneva that leading United Nations environmental scientists stated ". . . that talk of the death of the seas on a global scale is groundless." To the chagrin of the doom preachers, it appears that yet another of their predictions has come back to haunt them.

Let us look objectively at the oil spill issue. To put the subject in perspective, oil is frankly a nasty substance. The dictionary defines "nasty" as, "very dirty, foul, filthy, impure, disgusting, offensive" and this is indeed the essense of the issue. On the other hand, oil is not an insidious killer like pesticides or radioactive materials. Environmentally, it wreaks its damage in a physical, rather than a chemical sense.

Oil destroys basically because of its physical presence. Birds are particularly prone to this effect of oil, thus the reason they are held up as the symbol of ecological disaster by the anti-tanker groups. Marine life too, suffers much more so from the physical presence of oil than from toxicity. And of course man would be denied recreational use of beaches, if inundated with the gooey mess. In common with most substances (table salt for example), oil can be toxic depending upon concentration, exposure and other factors, but the adverse environmental effects of oil spills are almost exclusively of a physical character. It is this aspect to which the following comments are addressed in the hope of exposing more of the environmental hypocrisy.

Environmental Safeguard

It is well to remember that oil was, in the first instance, discovered oozing out of the ground, forming pools, ponds and streamlets of its own. It is thus indigenous to our environment. While somewhat hypothetical, it is worth reflecting that the very extraction of oil by man from the bowels of the earth could well represent, in the final analysis, a tremendous environmental safeguard against the possibility of a mammoth oil spill by nature through earthquake activity. Such an eruption would be many times more disastrous than the impact from the runaway well in the Gulf of Mexico in 1979 or from any tanker disaster.

In essense, the real issue of contention in dealing with an oil spill disaster is how to clean up the mess after the spill has occurred. Accidents are inevitable and while they can be reduced they cannot be eliminated because of human errors, carelessness, sabotage and natural phenomena.

Nowhere are greater precautions taken against accidents than in air transport, yet with disquieting regularity reports of air tragedies keep appearing. At least when an oil spill occurs, human life is seldom at stake, and to those of you who say, but what of fish and fowl, I ask, "Are you vegetarians, or hypocrites? Do you subscribe to the slaughter of billions of fowl, fish and animals to feed the human race?" Once, when I was addressing a group of biology students at a university seminar, it was put to me that streams rightfully belonged to microorganisms and that it was wrong to trade them off in the interests of the economy by using the streams for carrying off waste water. There was a knowing rumble of resentment from the audience but no verbal answer to my retort: "Are you a vegetarian?"

Torrey Canyon Spill

While oil spills are nasty, they are not permanent; another factor to be digested by those who scream of permanent environmental damage. The first of the major spectacular oil spills occurred in 1967 when the *Torrey Canyon* ran aground in the English Channel. At the time, it created havoc to a few miles of the local beaches and wild life. Fears that all natural life would be wiped out were hysterically broadcast. But today, nothing remains that even an expert ornithologist could use to prove that the area had ever been devastated, except the bird rescue centres built at the time, no doubt to appease an emotional segment of the population. All in all, many studies of so-called catastrophic oil spills show that there are no longterm effects to the environment. Total recuperation is certainly well within ten years. This has again proven to be the case with a more recent disaster when the tanker *Amoco Cadiz,* carrying 69 million gallons of crude oil, broke up on the rocks off the coast of Brittany.

With regard to the impact on local bird life, it is reported that many knowledgeable and humane people believe that the best way to deal with birds which have been assaulted by an oil spill is to put them out of their misery rather than attempt to rehabilitate them as the odds are against success.

Much oil is wasted and lost at sea. Many reports are available which document evidence of oil in the major shipping lanes. Much of the oil should not be there, as it was unforgiveably put there, deliberately in many cases, through ships pumping oil sludge from bilges or tanks as a routine procedure or as a safety measure when an overloaded tanker lightens cargo when hit by a storm. Such occurrences represent social and environmental abuses which should not be allowed and which no doubt contribute to the main evidence of oil along the shipping routes.

Fortunately, because of its organic structure, oil breaks down under the ever-present natural forces of sunlight, bacterial action and evaporation. In addition, gravitational forces will work to benefit in the oceans. Though the processes are slow, the inference is that oil is not likely to accumulate beyond a certain level. What is found in the oceans, at any given time, is probably there as a result of recent traffic. In time it will assimilate and be absorbed into the ocean environment. Of course, as it does so, more appears as a result of new traffic, but there is no evidence to show that such wastes are accumulating or that they remain for many years. The dissipation is like that of any other natural waste material but unfortunately with oil its physical presence can be temporarily detrimental to some life forms, as well as being an incidental nuisance to man and others. The basic problem is one of concentration. It is worth observing, in passing, that in some oil rich arid lands, oil residues are used to stabilize and condition soil when it is being reclaimed for vegetational purposes. So it obviously is not as diabolical as alarmists would like us to believe.

The facts of life are that we need oil; our society as it is structured today, cannot survive without a plentiful supply. When oil supplies diminish, society will of course undergo changes and new sources of energy will have to be utilized. In the meantime, how oil is brought from the oil field to the gas pump is purely a matter of economics. It is utter impertinence and unadulterated gall for environmentalists to discuss the pros and cons of supertanker design, or supertankers versus pipelines. Tanker design, size, loading, safety and navigational matters are for naval architects and experienced seamen to decide and pipelines a theme for engineers, certainly not for those with devious motives.

Greenpeace Blockade

I weary of hearing about the hazards from shipping traffic down the West Coast of British Columbia and within the Straits of Juan de Fuca. When compared with the English Channel and other such areas of sea commerce, it is as nothing. It is estimated that 300 ships a day pass to and fro in the English Channel while another 100 or so criss-cross it. If the dire predictions for the West Coast of B.C. by the doomspeakers are to be believed about the hazards in our coastal waters, then the sinkings between the coasts of France and England must be horrendous: strange, how little we hear of them. If the risks are so horrendous, why are we not having the same protests about the Eastern seaboard of our nation where tanker traffic far exceeds that on the West? In addition, the population likely to be affected on the Eastern seaboard greatly exceeds ours and their sea-front development is greater too. All but a few must see the hypocrisy in the hazard scenario on the West coast. It is sad to report that without exception the three major political parties which campaigned for election in the early 1980's agreed with the protesters — with the anarchists — who, in the form of the Greenpeace Foundation, are advocating the blockade of supertankers in the Strait of Juan de Fuca, waters in which the United States has sovereign rights.

While the Greenpeace threat was not an idle one, it certainly was meaningless. On January 23 and 24, 1981, specially controlled supertanker tests were undertaken in the American waters of the Straits of Juan de Fuca in an attempt to ascertain the manoeuvrability of these floating monsters under certain simulated events which could lead to accidents. Greenpeace opposed the tests, protesting that they served no useful purpose, that no catastrophe would occur in view of the extent of the special precautions taken, but that the tests would result in supertanker traffic being approved — in short, they saw the issue as *a fait accompli.*

Interestingly enough, they are right, for in truth, the real reason and *only* reason for the tests was to go "through the motions" as it were, to fulfill the nebulous demands placed on society by

environmentalism. Just as environmental impact studies serve little or
no purpose, so too did the manoeuvrability tests have little meaning,
other than to familiarize local tug-boat crews with the handling of these
floating monsters and to demonstrate before the public what is already
known to the tanker elite.

Of course, the media was there, "a small army of mike-
brandishing, camera-lugging newsmen" to record the day Greenpeace
"took on the U.S. Coast Guard and harass the 188,000 deadweight
ton *B.T.San Diego* on its first day of a four day supertanker test."
That the media reports ignored reality, were hysterical and biased should
not surprise the reader.

Exploded on the front page of the *Times-Colonist* of January 24,
1981, was a large, distorted, telephoto picture of the supertanker
B.T.San Diego with a circle around a diminutive (invisible, in fact)
Greenpeace zodiac boat under the bow; there was a massive double
line headline, a lengthy write up, with more pictures on page three *et
al*. At the bottom of the same front page under a much, much smaller
headline was the caption, "Huge coal pact will put $877 million in B.C.
coffers". The article stated that some 9,000 permanent new jobs would
be a direct effect, with more than double this as a result of spin-off
activities and service industries. The Minister involved said it would
"eclipse all previous resource developments in British Columbia".

Serve Little Purpose

That this major event was, in the estimation of the media, eclipsed
by the ridiculous antics of a few egoistic publicity-seekers confronting
a 188,000 ton tanker, should raise questions in the minds of every
concerned citizen on the role and credibility of the media and the
problems it is creating for society through distortion of realities, and
ill-conceived support for radical causes.

To facilitate the safe execution of the tanker manoeuvres, shipping notices were issued by the U.S. Coast Guard to stay clear of the
test area. As a result of Greenpeace's flagrant violations, some twelve
participants were arrested and charged. As demonstrated throughout
this text, here again, the link with socialism surfaced. A resolution was
presented to Parliament calling for funds to defend the law breakers.
The call, as the reader should now suspect, came from the political far
left — the N.D.P.

Every now and then the media confounds us all with words of
wisdom in these days of anarchy. In the *Times-Colonist* of January
29, 1981, there appeared in the editorial column under the caption, "A
silly protest", the following astute observations:

> "The purpose of the tests was . . . intended to provide data
> on which to base safety regulations for tanker traffic in the

strait. . . So why the protest? It is clear the whole thing was a contrived media event with little or no practical purpose. . . Canadian members of Greenpeace who were arrested and charged should be reminded they were in U.S. waters. As aliens they were lucky to have been treated as well as they were. . . ''

Acts Meaningless

Upon reading the editorial comment, one may in a moment of compassion be prepared to pardon the press for its transgressions, but the simple truth is that without the headlines, the cameras and the mikes, these acts of anarchy would indeed be so meaningless that they would cease. The paper, of course, did not, in effect, apologize for its earlier build-up to the whole event when the front page was used to announce "Supertanker battle round 2 starts today", or the headline on page three, "Oily Boid Day was unique Greenpeace media event".

It is interesting to ponder why the eco-freak, who is violently opposed to any disturbance of the landscape every time new development is proposed, should be so much in favour of pipelines over supertankers since a pipeline several thousands of miles in length unquestionably disturbs one hell-of-a-lot of natural landscape, whereas the tanker does little in this regard. Perhaps the answer is easy: tankers don't require funded studies as can be demanded in regard to a pipeline route, thus the academic pseudo-expert is quite happy to take his fee to determine which pipeline route is likely to cause least environmental damage, an exercise which at its best can be dismissed as futile. Hidden too, in the anti-supertanker issue, is the insidious presence of socialism and anarchism interferring with the sovereign rights of other nations.

New Ice Age

Over the past two decades, our intelligence has been assaulted and insulted with many doomsday theories. The carbon dioxide theory was to increase the temperature of the earth, melt the ice caps and bury our civilization under the resulting elevation of the seas. Others use the same data to tell us that a cooling effect would be caused, which would bring about another Ice Age. Take your choice of those theories before considering this one. We are now told that an oil spill in the Arctic could trigger a new Ice Age. This dire warning made the usual spectacular headlines:

"Oil-darkened ice, having lost the ability to reflect sunlight would absorb heat and melt. An Ice Age chain reaction would begin because the present dry Arctic winds sweeping down into Siberia, Canada and Northern Europe would pick up additional moisture. This moisture could produce additional ice south of the Arctic."

Such is the off-the-cuff humbug that environmentalists thrive on. Perhaps someone could explain who-the-hell spilled the oil that started the last Ice Age? Historically speaking, in geological terms, the earth has gone through a multitude of physical and climatic changes far exceeding anything which we today can envisage and all, I must add, long before man liberated himself — with his much castigated technology — from the bonds of his animal environment. To be intelligent, environmental issues must take into account reality, economics and history. If commonsense does not prevail, chaos and social nonsense results.

What must be resolved, and this can be done best with the people in the business, is to determine what measures can be taken to reduce the occurrence of spills and waste and minimize the impact of such spills when they occur. As far back as 1964, I attended study sessions in the United States where cleanup techniques for oil were discussed. My notes of that meeting show that absorbents, emulsifiers and skimming techniques were all being used. Unfortunately, no more sophisticated methods have since come to light. In the final analysis, time and nature are our best allies. As damage will occur when there is a mishap, the matter of equitable compensation to those injured must be made an integral part of any preventive program.

Santa Barbara Spill

While the *Torrey Canyon* grounding was a milestone in tanker spills, the Santa Barbara offshore oil drilling blowout was a peak in environmental hysteria. At the time, one would have thought the end of the world had arrived, certainly as far as the Californian Coast was concerned. Whereas, in fact, nothing worse than a leak of nasty gooey oil was at stake. In retrospect, it is much easier for the uninformed reader to now appreciate the rationality of the position as stated by the industry at the time.

Here is a portion of a statement from the *Oil and Gas Journal* of 1969 under the heading, "Calm Appraisal is needed to end Santa Barbara Hysteria":

> "The Hysteria whipped up over the Santa Barbara Channel blowout is beyond belief. Descriptions of the unusual accident by the general news media as a disaster and a tragedy are just out of touch with reality. The demand by some politicians for punitive moves against the entire oil industry is self-serving at its worst.
>
> "A disaster — it wasn't. No lives were lost, no extensive destruction of property occurred. A regrettable mess — of course. Expensive — very. But the resulting pollution is something that can and is being cleaned up. Any damage to

shipping or installations can be repaired. Everyone deplores the loss of seagulls and other birds. But the first dead fish is yet to be discovered, and the strict use of approved cleanup materials should prevent damage to the marine ecology of the area.

"The government doesn't ban commercial flying in this country after tragic air crashes. It doesn't halt highway travel even though thousands consistently die in accidents every year. Yet the first serious accident among some 1,100 wells drilled off Santa Barbara County and hundreds more in other waters inspires a cry for halting offshore drilling.

"The Company and its industry associates deserve praise — not malignment — for their efforts under difficult circumstances. They strained every muscle to plug the leak, prevent spread of the slick, and clean up the mess. They showed genuine concern and a high sense of responsibility. A full inquiry into the blowout ordered by the President should now give a calm evaluation of the whole problem. . . "

When placed against the awesome natural catastrophies in recent times in Bangladesh, Pakistan, India, Guatemala and many parts of Africa and South America, where human life losses were in the millions, and where human suffering can today be counted in the hundreds of millions, the emotional outbursts in the name of man-made environmental issues are as nothing.

Mackenzie Valley Pipeline

In 1977, in response to his assignment by the Federal Government, Judge T.R. Berger, a former leader of the socialist party (N.D.P.) in British Columbia, made public Volume I of his Report of the Mackenzie Valley Pipeline Inquiry. The Report, a document of questionable value, epitomizes the whole confrontation of oil versus the environmental issue. At best, Berger's Report simply furthers the socialistic goals of his political beliefs. There is little doubt that the Report fails to meet the intent of the terms of reference to ascertain what conditions should be imposed to meet social and environmental needs, if a Mackenzie Valley pipeline were built.

To suddenly conclude, as the Report does, that a ten year moratorium be placed on the pipeline development, until native land claim issues are settled, is nothing more than a piece of ill-conceived socialism. It is not insignificant to point out that in the minds of many, the claims of native people are, at the best, tenuous. The Report does nothing more than raise unrealistic hopes for certain native people, whose only real chance of survival is integration into the social structure which has virtually enveloped them. No doubt, some see themselves as the Arabs of the north, with hopes of participating in the now popular oil ransom game. Society cannot allow itself to be put in any such compromising position. It is in such critical issues as this, having an impact on the whole of society, that pressure group interests, no matter how strongly felt, cannot be accepted.

To suggest that the pipeline would create havoc, is without foundation. Years of experience, all over the world, as well as throughout Canada, has proven that construction of pipelines do not create the catastrophic effects implied by Berger and the environmentalists. There its little doubt that Berger, either from the outset, or as the inquiry proceeded, decided to seize the opportunity to produce an argument against the pipeline on behalf of socialism and the native people.

Here again, the Berger incident produces further evidence of the link between socialism and environmentalism. In May 1978, the Sierra Club awarded Berger the Club's distinguished achievement award. It was presented for "sensitive and thorough conduct of the Mackenzie Valley pipeline Inquiry" and for transforming "a technical analysis into a soul-searching evaluation of social, moral and environmental responsibilities."

Feds Needed Berger

In other words, like the ecological gods, Berger was not to be confused with technical facts while fostering the ends of environmentalism and socialism. It is of some significance to point out that at the time of Berger's appointment by the Federal Liberal Government, the Liberals were in a minority position in the 'House', needing the support of the Federal NDP socialists to govern.

It is common knowledge that Berger's former colleagues, for political reasons, were opposed to the idea of a pipeline. The leader of his former party went so far as to advocate the building of a railway to carry oil and gas from the Mackenzie Delta because it would not be so damaging to the environment. Have these people never once, just once, walked along a railroad? To suggest that such would disturb less of the natural environment than would a pipeline, is drivel. This is all quite incidental to the Mackenzie Valley issue, of course, since it was intended, in any event, to ultimately provide a transport corridor down the Valley which would have included a highway and possibly a railway, as well as a pipeline.

The only thing of value to come out of the Berger Report is that it quickly cleared the way for the alternative Alcan route. There are some who feel that the Berger Inquiry was simply a red herring. Had the Alcan route been subjected to the same type of nonsensical study, industry would have had no choice but to go the tanker route. The economic and social loss to the Mackenzie Valley will one day come home to its people, who will, when the realities of the situation dawns on them, question the wisdom of Berger. Indeed, in November 1979, there appeared the following in the Canadian Press:

> "Severe economic recession as a result of the Berger era is still evident in the Northwest Territories, the eighth national northern development conference was told. . . there has been no change in the 'economic stagnation' in the N.W.T. since 1976. . . the 'no development' era characterized by Mr. Justice Thomas Berger's Mackenzie Valley pipeline inquiry. . . "

Conflict of Interest

To put the Berger report in honest perspective, the question of "conflict of interest" cannot be ignored. Everytime an inquiry is called involving government activities, large corporations, or resource issues, the socialists in our midst raise their age old cry of "conflict of interest", if those chosen to conduct the proceedings could in any way be tainted through past association.

In August 1980, Berger was responsible for making a critical resource management decision on the maintenance of water levels in the Nechako River. The court case arose following a dispute between the Federal Fisheries department and the Aluminum Company of Canada. Berger found in favour of Ottawa. One must surely question the wisdom of having him adjudicate on critical resource matters because of his long-standing political associations. Had a judge of a different, but equally active political persuasion been chosen to conduct the Mackenzie Valley inquiry, with all of the political ramifications involved, the socialists, with little ado, would have adopted their all too familiar posture of outrage with accusations that the proceedings were a "whitewash".

Since writing this critique on Berger's activities in the environmental arena, he has of his own volition stepped down from his judgeship, on what can only be described as a conflict of interest over his dedication to socialism, as he was reprimanded for being "indiscreet" by expressing publicly his personal feelings on issues involving the courts of the land. It is pertinent to note that he now proposes to continue his career within the academic world, where, no doubt, he will find naive young minds receptive to his socialistic philosophies. An editorial put the matter this way, "Berger was, is and always will be a political animal. . . "

Of the Berger Report, others have said:

> ". . . the report is not to be believed, it is of little value to the people of the North,. . . Berger was appointed when Ottawa required the support of the socialists to give them the balance of power. . . the document is political not

factual. . . it is a classical example of southerners who invade the north to conduct studies. . . Berger doesn't have to live with the recommendation. . . his mistakes. . . You would think this was the first damn pipeline that man had ever built. . . there are thousands of miles of pipelines. . . How do you think the oil and gas is transported today?. . . Do you think we are bringing it down in buckets?. . . Environmentalists are all hypocrites. . . "

One oil industry executive put the media aspects of the subject this way:

"There is no possible way to compete for sensationalism with all the addled-brained, irresponsible charges, claims and demands which seem to occupy so much of our newspapers and television. The amount of newspaper coverage appears to be in direct proportion to the irresponsibility of the statement and lack of knowledge. Anyone who attempts to answer with reason and logic, is lost."

And here is the addle-brained proposition of one politician:

"Public interest groups should have equal time on television to counter advertising by oil companies. . . "

Anyone with an ounce of wit realizes that the present advertising done by industries is only an attempt to counter the hysterical, misleading nonsense carried on day in, day out in the media, as earlier exemplified. Be assured of one thing though, while the oil will come south, be it by tanker or pipeline, the cost will be higher, much higher, because of unreasonable and unrealistic environmental attitudes.

Chapter Thirteen

AN ORDER APART

Society must no longer delay in informing itself of the chaotic consequences of the course of action it now follows. The new environmental cult, which is rife across this land threatening social order, must be challenged. We must quickly re-establish the habits on which our order was founded, or be prepared to face the consequences of the subtle and subversive revolution which has overtaken us.

Those charged with the growth, development and survival of our society must be cognizant of the fundamentals of ecology, just as there was a need, only a century ago, to recognize the fundamentals of communicable diseases. But just as the problem of communicable diseases was put in practical perspective, so must the ecologist approach environmental issues which may well have serious repercussions on our future well-being.

It is somewhat ironical that improved public health has contributed to another social problem — population growth. Food production is going to be the most critical problem facing society in the future and here, more than anywhere else, will be needed all the prowess of the agriculturally-oriented ecologist, to help feed a possible world population double the present. There can be no question in any rational mind that this can only be done with the aid of pesticides. Just as we have learned to use fire without getting burned, so too must we learn to use our chemical killers. If ecologists are to secure a respected place in society, they will have to abandon their *"no change to the natural environment"* philosophy. They will have to accept the more practical ideal of the engineering charter and help *direct the great sources of power in nature for the use and convenience of man.*

Facts Not Freaks

If ecologists are to be a part, small albeit, of the decision-making process, they must align themselves with facts, not freaks. They must confront the heresy of the environmentalists. Environmentalism is being portrayed as a science. In truth, it only uses the language of science to confuse and confound. To underscore the shortcomings of the modern day environmental attitude of "wait until all the facts are in", it is worth looking at the position taken in the cancer research field. Often, a calculated risk is taken with humans, once research shows that something appears to work with animals, even though the reasons are not understood. The situation is evaluated this way and I quote from a prominent researcher: "The mechanism is not totally clear, but that is secondary to whether or not it works. We'll worry about the mechanism later". It is time ecologists saw the ways of such wisdom and their own shortcomings when dealing with the natural environment, where the hazards are not as traumatic as they are when human life is involved.

The environmentalists, who are claiming to save the world, are in fact, undermining the order in our whole society. They are radical and anarchical forces. They are all part of the aftermath of the academic and social unrest of the Vietnam war. Just because the Americans had the misfortune to blunder into a war in Vietnam that upset their youth, is no reason why society at large should tolerate the subversive confrontational activities generated in the American Universities in the 60's. It was during those years, with the support of the academics, that environmentalism gained momentum and began its subversive attacks on the Establishment.

Ecotactics

Revolutionaries have always exploited the misgivings and insecurities of youth to further their own ends. The Sierra Club puts it this way:

> "So we are cheering. We are cheering at the sight of fresh reinforcements from the nation's campuses. And we are waving a new flag. It is this handbook. . . "

The book referred to is titled *ECOTACTICS*. In the editorial introduction, the book says with reference to its writers:

> ". . . they are. . . very young. . . More than half are under 30. I mention this for several reasons. First since it is the earth environment that concerns us here, then youth must be heard. This is their earth more than anyone else's. . . "

There is no doubt that in the Western society, privilege has gone to youth; it is no longer bestowed on the aged. Yet, in truth, it is the older people, those who have made an honest contribution with the sweat of their brow, those who have struggled to their twilight years, with perhaps little to show for it, because of the hardships which confronted them, who should have a prior claim to the earth and the better things therein. They have made their contribution; they have prepared the way for others to follow, like the pioneers who opened up the land. They have paid their dues and are entitled to a dignified end. Shame on those who now say that the social handouts should go to the young, who feel that the Establishment owes them a living. Such claims are the spores of socialism. But the politician, all too willingly goes along with this attitude, because statistics show that there are more young votes than old votes. Political platforms are tailored to suit vote-gathering not sound government. Such is the hypocrisy which envelopes us.

The editorial in "Ecotactics" goes on:
"The youth of our contribution has something else going for it. . . their ideas and materials are fresh. . . "

Have the realities of life totally escaped the authors of such ideology? All were young, once upon-a-time, or does it better suit the deception to forget, to pretend that the youth of today have the power of clairvoyance? I recall well in my youth having all the ideals that go with the exuberant state of life. I too thought I had the answers to all the world's problems. From a rather narrow point of view, I felt I had the answers to the tragedy still going on in the land of my birth, Ireland. Now, in hindsight, I realize that what I thought would have solved the problem from my young and highly idealistic point of view could not have worked, an ideal influenced by the environment in which I grew up and would have served best only one point of view.

Self Interests

And so it is with today's young environmentalists. They wish to change the world but only to best serve their own interests. They have not seen all the pieces of the puzzle; they are not truly aware of all the factors affecting the total life of man. And more importantly, they are unaware that they are being duped by the activists within the academic world.

The role played by the academics in shaping the political attitudes of students is put in good perspective in an article from the pen of columnist Lubor Zink in Ottawa. The article reviews a survey of attitudes of students to political and economic matters:
". . . The result reads like old socialist propaganda,. . . the students could (not) have picked up this naive nonsense from our official socialists because most of them discarded it a long time ago. So the source of their befuddlement,. . . must be the school and the media. . . Since such views and attitudes

cannot be based on personal experience or solidly founded evaluations, they obviously reflect the views and attitudes of whoever had the greatest mind-shaping influence through the formative years. That means teachers. . . No one has told them that free enterprise is the economic dimension of all the liberties they enjoy and take for granted.''

Having lived and worked in both New Zealand and Great Britain, I have no illusions about the claims of socialism. It serves best those whose salaries are paid from taxes. Sir Winston Churchill said:

"I do not believe in the power of the state to plan and enforce. . . they (socialists) cannot approach the high level of internal economic production achieved under free enterprise. Personal initiative. . . constitutes the life of a free society. It is this vital creative impulse that I deeply fear the doctrines (of socialism) have destroyed.''

As much of the cause of the youth of the sixties related to the rights of the individual, civil liberty subversives were allowed to run roughshod over the *rights of society*. We are now reaping the ills of the over-tolerance of that era, which has given the drug pusher, subversive elements and criminals the same hard-earned freedoms accorded decent, law-abiding citizens. The time is long past to reestablish the ground rules. In our social structure the right of an *individual* cannot be allowed to override those of individuals who collectively make up a society and make the laws; if it be otherwise, we have anarchy.

Nobler Efforts Required

Man's real problems will not be solved with needless ecological studies and environmental confrontations. Man must first come to grips with much more important issues, namely, how to control population growth, not deter national productivity; how to feed the world population, not just the affluent; how to bring about a fair distribution of the things that go to make a quality life; how to bring equity into resource distribution on a global scale. These contingencies will require every bit of the nobler efforts of those who are genuinely concerned about the destiny of the earth environment.

Many horrifying scenarios have been published in the past two decades about the degradation of the environment. To seek perspective, let us assume that there were, in fact, a handful of deaths due to misuse of toxic chemicals. On the other hand, how does one estimate the thousands of lives that may have been saved through the suppression of disease-carrying pests, as well as the infinite benefits from increased food production? We have been given the message over and over again, that dioxin is the most deadly substance on the face of the earth. Yet, the record of human deaths attributable to dioxin is sparse. Compare this with the tens of thousands of deaths recorded annually on the highways and one is surely forced to pause and ask what is the real perspective of the horror stories about the chemical industry. In truth, these stories take scientific facts and distort them to bring out only the adverse effects of society's efforts to provide a life base for 5 billion people, instead of a fraction of that, which would be the case if we lived only by nature.

Who Killed Terry?

There certainly appears to be no limits to the deceptions fostered by the environmentalists. A most extraordinary example appeared in the press in mid 1983, under the headline, "Who Killed Terry". Upon further reading, I was aghast to find the reference was to Terry Fox, that heroic young man who gave all he had. The article, without so much as *one iota of evidence,* pronounced that Terry was, in all probability, killed by industrial pollution. Here is the case as presented by one of our modern day socialized university professors, though not of the sciences:

". . . what could please the polluters more than Terry's career and the growing legend that surrounds it? All that money for cancer research. Great! That will keep the people quiet for a while; they will bask in the conviction that "something is being done," that 'cancer is being beaten.'. . . That will keep the public's eye off the captains of industry while they, with the blessing of government, pour their poisonous chemicals into the lakes, streams and oceans, belch their poisonous smoke into the atmosphere. . . Nor did Terry himself see the issue. Lurching in agony past the very forces that may have contributed to his misfortune, Terry, a good Canadian, kept his eyes on the road, not looking to the left or right, never questioning the order, the industry that polluted his body."

How is that for a horror scenario?

If the earth did not harbor such a highly intellectual species as man, then no one would, in truth, disagree with the ideology of leaving nature alone to work out its own destiny, just as it took care of the dinosaurs and those thousands of other extinct species, lost without the interference of man. But man is a breed apart and because of his intellect, has needs over and above those of the pure animal kingdom. The inevitable truth is that we have an intelligent society and its needs must be given priority over the laws of the jungle.

If one can stop the growth of population and the ever-expanding demand for luxury goods now sought as a result of affluence and establish a status quo, then the case to limit exploitation of natural resources in the interests of lower forms of life might well become a consideration, though an irrational one, as nothing is more rapacious to lower forms of life than other lower forms of life. Nature left to her own devices kills and destroys without sentiment, consideration or planning. As the equation stands today, in the overall interests of mankind, we must have policies and philosophies which encourage and allow the maximum intelligent use of all our resources, otherwise hundreds of millions are doomed to lives of meagre existence, which need not be.

Any level of environmental protection can be built into any development. If the terms of reference laid down by society on the basis of its priorities requires that the works be embellished, that a landscape be left untouched, then it can be so. After all, we can all live underground in caves, if it must be. But in order to ensure that priorities are kept in proper perspective, the fundamentals of engineering science, not ecological surmise, are a prerequisite to the decision-making process to avoid the economic insanity of the environmentalists. Environmental concerns have a place in the decision-making process, but not as a self-serving device ahead of society's needs; they must *not* be given veto status, the present intent of the radical elements of the cult.

Had the environmentalists been around when man decided to abandon his caves, we would still be there. The environmental case against constructing cities would be overwhelming. If one is to accept at face value the cries of permanent damage, ecological destruction and other such doomsday wails, then no city, town, village, or community could ever have been erected. Yet, thank God, man in his ignorance pressed on, with the result that today we enjoy a way of life that is inconceivable by comparison to the nomadic or caveman existence. The time lapse since the rise of the modern day environmentalists is such that their "doomsday" claims can be shown to be without foundation. If there is evidence to the contrary, it has not been presented. To this date, we have only been given surmise, and that embellished with much emotionalism, which now leaves the real decision-maker, society, with no alternative but to press on with the ways that have stood the test of time.

Since the rise of the computer age, a new disconcerting dimension has entered the decision-making process. It is now the practice to place as much available information as possible into computer data banks. But what is overlooked, and this is particularly true with the intangible environmental field, is that much information stored may not only have a bias but be erroneous. Just as the written word carries with it an aura of credibility, so it is, today, with computers. Unless the material stored is credible, the system lends itself to manipulation by those seeking to support an illogical position contrary to the facts — 'tis but more shades of Orwell's 1984.

Order Founded on Logic

The practical relationship of man to his environment was put very realistically by philosopher and writer Eric Hoffer, in a down-to-earth article in which he reminded us of how inhospitable nature can be, how her bugs and burrs, her poison oak and ivy can all combine to make an adventitious sortie into the outdoors a veritable nightmare. He goes on to remind us of the awesome power of nature to wreak havoc through floods, tornadoes, earthquakes, plagues and the like and of man's unending struggle to protect himself against such forces. He concludes:

> "If history is to have meaning, it must be the history of humanization, of man's tortuous ascent through the ages, of his ceaseless effort to break away from the rest of creation and become an order apart."

If we are to have an order apart, it must be founded on logic. We must remember when we are dealing with society, we are not looking at a biological evolution, but at a cultural evolution. It would appear that the environmentalists want us to run a cultural regime using biological rules, which just don't apply. While it is very democratic and tolerant to allow the adversary to have his way, our society cannot much longer allow such idealism to undermine our way of life.

To restore order to the decision-making process, clearly defined policies and commitments must be made at the political level. To rid ourselves of the environmental dilemma, we must, without further delay find some way to define the jurisdictional roles of the Federal and Provincial Governments to ensure no overlap or duplication of authority or effort. We must weed out the parasites feeding off our taxes. Priorities for the overall betterment of society must be put in perspective.

Until politicians realize that they are not elected for their own gratification (nor to pound benches and jeer like idiots to mask their dismal performances in the "House") but rather, to administer, with dignity, the affairs of the country on behalf of the people, chaos will remain. Politicians must, in the exercise of their obligations, ensure that the bureaucracy does its duty and does it efficiently. After all, the politician is the "manager elect" of the people. Regrettably, there is much truth in the saying — politicians are not running the country, the country is running them.

If the present accelerating drive of the bureaucracies towards autocracy is not checked, the potential power of the public service to serve society will be lost. It presently chooses to serve first its own ends. Changes are direly needed and without delay. A fundamental change in philosophy is required. Since industry is the life force of our society, it is beholden on government, any government, to establish a relationship with industry conducive to economic and social stability. Whatever the outcome, every effort will be needed to prevent the continued destruction of the initiative inherent in most individuals, particularly in the producer, that priceless creature upon whom society depends.

In this criticism of the politician, let us not forget, for one moment, the role played by the media and the sabotage it wreaks in the political arena. It is nothing less than disgraceful the way the electronic media is allowed to harass those holding public office, particularly those in Cabinet positions. The evidence is there each evening on the magic tube for all to see. It is iniquitous that elected members are expected to respond, off-the-cuff, to manipulators equipped with microphones asking questions designed to ridicule (have you stopped beating your wife, etc.). It is time legislation was enacted to rid us of these louts serving the ends of socialism through the creation of public mischief. If more courtesy and respect were shown to public office, a better calibre of candidate would come forward; but the socialists in our midst don't want this; they prefer the establishment to make its choice from among its lessers, rather than from the talented. Many of the capable who have tried in recent years have left in disillusionment.

Charges of Collusion

Since industry is the economic force in our society, it follows that our bureaucracies must be geared to help industry. Those who followed such a philosophy during the 1960's were accused of being in collusion with industry, a situation which prevails to this day. The charges of collusion by the pressure groups has resulted in the present bureaucratic, red-tape, duplicating nonsense now rife within the public services which has brought much economic development to a frustrated halt. while aiding and abetting an uncontrolled growth in the public service. In 1971 in a letter to a member of the University of Victoria regarding my participation in a seminar for biologists, I wrote:

> "While some may wish to curb our growth, it is more realistic to recognize the inevitable and prepare for it in a practical way which ensures the most good for the most people. In our democracy, such decisions depend on the wisdom of our elected leaders. It is vital that we lay before them tangible facts with which they can work on our behalf. You may recall that my prescription for decision-making was that commonsense must at all time prevail and experience must be recognized and used."

Unfortunately, we cannot be too optimistic that our elected leaders will do that which best serves the country. It is a sad fact, but all too true, that politicians, as has been demonstrated on a number of occasions throughout these pages, prefer to use the Public Service to further their own ends.

An Evil to be Shunned

Because of the affluence in the 1960's, the environmentalists got away with their false doctrines and nonsense. They made much of the fact that economics "over-influenced" decision-making in our society. They portrayed economics as an evil to be shunned and in its place erected their ecological idols. Like it or not, it is an undeniable fact that economics has had much to do with the evolution of our society; it has determined our present high quality of living and will continue to be the controlling influence for eons to come, when many of the environmental fads of today are long forgotten.

That the environmental anarchists won the confrontation of the 60's is indisputable. I recall well, the Minister in charge of environmental issues in those days, in a moment of exasperation saying, "I quite honestly don't understand what is going on any more." Is not this the intent of the activists? Create controversy, confusion and distrust — then take over. On certain occasions, when situations were blatantly misrepresented, the author suggested that charges of causing public mischief be laid, but the idea fell on deaf ears. Politicians shun such confrontation with voters. They prefer to pay lip-service to the wailings of the uninformed, making little effort to enlighten them because the vocal minorities will create controversy out of any statements made, if not by their own efforts, then by the efforts of the media. This reluctance to do battle has some very disquieting ramifications. Every time an honest attitude of the majority dealing with realism is presented, it is instantly put down as discrimination against some obscure group or creature. How much longer can we survive this disembowelment of our system is a question needing an answer.

An ex-Minister of Environment (he had to be "ex" or he daren't say it) put it this way at a luncheon address to the Association of Professional Engineers in 1983, in talking about environmental pressure groups and their causes:

> ". . . if the fish aren't there, it's the fault of almost everybody else except other fishermen who may have taken the fish. It's certainly the fault of B.C. Hydro, of the Federal Fisheries Ministry, of the Ministry of Environment, of any mine in the area, any highway project, or any damn other thing. What I am telling you is that I gave up trying to please them and I gave up trying to do anything for them because no matter what I did I was wrong. . . ."

How true; how true; well said Sir!

Paternalistic and Unreal

Most people readily acknowledge that environmentalism is somewhat of a motherhood issue. There is little doubt that the ecological gods prey on such instincts to achieve their ends. In the 1960's there was a court decision adjudicating on a case involving waste discharge, which puts these attitudes in some perspective. The decision of the presiding judge in dismissing the case was:

> ". . . to seek to protect the public in a contingency that may never arise, is too paternalistic and unreal . . ."

Had our society vigorously adhered to paternalistic philosophies we would still be back in The Dark Ages. The problem with paternalism is that only in a very few cases will the feared "catastrophe" occur. To take precautions to absolutely guarantee that a misfortune will not occur is an expense and luxury society cannot afford. In any event, overcaution is not in keeping with nature's law of chance over life and death. Instead, society adopted the philosophy of compensation, which is well illustrated by consideration of the automobile, which is responsible for thousands of tragic deaths each year, not to mention the awesome number of injuries, leaving many maimed for life.

There is no doubt that most highway accidents could be eliminated, if speed limits were posted and enforced at, for example, 20 m.p.h. But such action would nullify most of the benefits of the auto, and so it is that society undertakes to run the risk by providing compensation through insurance. There just is no other practical solution. To enforce a 20 m.p.h. limit "is too paternalistic and unreal". And so it is with the highly intangible issues of environmentalism. What we need is a well devised system of compensation to meet those unforseen calamities *which will occur.*

Mercenary Market Value

It is an inevitable fact of life that certain people must step aside to let society progress. Neither individuals, nor minorities, can be allowed to hold up what is to benefit the majority. But, where such are affected, then equitable compensation must be made, not just for the mercenary market value of the real estate or business involved. To get recompensed for such is no less than one's mere rights. It does not compensate for a lost way of life, for the security one may feel by having roots, for nearby friends who can be depended upon to lend a hand when ill befalls, or to know you will never be alone in a day of need. Here is an extract from one of those dubious environmental studies carried out for B.C. Hydro:

> "An additional 20 families in farmsteads and rural dwellings would be required to relocate. Many of these people are members of long-established farm families and they would likely experience severe social strains as a result of forced relocation."

To arrive at an equitable solution is a most difficult undertaking.

Value on the open market can only establish a rudimentary basis of compensation as such only establishes what the property is worth to *someone else*. It does not account for the heritage values which an owner may feel very strongly. Of course, while such special values must be given every reasonable attention, they cannot be allowed to be used to blackmail. The objective of all parties is to arrive at a solution which will ensure that those displaced can continue to enjoy the life-style to which they have become accustomed and to maintain the same level of security for the future which their present status offered them.

During my years of exposure to public concerns and attitudes on environmental issues, it was all too obvious that many were aggrieved solely because they felt entitled to compensation, which had not been forthcoming. I reviewed many cases which I considered valid. Some related to oyster growers, where water quality had, in truth, deteriorated to levels which affected the oysters; others related to property owners where increased industrial, commercial and civil activities had produced an undesirable impact. There were of course many false claims, but, all in all, there were those that had a case.

Unfortunately, court actions, more often than not, fail to bring about the desired result. As monies for legal fees can be extortionary, many can do little but protest through whatever channels are available — thus the rise of pressure groups. Indeed, it is the dismal failure of the legal system to function with anything approaching effectiveness, that has given rise to many of society's problems. There are many cases where compensation is warranted and because it is not forthcoming, such people with axes to grind join ranks with the environmentalists, which creates the illusion that environmentalism shares the mantel of justice.

No Monetary Stake

On the matter of compensation, it is intriguing to note that environmentalists are forever interfering with land developments, in which they have no monetary stake, for such nebulous reasons that the area is a "hiker's paradise", an "ecological jewel", a "wildlife santuary" whose primary purpose seems to be to raise live targets for hunters. Perhaps there are, indeed, some areas where the claims are justified. But somewhere, the realities of life must take over. Are the environmentalists prepared to have compensation paid to those who don't want hiking in the area, with the litter and vandalism that often goes with it, or who don't want a mosquito swamp at the foot of the lot, or whose investment opportunities are diminished by declaring the area a sanctuary of one kind or another? Such situations, too, require compensation, but the unanswered question is: who pays?

It is with regret that the author noted throughout his years of involvement with the environmental issue, that the whole spectrum of industry, like the engineering profession, tended to assume a guilt complex, shrugging shoulders and simply passing on the inevitable increased costs to the unsuspecting purchaser, in the hope that the problem would go away. Granted, during the rise of environmental hysteria, big, bad industry was alienated and pilloried as a scapegoat. As explained, the Minister of Environment Canada made it quite plain, in the early 70's that the Government would not be sympathetic to "industries' pleas", with the inevitable end that problems were not being brought out into the open for honest discussion and partial solutions were all too often simply implemented as a sop to appease critics. Realism did not prevail.

Industry should have been coming forward with a united front to point out the consequences — who would gain? — who would lose? — and to lobby against the environmental movement being given what was tantamount to a veto in the decision-making process. It is imperative that the business community fight to ensure that legislative requirements are for the betterment of our society, for be assured, the forces of the left are at work to enslave us with more taxes, more bureaucracy and more government control.

A Royal Commission?

The primary question raised by this book is, can the environmental record be set straight? Under normal circumstances the panacea would be to order a Royal Commission. Such an investigation could lay to rest the environmental bogeyman, *provided it is not just another piece of hypocrisy* like the various hearings described earlier.

But many would challenge the effectiveness of such a Commission, as all too often such efforts have come to nought in the past. A well known Victoria columnist puts the matter this way:

> "If you strung all Royal Commissions end to end, they would form a blacktop of broken dreams and pigeon-holed promises. Commissions sit, papers are written, they receive the momentary glare of publicity and are relegated to the dusty, musty public archives."

So much for that proposal. Perhaps this book alone may prove to be the antidote needed. In any event, we must create a forum to find the truth and dispense with the destructive forces promoting environmentalism as the end-all of civilization. But above all, we must find some way to return the decision-making process to those who are capable and equipped to make decisions. And, we must do it now!

Something said many years ago by Walter Lippman, renowed journalist, author and sometime advisor to Presidents, is worth repeating to round out this story:

"What is left of our civilization will not be maintained, what has been wrecked will not be restored, by imagining that some new political gadget can be invented, some new political formula improvized which will save it. Our civilization can be maintained and restored only by remembering and discovering the truths, and by re-establishing the habits on which it was founded. There is no use looking into the blank future for some new and fancy revelation of what man needs in order to live."

THE AUTHOR

Charles Keenan, a professional civil engineer with 30 years experience, has been an environmental consultant to major resource industries in British Columbia for many years. In addition, he has served in various senior technical and administrative capacities with the British Columbia Government in the now-named Ministry of Environment and in the Ministry of Health. He was chief technical adviser to the Pollution Control Board for many years before becoming Director of Pollution Control. He has been intimately involved with the drafting and development of environmental legislation and has served on National and International environmental committees. His knowledge of the environmental scene is extensive.

CAPPIS PRESS   **ISBN 0-919763-08-1**

NOTICE TO READERS

If you are unable to find your own copy of ENVIRONMENTAI
ANARCHY at your library or bookstore, please write t

CAPPIS PRESS, PUBLISHERS
252 Superior Street
Victoria, British Columbia
Canada   V8V 1T3

Ask for our book list